The College Cost Disease

Higher Cost and Lower Quality

Robert E. Martin

Emeritus Professor of Economics, Centre College, USA

Edward Elgar
Cheltenham, UK • Northampton, MA, USA

Published by
Edward Elgar Publishing Limited
The Lypiatts
15 Lansdown Road
Cheltenham
Glos GL50 2JA
UK

Edward Elgar Publishing, Inc.
William Pratt House
9 Dewey Court
Northampton
Massachusetts 01060
USA

Paperback edition 2012

A catalogue record for this book
is available from the British Library

Library of Congress Control Number: 2010932053

ISBN 978 1 84980 616 9 (cased)
ISBN 978 1 78195 338 9 (paperback)

Typeset by Servis Filmsetting Ltd, Stockport, Cheshire
Printed and bound by MPG Books Group, UK

Contents

Figures

A note for readers

I intend this book to be accessible to anyone with a basic understanding of economics and enough interest in the topic to do a little work while reading the book. The target audience includes faculty members, administrators, governing boards, public policy makers, members of the education reform movement, and my fellow economists.

Economists are sometimes accused of writing only for each other and it is thought this tendency reduces the impact economics has on public policy issues, such as higher education reform. Writing for both a technical and a nontechnical audience is an ambitious endeavor; one can simultaneously disappoint your technical audience and confuse your nontechnical audience. A glossary of economic terms is provided for my non-economist readers in the hope it will facilitate your understanding. I leave it to my readers to decide if I have succeeded in this attempt; if not, I apologize to my fellow economists for extended explanations of economic concepts that appear obvious and to my non-economist readers if the explanations are not transparent.

Preface

My purpose here is to apply formal economic theory to higher education. The uniquely high cost and quality issues in higher education lead me to a critical evaluation of the academy. I know these criticisms are difficult for members of the academy to accept and I hope my colleagues realize I undertake this project because I am dedicated to what higher education can and should be.

The problems come from the network of incentives within the academy. These incentives are not properly aligned with the public interest. The incentives create the problems. The incentives can make it appear members of the academy are engaged in collusion. Nothing could be further from the truth; there is no conspiracy; people follow where the incentives lead. The vast majority of faculty members, administrators, and board members are sincere in their belief the actions they take are in the public interest.

The misalignment of incentives leads to extravagant increases in cost per student and a secular decline in quality. Because the public is uncertain about value added per individual institution, they choose cost as a proxy for quality; the assumption is, if it cost more, it must be higher quality. The value added uncertainty also explains why reputations are the primary means of competition among higher education institutions. The association of cost with quality creates a perverse incentive for colleges and universities to spend as much as they can per student. The competition has no limit; there are always projects that conceivably could improve "quality." Hence, reputation competition among higher education institutions is a race to spend as much as possible per student.

As they are nonprofit institutions, their ability to spend is capped by available revenues, so any increase in revenues drives costs higher in an unending spiral. Even the richest institutions never have enough money; they are always in fundraising mode in order to lift the cap on expenditures. The wealth accumulated by colleges/universities and the amount they spend per student are barriers to competition from less well regarded institutions. The faster a top tier institution can raise its expenditure per student, the less competitive threat there is from lower tier institutions.

Reputation competition is efficient when consumers make frequent repeat purchases, they can easily evaluate quality after purchasing the product, they immediately abandon producers who cheat on quality, and there are no third parties in the transaction. None of these conditions exist in higher education. Reputation competition in higher education is inefficient, quality uncertainty is a financial advantage for institutions, quality cheating is a constant problem, costs are chronically high, and the institutions are subject to significant principal/agent abuse.

There are few constraints on principal/agent abuse in higher education and agency problems always lead to costs that are higher than necessary. The decades long history of exceptional cost increase is the product of reputation competition and serious unresolved agency problems in higher education.

The importance of academic reputations means administrators and governing boards are narrowly focused on public relations and they scrupulously avoid all controversies. As conditions change, they do not attempt to reallocate resources; instead, they seek to solve all campus problems by raising more money. This public relations mindset adversely selects for lower academic quality. Administrators divert resources from real quality because those programs are slow to develop, the benefits are difficult to measure, and the results are most likely to be realized during the next president's tenure. Instead, administrators prefer projects with immediate public relations value and obvious tangible results, such as facilities competition and media events.

Since attempts to control cost are always controversial and controversies damage reputations, administrators and governing boards will not voluntarily reform. There is a bias against real reform among administrators and governing boards. The college access problem cannot be solved until colleges and universities control their costs. The bias against reform among administrators and governing boards insures that true reform will not come from within higher education.

There is a robust market for senior scholars and no market at all for senior teachers. This is an anomaly because the public values quality teaching and is indifferent to research; economic theory suggests there should be a vigorous market for senior teachers and an indifferent market for senior scholars. There is no market for gifted senior teachers because colleges and universities refuse to measure teaching value added. Maintaining uncertainty about teaching value added is a financial advantage for colleges/universities; quality uncertainty makes the demand for services more price inelastic and it strengthens the institution's negotiating position with respect to teaching faculty. Median faculty members also benefit from quality uncertainty; when teaching productivity is not measured, low productivity faculty are paid a premium and high productivity faculty are paid less than their true contribution. Unfortunately, this adversely selects for poor teaching and people who prefer that rewards are disconnected from productivity. Further, the incentive imbalance between teaching and research creates one-dimensional faculty members who are too intensively focused on research; when you are rewarded only for more research output, you neglect teaching. The neglect of teaching leads to a secular decline in quality.

Acknowledgements

I dedicate this book to my grandchildren: Chloe, Arianna, Travis, Connor, and Nicholas. I would also like to thank my patient, loving wife, Marlene, who tolerated my compulsive behavior during this manuscript's preparation, and the Hub Coffee Shop posse, who endured too many pedantic monologues on this topic.

In addition, I am indebted to the John William Pope Center for Higher Education Policy for partial financial support and to the Cato Institute for hosting presentations of some of this research.

Finally, I thank my daughter, Amy Martin, who designed the cover for this book. Also, I just plain thank her for being my daughter.

1. Cost, quality, and anomalies in higher education

1.1 INTRODUCTION

Polls reveal students and parents are very concerned about college costs, although they tend to give higher education good marks on quality (Bok, 2006; Wadsworth, 2005). Concern about quality seems to increase with proximity to and familiarity with higher education. Polling results from Public Agenda and the Center for Public Policy and Higher Education reveal parents and students are "squeezed" by the importance of higher education and their perception that the opportunity to attend college is declining (Immerwahr and Johnson, 2010).

Of those polled, 74 percent think higher education costs are rising as fast as or faster than health care costs[1] and 83 percent think students have to borrow too much to go to college (Immerwahr and Johnson, 2010: 11). A plurality, 60 percent in 2009, believes colleges and universities are more concerned about their own financial interest than the quality of the education students receive (Immerwahr and Johnson, 2010: 12). During the current recession, higher education institutions continue to significantly increase tuition and fees (College Board, 2009) and some public institutions plan to restrict enrollment in response to budget cuts. These actions are consistent with the pursuit of self-interest rather than the spirit of public service and shared sacrifice. The public thinks higher education is simply another vested interest group and the academy does little to dispel that perception.

The public's concern is also reflected by numerous studies, commissions, and books dedicated to cost/quality issues in higher education.[2] The consequences are also well documented: rising cost reduces college access, lower access reduces economic mobility, and declining quality threatens national competitiveness and contributes to a relentless widening in the distribution of income (Furchtgott-Roth et al., 2009; Mehta, 2000).

The measurement of cost increases is well and truly covered by other scholars. My purpose is to look inside the higher education "black box" in order to identify what drives the well documented cost/quality problems. The cost and quality problems are symptoms of an underlying "disease" that cannot be cured by treating the symptoms. The root cause of the "disease" is the network of incentives that create the problems we observe. Treating symptoms without changing incentives has unintended consequences that very well may make things worse. Meaningful reform will come from an understanding of the incentive system responsible for the cost/quality problem. Understanding the incentive system also reveals why the college access problem cannot be solved unless cost control reform is successful and why reform will not come from within the higher education community.

When people follow an incentive system, their collective behavior can give the appearance that some "conspiracy" exists to take advantage of others. For example, the incentives embedded in competitive markets lead individual firms to set prices that appear to be uniform. The incentives lead to uniform prices. Alternatively, if firms collude to preserve market share, prices will also be uniform. Parallel behavior may be the result of collusion or the result of system-wide incentives. If any passage in this book gives the impression I think such a conspiracy exists in higher education, that impression is false. Members of the academy follow what the incentives encourage them to do. Members of the academy try to "do good"; since the incentives are not aligned with the public interest, the results are in conflict with the public interest.

This book is a candid discussion of major issues in higher education. It is a critical analysis of what is and a hopeful analysis of what might be. While there are some hard truths the academy needs to face, some things work well in higher education. The scope and quality of scientific research are a national treasure that makes significant contributions to our health, wellbeing, and culture. It is important that reform not harm the core of that research output. Further, there are individual programs and institutions that do a conscientious job in maintaining teaching quality and containing cost; on the average, however, this is not true.

Nothing I say here should be construed to be a template that fits all institutions. There are significant differences in cost control records between private and public institutions; surprisingly,[3] the public institutions do a better job controlling costs than do the private institutions. Further, the behavior and the problems vary considerably between institutions at the top of the quality hierarchy and those at the bottom of the quality hierarchy.

The following chapters contain considerable discussion of "faculty productivity." Unless otherwise specified, this phrase refers to faculty teaching productivity, since that is where the productivity problems reside. There are few problems, other than the balance[4] between research and teaching, with faculty research productivity. That fact is encouraging, since it means faculty members respond to incentives, as Levitt and Dubner tell us we should expect (2009). In other words, if reform leads to a set of incentives compatible with the public interest, the force of competition will correct most of the problems and direct regulation will be unnecessary.

Finally, this book is not an empirical study. The statistics I report are for the purpose of illustration and should not be considered conclusive. I would like to say the book is a behavioral theory of higher education; honesty prevents me from making that claim. Since I draw from existing economic theory regarding asymmetric information, reputation markets/ experience goods, the principal/agent problem, and nonprofit institutions, the book might best be described as a "meta-analysis." The analysis leads to a variety of empirical hypotheses that I do not test. It is my hope that others will test these hypotheses and find them either correct or wanting in empirical support. I welcome those studies.

1.2 DRAWING INSIGHTS FROM ANOMALIES

An anomaly is "a discrepancy or deviation from an established rule or trend."[5] In this case, we consider economic anomalies: behavior that appears to be at odds with what traditional economic theory suggests we should observe. I contend that a close inspection of these anomalies provides important keys to understanding higher education's cost and teaching quality problems. The anomalies point to the source of the problem.

The Chivas Regal Anomaly

Normal demand theory states the quantity demanded declines as price increases; demand curves slope downward. The Chivas Regal anomaly arises when consumers associate higher price with higher quality and in its extreme form it occurs when a firm raises its price and the quantity demanded increases, causing the demand curve to appear to be upward sloping in price. The extreme form of the Chivas Regal anomaly is rare in the for-profit sector. In contrast, the extreme form is common among elite higher education institutions. Indeed, it is an integral part of some institutions' marketing plans (Larson, 2001; Wang, 2008).

A necessary condition for the Chivas Regal effect is that consumers are uncertain about product quality, so they use price as an indicator (a proxy) for quality prior to purchasing the product. If consumers know quality prior to purchase they have no need to rely on price as an indicator of quality.

The primary objective among higher education institutions is to build academic reputation (H.R. Bowen, 1980; Brewer, Gates, and Goldman,

2002; James, 1990; Martin, 2005). Like using price as an indicator of quality, reputation competition only makes sense if consumers are uncertain about the quality provided; if consumers are certain about quality prior to purchase, the quality provided in the past is irrelevant. Both reputation competition and using price as a proxy for quality are characteristics of markets for experience goods. An experience good's quality cannot be determined prior to purchase, and the consumer must buy the product or service before he can determine its quality; that is, the consumer can evaluate quality only after he has "experience" with the good or service, hence the name (Nelson, 1970).

Chapter 3 contains an analysis of the economics of experience goods as it applies to higher education (Grossman, 1981; Holmstrom, 1999; Hörner, 2002; Klein and Leffler, 1981; Lutz, 1989; Martin, 1986; Nelson, 1970; Shapiro, 1983; Spence, 1977). Asymmetric information (where providers have more information than buyers) can lead to market failures (Akerlof, 1970; Holmstrom, 1999: 169). Reputation competition is the market's solution to asymmetric information problems. The reputation mechanism works well when consumers purchase the product frequently, when they can readily determine quality after purchase, when they abandon quality cheaters quickly, and when there are only two parties to each transaction. Whenever reputations play an important role in any market, it follows the providers sell an experience good or service and consumers are uncertain about quality.

Higher education services are perhaps the most complicated type of experience good. Students and their parents make these purchases once per student, they may not know what they bought until years after the purchase, when they commit to one provider it is expensive to shift to another provider, and the transaction frequently involves a third party payer. In addition, it is very expensive and students cannot exchange the service among themselves after the purchase; the service is personal and cannot be resold to others. These characteristics suggest the reputation mechanism may not work very well in higher education.

The theory of experience goods reveals that quality cheating by providers is always an issue, costs are higher than costs would be under full information, the more uncertain consumers are about quality the higher is the cost, and providers have an incentive not to provide full information about quality. Chapter 3 explains why colleges and universities place so much emphasis on reputation. It explains why quality is an issue and why colleges and universities are so ambiguous about the value they add. Finally, the Chivas Regal effect links expenditure per student to reputation, so reputation competition becomes a race to spend the most per student in a contest with no upper bound.

The Separation of Pay and Productivity

Among for-profit firms, real wages rise as productivity increases. In the macro-economy, if nominal wages grow faster than productivity, prices rise such that the rate of increase in real wages is limited by the rate of productivity growth. William J. Baumol noticed that real wages tend to rise in service industries even though productivity does not increase in those industries (Baumol and Bowen, 1966). This observation became known as "Baumol's cost disease."

Baumol argues real wages rise in higher education even though productivity does not rise, or even declines, because opportunity wages are rising in the rest of the economy. It is important to note the potential for adverse selection in terms of labor quality when real wages and productivity rise in the general economy while real wages increase in education at the same time productivity declines (Hoxby, 2004; Roy, 1951). Self-selection among workers in the macro-economy leads to a disproportionate number of people choosing academic careers who expect real wages to increase without any increase in productivity; they expect their real wages to rise regardless of personal productivity. This sense of entitlement is an adverse selection effect from the disconnection between real wages and productivity. The disconnection insures real cost per unit will rise in higher education. This disconnection is due to principal/agent problems (Holmstrom and Milgrom, 1991; Mas-Colell et al., 1995: 471–510) in higher education (Chapter 4).

The "Higher Revenues Drive Costs Higher" Anomaly

Consider the for-profit firm. In order to raise more revenue the firm must sell more product or service. In order to sell more, it must produce, package, and distribute more product. If it is producing at capacity, it must also expand capacity before it can sell more. Among for-profit firms, increases in cost tend to precede increases in revenue. If the firm's production is characterized by increasing returns to scale, average cost per unit declines as output increases.

In higher education, when enrollment demand increases, revenues rise, and cost per student increases, even though higher education appears to be subject to increasing returns to scale and scope (Brinkman, 1990; Cohn et al., 1989; Johnes, 1997; Koshal and Koshal, 1995, 2000). An increase in revenue per student is not taken as profit in order to efficiently expand output; it is taken as increased expenditures to benefit faculty members, administrators, and trustees. In higher education, revenue serves as a cap on expenditures; more revenue drives cost higher. This anomaly is known as H.R. Bowen's "revenue theory of cost" (1980).

Higher revenues drive costs higher because of nonprofit status, the principal/agent problem, and the fact that education is an experience good. Chapter 4 contains a comparative analysis of the principal/agent problem in nonprofit and for-profit firms. The principal/agent problem exists everywhere. Voters have an agency problem when they vote for politicians who do not honor campaign promises. Patients have an agency problem when doctors practice defensive medicine. Clients have an agency problem when lawyers serve their own interests at the client's expense.

In each case, a principal/agent problem leads to costs that are higher than necessary. When public servants misbehave, the cost of government is higher than necessary. When for-profit managers take decisions in their own interest at the expense of stockholders and bondholders, the firm's costs are higher than necessary. The same is true for higher education: agency problems lead to higher cost. The long record of rising real higher education cost per student is strong empirical evidence suggesting significant agency problems in higher education.

The public is reminded regularly about for-profit firm principal/agent problems. The latest reminder is Bernie Madoff and his Ponzi investment fraud. Principal/agent problems are at the heart of the sub-prime mortgage problem; since loan originators were not the same people as the ultimate lenders, the originators were acting as agents for the ultimate lenders. More typical is the set of corporate scandals that followed the dotcom stock market bubble; corporations such as Enron come to mind. These scandals led to renewed regulation, just as the current banking crisis will lead to new regulation.

These problems surface regularly despite the fact there are numerous constraints on agency problems among for-profit firms. For-profit firms are highly regulated by both the federal government and state governments. Similarly, there are numerous private groups who oversee firm behavior. The stock exchanges oversee firms, and financial analysts, banks, investment bankers, and individual investors are constantly analyzing firm activities. Finally, the "market for control" of firms constrains agency behavior. Despite all of this regulation and oversight, agency issues are a constant problem among for-profit firms. Indeed, the agency problem may be capitalism's "Achilles' heel."[6]

In higher education, the principals are students, parents, taxpayers, and donors and the agents are faculty members, administrators, and trustees. Nonprofit organizations are subject to very little regulation and there are very few private groups who exercise effective oversight. Most nonprofits are regulated by the states; the exception is the Internal Revenue Service, which is charged with enforcing regulations for tax exempt status. Owing to the assumption that nonprofits seek to "do good," the IRS tends to give nonprofit organizations a pass (Fremont-Smith, 2004). Similarly, the press tends to give higher education a pass out of misplaced sympathy (Maeroff, 2005); on the other hand, the press loves a juicy for-profit principal/agent story. Finally, there is no "market for control" of nonprofit institutions, so there is no natural constraint on agency problems in higher education.

The "Business Model" in Higher Education

Bok (2003), Kirp (2003, 2005), Massy (2003), Tuchman (2009), and Weisbrod (1998), among others, argue that commercialization of higher education leads to rising cost and declining quality. The anomaly here is: over the past century the business model clearly led to lower costs and higher quality in the rest of the economy. Why would such an obviously successful model fail so miserably when applied to higher education? Has higher education really adopted the business model? This issue is explored in Chapter 5.

A careful analysis of campus commercialization problems in research, teaching extension programs, sports, and faculty professionalism reveals the problems have an internal origin; they are not the result of an outside influence. Indeed, they are the result of unresolved agency problems.

Higher education did not sell its soul to capitalism; it sold its soul to public relations, since that is how one manages reputation (Chapter 3). Rather than the "corporate model," the political campaign is a better analogy: raise all the money you can, do not worry about cost, and scrupulously cultivate an image, regardless of what the reality may be. The reason why this particular devil had its way with higher education is because public relations builds reputations and more money leads to more benefits to the agents responsible for managing higher education. Again, this does not imply a conspiracy; insiders are simply following where the incentives lead them. The new expenditures always have some impact on education quality and are easy to rationalize in that regard.

There is a persistent bias against capitalism in higher education and that makes the academy ready to blame its failures on an "outside agitator" like corporate America. Pursuit of self-interest is a basic human failing; it is not something unique to capitalism. The difference is the business community is more honest about its intentions than are either politicians or members of the academy. Self-interest drives behavior in the Iranian theocracy and it drove behavior in the former Soviet Union. We find corruption everywhere, regardless of ideology. The conflict of values represented by "the commercialization" of higher education has nothing to do with capitalism or the business model. The conflict of values is between traditional academic values and the values inherent in "public relations."

The Missing Market for Senior Teachers

In normal economic theory, the demand for resources to produce a product is said to be "derived" from the consumer's final demand for the product produced by those resources (derived demand theory). The amount producers are willing to pay for a resource depends directly on the intensity of the consumer's final demand for the product produced by those resources. "The price of land to grow corn is high because the price of corn is high."

Those who pay for higher education, parents, taxpayers, and donors, have an intense and well funded demand for high quality teaching. On the other hand, most parents and taxpayers have only a casual interest,[7] at best, in the research produced by faculty members. Derived demand theory suggests there should be a brisk demand for seasoned teachers and a weak demand for seasoned researchers. The anomaly here is that we have exactly the opposite situation in higher education: there is a brisk and lucrative market for senior scholars and no market at all for senior teachers (Bok, 2003; Kirp, 2005; Ransom, 1993). Mobility (the ability to get another tenured position at some other institution) depends exclusively on research productivity. Even at ostensibly teaching institutions, colleges do not hire with tenure on the basis of teaching productivity alone. Chapter 6 considers the absence of a market for high quality senior teachers. Why does this market not exist?

1.3   HOW DO WE KNOW THERE ARE QUALITY PROBLEMS IN HIGHER EDUCATION?

American colleges and universities are held in very high regard by the rest of the world. The number of foreign students who study here is evidence of this high regard, as are polls regarding the quality of US higher education. In that sense, foreign students vote with their feet when they come to the US to study. The scientific accomplishments and technical dominance of our industry reveals something must be working well in higher education. Therefore, it is fair to ask: why would one think US higher education has quality problems?

Our first indication something is wrong comes from inside the academy. Derek Bok's book *Our Underachieving Colleges: A Candid Look at How Much Students Learn and Why They Should be Learning More* (2006), Harry Lewis's book *Excellence without a Soul* (2006), William F. Massy's book *Honoring the Trust: Quality and Cost Containment in Higher Education* (2003), and Richard Hersh and John Merrow's book *Declining by Degrees: Higher Education at Risk* (2005) all explore quality problems in higher education. There are many other authors who express real concern, while I am aware of no one who makes the case that the quality of undergraduate education is increasing.

Consider the core academic activities: undergraduate education, graduate education, and the discovery of new knowledge, most importantly new science. As we see in Chapter 2 the quality indicators for undergraduate education, such as graduation rates, retention rates, grade inflation, and student study time reveal teaching quality is in a secular decline. The output of new science and the quality of graduate education are not yet the issue. Since value added in undergraduate education is hard to measure, academic reputations at the major institutions are driven by the quality of their graduate programs and their output of new science (research). Indeed, the quality of our graduate programs draws the world's best graduate students; those students stay here, create new science themselves, and work for our industries. We have a technical advantage over the rest of the world primarily because we attract and retain the world's best people.

It is not unusual for over 50 percent of each graduate student cohort to be composed of foreign students; this is particularly true of graduate programs in the hard sciences, where fewer and fewer native born students are well enough prepared to attend these programs. As the rest of the world prospers, domestic opportunities for foreign students educated in the U.S. rise and the number of those students who take up residence in the U.S. will decline. The U.S. is then stuck with a failed undergraduate system that cannot prepare our young people for the knowledge-based careers that drive international competition.

The glow from graduate education and the output of new science has a halo effect on all of higher education. Further, as we discover in Chapter 3, academic reputations are extraordinarily durable, since they take a very long time to establish and quality indicators are hard to measure. The decline in K–12 quality is well documented and it has continued for decades, despite our attempts to arrest that decline. We should not be surprised to find that those problems have infected undergraduate education in America.

Jonathan Grayer, CEO of Kaplan, Inc. and a member of the Spellings Commission, argues the quality distribution that makes up U.S. higher education is strictly bi-modal;[8] it is composed of a large number of relatively low quality institutions and a very small number of high quality, or elite, institutions (Zemsky, 2009: 121–4). Grayer's point is the country's international reputation for quality is driven by the elite institutions and in turn the reputations of the elite institutions are driven by world class scholarship, rather than the quality of their undergraduate programs. Zemsky writes "Most observers of American higher education would argue that the quality of student inputs remains more important than the quality of the educational process" (2009: 122). In other words, the perceived quality of undergraduate programs at the elite institutions is driven by the quality of the students they attract (selectivity) rather than the value added by these institutions after they enroll.

If this is true, the elite institutions create very high opportunity costs by not maximizing the educational experience they offer these gifted students. This may explain why the elite institutions refuse to participate in the National Survey of Student Engagement (NSSE) (Zemsky, 2009: 86), which measures the conditions that promote positive educational outcomes. Since these institutions are regarded as the highest quality institutions, they have nothing to gain by first discovering problems (the principal/agent problem in Chapter 4) and secondly revealing quality information to the public (reputation competition in Chapter 3).

1.4   HOW DO WE KNOW COSTS ARE "TOO HIGH"?

Since 1980, annual increases in tuition and fees at public and private four year institutions have been at rates considerably faster than the general inflation rate and the inflation rate in the service sector, and on a par with the rate of increase in health care costs. This trend is also true for the net price of attendance.[9] Each fall one can count on multiple popular press articles about the high and increasing cost of college. The fall of 2009 was no exception, even though the economy was in "the worst recession since the Great Depression." Tuition and fees at public four year institutions increased by 6.5 percent for the academic year 2009–10, while tuition and fees at private four year institutions increased by 4.4 percent (College Board, 2009). It is noteworthy that the consumer price index *decreased* by 1.2 percent during this period. Hence, while the rest of the economy was busy laying off workers and cutting prices, higher education was raising its prices. Further, the real increase in public tuition and fees was approximately 7.7 percent and the real increase in private tuition and fees was 5.6 percent. The lower percentage for private institutions does not mean they behave more responsibly, since average tuition and fees for private institutions is almost four times as high as those of public institutions. For every dollar public institutions raised their tuition, private institutions increased their tuition by almost three dollars.

Increasing Demand

The difference in median incomes for the high income quartile and the low income quartile represents the expected return one could obtain by following labor market signals. Following labor market signals creates economic mobility. In order to follow the path to higher incomes, one must acquire marketable skills. If there are no barriers and the path to higher income is open, the gap between high and low income groups will close and there will be a steady rise in real incomes across the entire income distribution. When the demand for skilled labor increases, the gap rises, and when people respond by acquiring the skills, the gap contracts. For the past three decades, the income distribution has continued to widen. The persistence of that gap is troublesome.

Higher education is a critical bottleneck on the path to marketable skills. The successful participant in the knowledge economy must go to college. The fact that the real cost of college has increased dramatically over the last three decades, during the same time that the gap between high and low income families increased, suggests the cost of college is a barrier to economic mobility (Furchtgott-Roth et al., 2009).

Some argue increases in real cost per student are due to increased demand for higher education (Clotfelter et al., 1991). The increase in demand comes from higher returns on investment in education (Brewer et al., 1999; Ehrenberg, 1989). This is a "derived demand" argument. However, increases in demand do not necessarily raise price;[10] the outcome depends on competitive conditions on the supply side. Since monopolies create artificial shortages, an increase in demand in a monopolistic industry will increase the cost of the service. Similarly, if the industry is a competitive increasing cost industry, an increase in demand will increase the cost of the service. Alternatively, if the industry is a constant or decreasing cost competitive industry (like the electronics industries), an increase in demand will not change or it will decrease the cost of the service.

If higher education is a competitive industry, its cost history reveals it must be an increasing cost industry with a steeply rising long run supply curve. Since higher education has the worst cost control record in the economy, there have to be very powerful factors causing industry-wide costs to rise the way they have over the past three decades.

Whether a competitive industry has increasing, constant, or decreasing cost depends on how industry output affects its resource costs. If increased output drives up the cost of raw materials or labor, then it will be an increasing cost industry. Ph.D. faculty members are the only resource unique to higher education;[11] the other resources employed by higher education come from resource markets shared with the rest of the economy. If higher education is a uniquely high increasing cost industry, the effect of increasing industry demand has to work through faculty labor markets.

The market for tenure track faculty varies considerably by discipline. The market for faculty in medicine, engineering, and the hard sciences remains tight, while there has been chronic and periodic excess supply of new Ph.D.s in the market for some sciences, the social sciences, and the humanities (Ehrenberg, 2002, 2004). There is chronic excess supply in the humanities and periodic excess supply in some sciences and economics. The personal cost of chronic excess supply of humanities Ph.D.s is discussed by Benton (2010), where he describes graduate school in the humanities as a "poverty trap." Despite expectations that academic labor markets would lead to faculty shortages, this has not happened. As colleges and universities substituted instructors and adjunct faculty for tenure track faculty and as the number of foreign graduate students increased dramatically, the market for tenure track faculty has been in balance or excess supply. These labor market conditions are inconsistent with the notion that higher education is a competitive increasing cost industry.

Alternatively, higher education may be monopolistic. If higher education is monopolistic, supply will be inelastic and increases in demand will cause rapidly rising cost with little increase in output. Consider the history of the elite institutions. Over the past 50 years the U.S. population has grown significantly and along with that growth the number of really gifted students has also grown in number. Further, U.S. higher education's access to the international market for gifted students grew steadily. Despite the obvious increase in gifted students the elite institutions did not expand their enrollment significantly; instead, they took the opportunity to become even more selective, which further increased their market power (Hoxby, 2009). That is not behavior characteristic of a competitive enterprise.

Reservation Prices

Robert Zemsky, among others in higher education,[12] argues that the college cost problem is exaggerated, stating in an article in the *Chronicle of Higher Education* about his service on the Spellings Commission,

> Some of what I was hearing while serving on the commission I already knew a lot about. I had already pretty much concluded that the argument over higher education's affordability was something of a sham. Given the continuing growth in college enrollments, it is pretty hard to argue that a college education has become increasingly unaffordable. Expensive, yes, perhaps even too expensive, but not on the evidence unaffordable. (2007: B6)

Zemsky repeats this argument in *Making Reform Work: The Case for Transforming American Higher Education*, where he states,

> When something is unaffordable it means it won't be purchased. Health insurance – and with it access to health care – is now unaffordable for a large and growing number of American families. We know that to be the case because an increasing number of American families do not have health insurance. That seemingly is not the case for American higher education, given that in most years enrollments have continued to rise even as have the prices students are expected to pay. (2009: 111)

Zemsky's argument is college costs are "too high" only when students refuse to go to college.

Zemsky argues higher education is affordable since college enrollment is increasing, while health insurance is unaffordable because the number of people without insurance is increasing. Is the criterion for "affordability" the number of people who continue to purchase the service despite the higher cost or is the criterion the number of people who are rationed out of the market due to higher cost? The number of people with health insurance has continued to increase just as has the number of people attending college, and the number of people going without health insurance has increased just as has the number not completing college because of higher cost. There is no difference between higher education and health care in this respect.

From 2007 to 2008, the number of people with health insurance increased by 1.7 million, while the number without insurance increased by 0.7 million, and the proportion without insurance held steady at about 15.4 percent (De Navas-Wall et al., 2009). As the data in Chapter 2 reveal, total enrollment in higher education has increased, while five year college completion rates have declined (Bound et al., 2009). The objective data reveal that increasing numbers of people purchase both health insurance and higher education services each year. However, the number of people going without these services also increases each year.

Professor Zemsky's assertion that college costs are not "too high" if people continue to attend college is incorrect by virtue of objective evidence and it is conceptually wrong as well. The argument ignores "reservation prices," "competitive prices," and wealth transfers: Costs are "too high" because they transfer wealth from students, parents, taxpayers, and donors to members of the higher education establishment. Further, wealth transfers expropriate the benefits students should retain from the acquisition of marketable skills; this monopolistic expropriation reduces economic mobility. As a consequence, students have less financial incentive to invest in knowledge precisely at the time when global labor markets favor

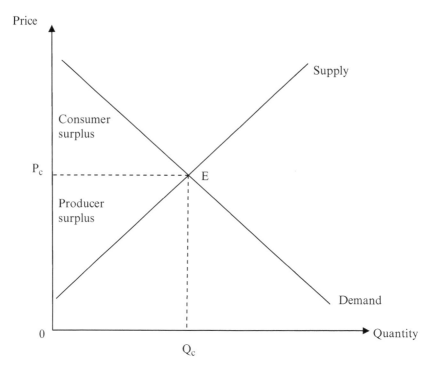

Figure 1.1   Reservation prices

knowledge workers at the expense of unskilled labor. Less investment in human capital reduces economic mobility and contributes to a persistent widening in the income distribution[13] (Mehta, 2000). Higher college costs are a barrier in the path to economic mobility.

The consumer's reservation price is the highest price he is willing to pay for that service. The consumer does not refuse to purchase the service until the price exceeds his reservation price. Alternatively, the competitive price is the price that would be charged by a competitive industry for that output/quality combination.

As in Figure 1.1, the market demand curve is a schedule of reservation prices, where the consumer with the highest reservation price is the first point on the demand curve, followed by consumers with successively lower reservation prices. Similarly, the market supply curve is a schedule of the producers' reservation supply prices, the lowest price producers are willing to take for the quantity supplied. The market price is established by the intersection of the market supply curve and the market demand curve. The market equilibrium creates consumer and producer surpluses since consumers pay the competitive price that is below their reservation price and producers receive a price greater than their reservation supply price. Thus, competitive market transactions are not a zero sum game; consumers and producers simultaneously benefit from the transaction.

The competitive solution reveals a financial incentive to monopolize the market. Assume ownership of all the firms is transferred to a single owner who knows each consumer's reservation price. Nothing real has changed thus far; the only thing that has happened is all legal titles have been transferred to a single person, the new monopolist. Since the new monopolist knows each consumer's reservation price, he moves down the market demand curve selling each consumer one unit at the consumer's reservation price. This price discriminating monopolist chooses the same output[14] level as the competitive firms. Since nothing has changed but the legal title, cost is the same. The difference is in the monopolist's revenue versus the competitive industry's revenue: The monopolist's revenue equals the area under the demand curve up to the output level, while the competitive industry's aggregate revenue equaled the competitive price times the same output. Hence, the price discriminator earns monopoly rents that are not available to the competitive firms and he does this by capturing the entire consumer surplus. Note also that the monopolist has converted what was a mutually beneficial exchange into a zero sum game: only the monopolist benefits.

None of the consumers refuse to purchase the product because the price equals their reservation price. Therefore the fact that consumers continue to purchase the product implies only that the price is less than or equal to their reservation price; it tells us nothing about whether or not the price is "too high." The price is "too high" when the average price charged all consumers exceeds the competitive price, which it assuredly does when the monopolist exploits the consumers' willingness to pay.

In 2000 the proportion of those polled who think higher education is essential for personal success was 31 percent; in 2009 that proportion was 55 percent (Immerwahr and Johnson, 2010: 4). This is a significant shift in the perceived importance of higher education for a nine year period. Reservation prices and the perceived importance of a college degree are positively related. The more a person believes success depends on a college education, the higher their reservation price will be. Higher reservation prices mean increased willingness to pay for college and a higher financial gain for colleges and universities who exploit willingness and ability to pay. A college or university's market power increases the more success depends on advanced education.

Monopoly power leads to wealth transfers from consumers to the monopolist in the form of prices that exceed the competitive price. These monopoly transfers were the source of dynastic wealth accumulations in the railroad, banking, oil, and steel trusts of the late 1800s, and those wealth transfers led to U.S. antitrust laws, beginning with the Sherman Antitrust Act of 1890. Consumers did not refuse to ride railroads, consume oil, use steel, or patronize banks during that period, although it was clear to the public the prices charged by trusts were "too high." Public policy is supposed to protect consumers from monopoly wealth transfers. It should not matter whether the transfers arise among for-profit firms or nonprofit firms like higher education.

1.5 TRADITIONAL EXPLANATIONS FOR RISING COST IN HIGHER EDUCATION

Getz and Siegfried (1991: 263–8) identify six explanations for higher cost in colleges and universities, while Breneman (1996) argues there are two competing theories that explain cost increases in higher education. In this section, I explain why Breneman's two theories of cost are not competing theories and why Getz and Siegfried's six theories are in fact just Breneman's two cost theories plus two additional theories that cause costs to rise in higher education. The four theories are noncompeting in the sense they all cause costs to be higher; the existence of one does not preclude the existence of the other. It should be no surprise that something as complex as higher education costs cannot be explained by a single theory or cause. Multiple factors drive costs higher.

Breneman identifies "Baumol's cost disease" and "Bowen's revenue theory of cost" as the two "competing cost theories" (1996). Baumol's cost disease was first applied to the arts as an explanation for why costs rise even though productivity does not increase in the arts (Baumol and Bowen, 1966). Traditional labor theory suggests real wages should rise only as fast as labor productivity rises, while in fact real wages rise in the arts while productivity does not change. Note that Baumol's attention was drawn to what is in fact an anomaly in the arts and in higher education (the disconnection between pay and productivity). Baumol argues that opportunity wages for those employed in the arts increase because productivity is rising in the rest of the economy where they could be working if they were not working in the arts. Therefore real wages rise in the arts, despite the lack of increased productivity, since the opportunity wage is always rising. The same argument can be made for faculty salaries in higher education.

In addition, Baumol explains why productivity does not increase in the arts and higher education. He argues production technologies in the arts and education are characterized by fixed proportions; a string quartet requires four musicians and each classroom requires one professor. The fixed proportions production technology is thought to limit productivity increases, since it means input substitution is not possible.

The cost disease argument makes considerable sense when applied to some faculty salaries. Medical, legal, engineering, and business school faculty members have ample employment opportunities outside of higher education. If they choose to become faculty members they forgo higher incomes. As this opportunity cost increases, colleges and universities must pay higher wages to attract and retain faculty. The argument seems weak when applied to faculty in the humanities and the arts.

Baumol's argument explains why real wages rise while productivity does not; but it seems incongruous we would find real wages rising while productivity is declining (as the data in Chapter 2 reveal is the case). It is particularly incongruous since administrators and trustees chose to reduce teaching productivity over the past three decades; they reduced student/faculty ratios and teaching loads. Why would they choose to lower productivity while raising real wages? The cost disease argument does not explain why cost increases in higher education have significantly outpaced cost increases in the rest of the service sector (which experiences similar productivity and technology issues) or why they have outpaced health care cost increases.

Since Baumol formulated this hypothesis in the 1960s there have been significant unforeseen technological developments that increased service productivity. Triplett and Bosworth (2003) provide evidence that service industry productivity increased substantially after 1995 owing to IT investments and improvements in multi-factor productivity (network effects). The improvement was sufficient for them to declare "Baumol's disease has been cured" (2003: 23). The argument that higher education is a victim of productivity improvements by others is unlikely to be the whole story.

H.R. Bowen's revenue theory of cost is derived from higher education's nonprofit status (1980). In order to survive, all nonprofits must balance their budgets; chronic unfunded deficits lead to extinction. On the other hand, nonprofits exist in order to provide as many services as possible to their clients or, in the case of education, their students. Therefore nonprofits spend all the money they have and expenditures are capped by the nonprofits' revenues. As a result, any increase in revenue leads to an increase in cost, and costs are driven by revenues.

Getz and Siegfried identify six reasons for higher cost:

1. Competition forces colleges and universities to add services beyond education that students demand.

2. Rising opportunity costs for resources cause colleges and universities to pay more for the resources they use.
3. There are very limited opportunities to substitute one resource for another in higher education.
4. The "leading position" of faculty members and administrators causes them to emphasize quality beyond what would be offered in a for-profit environment.
5. Colleges and universities do not minimize costs because of weak management and governance that does not emphasize cost control.
6. Government mandates[15] higher cost through regulation (1991: 263–8).

Reason number 1 reflects rising student demand for luxury living conditions, better food, more entertainment, and expensive overseas programs. In the past, dormitory conditions were basic, the food was institutional, students provided their own entertainment, and students traveled overseas at their own expense. These services are now bundled with the "college experience" and they have undoubtedly contributed to rising cost, although it is not clear the public interest is being served by "bundling" these services.[16] The bundled services provide significant benefits to faculty members and administrators in the form of food, travel, and entertainment.

Getz and Siegfried also argue the shift away from majors in arts and sciences toward majors in business and engineering from 1970 to 1985 contributed to cost increases. This does represent a shift in student preferences, but it raises the question why such shifts in consumer preferences, which happen all the time, do not cause similar increases in costs among for-profit firms. Why did colleges and universities not reallocate resources when student preferences changed?

Getz and Siegfried's reasons 2 and 3 are in fact Baumol's cost disease. Rising opportunity wages and fixed proportions production cause costs to rise in industries with little productivity improvement. Baumol uses string quartets as an example of fixed proportions production and the limitations on substituting say capital for labor. If "capital deepening"[17] were possible in the arts and education, then productivity would rise and real costs would not necessarily increase. Baumol's string quartet argument is restricted to live performances and that may be misleading. As he notes, travel technology makes it possible for the same four musicians to increase the number of performances per period (Baumol and Batey-Blackman, 1995: 5); but it is also clear that technical progress in digital recording, broadcasting, and virtual technologies increases the quartet's output substantially and increases their potential rewards accordingly. The same applies to education technology: the potential for capital deepening in education is unlimited, including virtual instructors who eliminate the need for faculty. Rather than a limit on resource substitution in higher education, a more appropriate question might be why do faculty members resist capital deepening? Is this a Luddite response?[18]

Getz and Siegfried's reasons 4 and 5 are H.R. Bowen's revenue theory of cost. Bowen's revenue theory of cost is due to the intersection of non-profit status, the principal/agent problem,[19] and the theory of experience goods.[20] Reason 4 concerns the dominant position that faculty members and administrators hold in campus governance. The dominant governance position allows them to direct resources to activities that serve their individual interests, which is the principal/agent problem. Reason 5 is also a principal/agent issue. Colleges and universities do not minimize costs or pay effective attention to cost control because it is not in the agents' interest to do so.

1.6   BOWEN'S REVENUE THEORY OF COST

H.R. Bowen summarizes the revenue theory of cost as follows:

> Colleges and universities have no strong incentive to cut costs in quest of profits because they do not seek profit. They are not forced by competition to lower costs in order to survive. This is so partly because they are subsidized by government and philanthropy and partly because they are shielded from competition by geographic location and by differentiation of services. It is so also because institutions know little about the relationship between their expenditures and their educational outcomes, and it is easy to drift into the comfortable belief that increased expenditures will automatically produce commensurately greater outcomes. Under these conditions, the unit costs of operating colleges or universities are set more largely by the amount of money institutions are able to raise per unit of service rendered than by the inherent technical requirements of conducting their work. Within wide limits, institutions can adjust to whatever amount of money they are able to raise. When resources are increased, they find uses for the new funds, and unit costs go up. When resources are decreased, they express keen regret and they protest, but in the end they accept the inevitable, and unit costs go down. This set of generalizations might be called the *revenue theory of cost*. (1980: 15)

The absence of a profit maximization incentive, the existence of subsidies from third party contributors, limited competition, and an unexplored connection between expenditures and outcomes lead to expenditures following revenues and a failure to minimize costs.

Bowen identifies five "laws" of higher education cost:

1. "The dominant goals of institutions are educational excellence, prestige, and influence."

2. In the pursuit of these objectives, "there is virtually no limit to the amount of money an institution could spend for seemingly fruitful educational ends."
3. "Each institution raises all the money it can."
4. "Each institution spends all it raises."
5. "The cumulative effect of the preceding four laws is toward ever increasing expenditure" (1980: 19–20).

Institutions measure excellence by the quality of the inputs, such as the quality of the students and faculty, while the relationship between these inputs and the output is unexamined and vague. The pursuit of excellence means institutions always need more money; even the rich institutions never have enough money. Bowen notes that fundamental questions like "what is the minimal amount needed to provide services of acceptable quality" do not get asked (1980: 20).

In the end, Bowen identifies three major findings:

1. There is a wide variance in cost per student among institutions, even within groups of similar institutions.
2. There is a wide variance in the allocation of resources across academic programs, where the "data give the impression of almost centrifugal randomness."
3. It is very hard to connect expenditures with value added (1980: 227–8).

If higher education institutions were minimizing costs according to a defined education technology, we would observe a clustering of cost per student around a mode that represents that technology. If expenditures are allocated according to a standard academic model, we would expect to see a consistent set of academic programs and a consistent distribution of resources across academic programs. Finally, if institutions minimize costs according to a production technology, it would be easier to connect expenditures to value added.

Bowen's three major findings are a puzzle. There is a studied lack of uniformity among similar institutions in terms of program offerings, staffing within the same programs across institutions, student services, amenities, and public service activities. This "centrifugal randomness" suggests a defined education technology is not being followed.

In order to understand this outcome, consider Figure 1.2. The set of possible activities the institution may engage in are represented by the different slices in the pie chart. Assume the institution is at the center of the pie chart contemplating the different activities where it can apply its resources. The institution can, at the same time, go in as many or as few

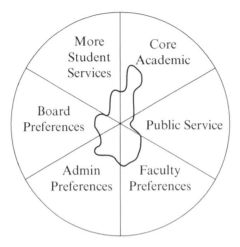

Figure 1.2   Activities

directions as it chooses. Beyond the core academic activities (teaching/research), it can choose public service activities, offer new entertainment, food, or accommodation services to students, pursue pet projects proposed by the board, undertake projects that enhance administrators' careers, or pursue personal interests favored by faculty members.

The for-profit firm would expand exclusively into "core academic" activities since that is the least cost course of action. For-profit firms focus on their core competencies in order to be as competitive as possible. The profit maximizing solution leads to a well defined production technology where expenditures are connected to value added.

The nonprofit higher education institution with shared governance expands its activities in multiple directions. Further, each institution chooses a different combination of activities based on different preferences and different political strengths between trustees, administrators, and faculty members. Ex post, the border of each institution across these multiple activities is different; the irregular shape in Figure 1.2 represents the border of one institution. The different border and different combination of activities creates the "centrifugal randomness" Bowen observed in costs and resource allocations. The border of each institution is a historical accident due to prior distributions of personalities and political influence among faculty members, administrators, and trustees.

Note that Bowen's description of the revenue theory of cost is an empirical description of what happens; it is not a true behavioral theory of cost. For example, what is it about the economics of higher education that makes reputations so important? Why does a commonly accepted model of higher education technology not exist? Why do higher education institutions habitually "know little about the relationship between their expenditures and their educational outcomes," a statement that is as valid today as it was in 1980 (1980: 15)? Why do higher education institutions not apply cost/benefit analysis to select the best programs from a portfolio of options? Why do colleges and universities rarely subject new programs to a detailed forensic audit to determine how well the program works? Since the purpose of higher education is to ask questions and to learn about the world around us, why have higher education institutions been so unwilling to ask penetrating questions about their own institutions? Why the studied lack of curiosity when it comes to our own house?

1.7   SUBSEQUENT CHAPTERS

In the chapters that follow, I provide a behavioral foundation for Bowen's revenue theory of cost. The foundation is based on the intersection of nonprofit status, the principal/agent problem, and the theory of experience goods. Chapter 2 contains a simple algebraic model of faculty teaching productivity and an empirical analysis of higher education productivity, cost, financial burden, and quality over the last three decades. The data reveal teaching productivity steadily declined, real faculty wages increased, real cost per student rose, the financial burden on society increased, and teaching quality declined.

As faculty teaching productivity declined, real wages increased until 1970, declined for a decade, and then began a steady rise after 1980. Real cost per student followed the same historical pattern. It is curious to note that grade inflation followed the same historical pattern: rising until 1970, declining during the 1970s, and then rising after 1980. Further, Harry Lewis reports the same pattern in the proportion of Harvard's undergraduates on the Dean's list (2006: 110). Higher faculty salaries are associated with worse grade inflation?

The theory of experience goods is explored in Chapter 3. This literature reveals that reputations matter only when customers are uncertain about quality before they purchase the service; the more uncertain they are the more important reputations become. The efficiency with which reputations resolve the information problem depends on frequent purchase, easy determination of quality after purchase, and easy shift to alternative providers if the provider cheats on quality. Higher education services are purchased once, they are notoriously difficult to evaluate, and it is costly to shift to other providers. Quality cheating is always an issue in experience goods markets. Providers have an incentive not to disclose quality. Entry is expensive and it can take a very long time to establish a reputation as a high quality provider. Consumers associate cost with quality (the Chivas Regal effect), which sets in motion the race to spend more per student in order to build reputation.

The relationship between nonprofit status and the principal/agent problem is explored in Chapter 4. Nonprofit status caps expenditures with revenues causing the revenue-to-cost spiral that plagues higher education. The principal/agent problem is universal; it is common in politics, for-profit firms, medicine, the law, and education. There are numerous constraints on the principal/agent problem in for-profit firms and negligible constraints on the principal/agent problem in higher education. The principal/agent problem results in costs that are higher than necessary, and higher education has a dismal cost control record. The principal/agent problem and nonprofit status lead to a separation between productivity and pay and cause cost per student to rise even though higher education may have considerable economies of scale and scope.

The extensive literature on "commercialization" or "corporatization" is considered in Chapter 5. This literature argues the pursuit of self-interest observed on many campuses is due to an alien corporate influence. In fact, the pursuit of self-interest is simple agency abuse, discussed in Chapter 4. The corporate model leads to low real cost and significant improvements in product quality. If higher education was taken over by corporations after 1980, why would real cost per student explode and quality decline? The real "alien influence" on campus is the public relations model. It is the public relations mindset that causes colleges and universities to ignore costs, raise all the money they can, and carefully manage their reputations. The problems we see come from the campuses; they are not imposed on higher education from the outside.

The missing market for senior college teachers is considered in Chapter 6. The market does not exist because colleges and universities do not explore the relationship between their programs and results. From Chapter 3 we learned why institutions prefer to compete on the basis of reputations rather than teaching value added per dollar spent. Since information about teaching productivity does not exist, colleges and universities do not make employment offers to senior faculty based on teaching. A vigorous market for senior scholars exists because scholarly productivity is readily observed. The anomaly here is that the public (who pays for higher education) is indifferent to scholarly output and most concerned about teaching productivity. The absence of a rewarding teaching career path creates numerous adverse incentives in higher education.

The working parts in earlier chapters are brought together in Chapter

7. Interactions between reputation competition, nonprofit status, the principal/agent problem, the missing market for senior teachers, and public relations are explored.

Information problems are a consistent theme throughout this book. There are two types of information deficits: The first is the information needed to constrain agency problems and the second is information about teaching value added. Principals cannot constrain agency abuse without the information needed to monitor agents' actions. There is considerable financial information available. The missing information concerns the history of nonteaching professional staffing patterns, nonteaching professional staff salaries, the history of faculty teaching loads, and the history of total contact hours per class per semester.

The second information problem concerns measures of teaching value added. There are two subcategories in teaching value added: measures that allow prospective students and parents to compare one institution with another and measures that are sufficient to establish a market for tenured senior teachers. Insiders will insist that measures of teaching value added need to be near perfect. A careful consideration of perfection, efficiency, and the information sufficient to establish a vigorous market for senior scholars reveals teaching productivity measures do not have to be perfect in order to be efficient.

Other topics considered in Chapter 7 are the role new technology can play in resolving the foregoing information problems and the critical role that elite institutions should play in higher education reform. It is argued that e-technology and the web can provide the critical teaching value added information and that reform is most likely to succeed if the elite institutions take the lead.

NOTES

1. This perception is consistent with the empirical evidence (Martin, 2005; NCPPHE, 2008).
2. For example, see Bok (2003, 2006), Hersh and Merrow (2005), Kirp (2003), and Massy (2003).
3. This result is surprising since private institutions do not receive as much public support as public institutions, they are not government institutions, and they sell their services directly in the market for private higher education. As they are closer to the market and not subject to as much government oversight, one would expect they would be more efficient than the public institutions. The cost per student record does not support this, however. It suggests more government oversight leads to better cost control. On the other hand, my limited personal sample suggests private institutions have fewer issues with teaching quality.
4. It is likely research marginal cost exceeds marginal benefit in many disciplines (Bauerlein, 2009). On the other hand, this is not likely to be the case in medicine,

engineering, and the hard sciences. Indeed, the research output of those disciplines is the source of our reputation for world class higher education institutions.

5. Wikipedia.
6. Modern capital markets depend on trust, or faith that money invested in the financial instruments traded on these exchanges has a reasonable probability of being recovered with a positive return at some future date. Anything that damages that trust lowers the value of the assets traded. When there is no rule of law, no respect for property rights, and no trust managers will take decisions in the shareholders' interest, capital markets collapse or cannot be formed.
7. This is not meant to diminish the social value of most research. It simply reflects the fact that, if you asked parents and taxpayers which is more important, teaching or research, most would say teaching is the more important.
8. The distribution has two separate peaks.
9. The net price of attendance is the total cost of attendance less scholarships and grants awarded to the average student.
10. As we will see in Chapter 6, the vigorous derived demand for high quality teaching has not increased the wages paid to senior teachers.
11. Note also that the higher education industry supplies its own unique resource through graduate education.
12. Some argue higher education costs rise because the return to marketable skills is high; so the reward to factors that produce those skills is high. The efficient theory of derived demand for factors that produce marketable skills assumes those factors are competitively supplied; they are not supplied competitively in higher education.
13. Mehta considers the relationship between secular changes in education quality and the income distribution. He finds that "increasing overall educational achievement is linked to increasing equality and growth in the primary sector, while falling educational achievement is linked to decreasing equality and growth in the secondary sector" (2000: 253).
14. As the monopolist moves down the demand curve, the marginal revenue he receives is the incremental consumer's reservation price. So marginal revenue is equal to marginal cost where the supply curve cuts the demand curve and profits are maximized at that point.
15. Government mandates are unlikely to play a significant role in the history of higher education cost increases since the government has not routinely added new mandates each year. Title IX stepped costs up when it became law, as did disability mandates, but we see a continuous increase in costs in the record.
16. Bundling food, housing, travel, and entertainment is similar to cable television bundling its channel offerings. Customers wind up paying for services they do not want and their choice is limited. Further, bundling by higher education is the opposite of "privatizing" government activities.
17. Capital deepening means giving workers more and/or higher quality tools to work with.
18. During the industrial revolution, workers responded violently to the introduction of machinery that reduced the demand for labor in the short run but increased labor productivity causing real wages to rise in the long run; factories were burned and machinery was destroyed. This myopic reaction has since been known as a Luddite response after the man who organized the workers.
19. The principal/agent problem arises when agents take decisions in their own interest rather than acting in their principal's interest. The principal/agent problem occurs everywhere: politics, business, medicine, the law, and education.
20. An experience good is a good whose quality cannot be determined until after it has been purchased. Reputations are the dominant means of competition in experience good markets; indeed, reputations are irrelevant unless consumers are uncertain about quality prior to purchase.

2. Statistical measures: teaching productivity, cost, financial burden, and quality

2.1 INTRODUCTION

This chapter contains descriptive statistics designed to establish a context for the cost and quality issues considered in the book. First, however, it is important to understand how administrative decisions regarding student/staffing ratios, average class sizes, and teaching loads directly affect cost per student and teaching quality. To this end, the simple algebra in this chapter makes the connection between administrative decisions and cost per student. In each case, I demonstrate what the algebra suggests will happen to productivity/cost as student/staffing ratios, average class sizes, or teaching loads change. Then, I use data from the National Center for Education Statistics (NCES) to confirm that, as colleges and universities lowered the student/faculty ratio, class size, and teaching loads, productivity declined and cost per student rose.

2.2 THE COST/QUALITY ISSUE

Higher education costs rose more rapidly than costs in any other sector of the economy, including health care, from 1980 to the present. If teaching quality and cost rose together, there would be less concern about this issue. The evidence suggests teaching quality actually declined, however. Technical progress in health care has been remarkable: new diagnostic procedures, less invasive treatments, and more effective treatments saved many lives. Unfortunately, technical progress in health care means higher cost as quality improves. This is not true for higher education for two reasons: innovation in higher education is very slow and quality is declining as costs rise. Thus, college cost is a serious policy concern. It appears students, parents, taxpayers, and donors are paying more for less.

For the last three decades tuition growth exceeded both the inflation rate and the rate of growth in median household incomes. As a consequence, the real burden imposed on students, families, taxpayers, and donors who support higher education increased steadily from 1980 to the present. Further, students graduate with record debt levels and those with majors that have limited income prospects are particularly burdened by this debt.

The burdens imposed by higher cost are part of the annual fall lament concerning tuition and fees (Wang, 2008). It is no surprise that surveys reveal the public thinks college costs too much (Crawford, 2003) and those perceptions are validated by several commission reports. The higher education cost issue is very well documented.

In 1997 the Council for Aid to Higher Education described the cost control issue as a fiscal crisis in higher education access. The National Commission on the Cost of Higher Education stated: "continued inattention to issues of cost and price threaten to create a gulf of ill will between institutions of higher education and the larger society" (1998: 1). Reports with similar themes come from the Lumina Foundation (Kipp et al., 2002), the U.S. House Committee on Education and the Workforce (Boehner and McKeon, 2003) and recently the National Center for Public Policy and Higher Education (NCPPHE) (2008). The NCPPHE report gave every state, except California, an "F" in affordability.

Data from the NCES reveal that the growth rate in higher education cost exceeds the growth rate in both service sector prices and health care cost (Martin, 2005; NCPPHE, 2008). Higher education has the worst cost-control record of any sector in the economy. The inability to control costs imperils low income college access and leaves those who find the means to go to college with record debt burdens after they graduate. The college access problem can never be solved without first solving the chronic college cost problem. No amount of money will solve the access problem without solving the cost problem first. In fact, more money just makes costs rise faster.

2.3 THE HISTORY OF PUBLIC/PRIVATE MARKET SHARE

Higher education services are provided by state sponsored public institutions, private nonprofit institutions, and a small but growing number of for-profit private institutions. In this book, I focus on public institutions and private nonprofit institutions. The public and private institutions are sufficiently different in terms of financing, scale, and governance that they should be considered separately. In the analysis that follows, results are reported for public and private institutions separately, wherever possible.

Figure 2.1 contains total enrollment in public and private institutions from 1947 through 2007. Beginning in the late 1950s public sector

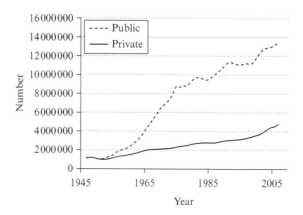

Source: NCES, *Digest of Education Statistics*, 2008, Table 189.

Figure 2.1   Enrollment: 1947–2007

enrollment began to diverge from private sector enrollment. This divergence resulted in a declining market share for private sector institutions. In 1947 private institutions accounted for 51 percent of total enrollment. By 1974 the private institutions' market share had declined to 22 percent. Private market share remained in that range throughout the period from 1974 to 1995. Since 1995, the private institutions' market share has increased to 26 percent in 2007.

The growth in enrollment among private institutions appears to be smoother than the growth in public sector enrollment. There are declines in public enrollment in the 1970s, early 1980s, and early to mid-1990s that appear to coincide with adverse economic conditions. Alternatively, private sector enrollment does not seem to be as sensitive to economic conditions. The sensitivity of public sector enrollment to economic conditions is probably due to lower family incomes[1] on average for those attending public institutions as compared to those attending private institutions.

The following sections contain simple models of labor productivity (faculty, nonacademic professional staff, and nonprofessional staff). The analysis reveals the critical administrative decisions that determine productivity and the link between productivity and cost. The purpose of the simple algebraic models is to show the direct effect of administrative decisions regarding student/faculty ratios, teaching loads, class size, and student/staff ratios on cost per student. These simple models predict that lower student/staffing ratios, lower teaching loads, and smaller class sizes must mean increases in cost per student. The data section that accompanies these algebraic models documents the connection between lower productivity and higher cost, just as the algebraic models suggest. The analysis reveals that faculty productivity has declined, while real faculty salaries have increased, and this has contributed to the dramatic rise in real cost per student which began in 1980 and continues to this day. Traditional wage theory suggests real wages should increase as labor productivity increases; the fact that faculty real wages continue to increase as productivity declines is the anomaly Baumol sought to explain (Baumol and Bowen, 1966). Much more dramatic is the decline in nonacademic professional staff productivity, which has made a major contribution to rising cost.

While instructional wages and salaries account for about a third of total expenditures per student, that proportion has declined slightly during the period under consideration. This reveals two things: first, while real faculty salaries have increased, although productivity has declined, real faculty wages and salaries have not grown as fast as have real expenditures for other activities; and second, the dramatic decline in nonteaching professional staff productivity accounts for the other two-thirds of the real increase in cost per student. Colleges and universities are doing a lot more today than just teaching and they are doing it with more professional employees. The nonprofessional employee ratios (student to employee) have increased significantly, suggesting significant improvements in their productivity. Interestingly, the low pay afforded nonprofessional staff on college campuses is a common campus issue.

2.4 FACULTY AND STAFF TEACHING PRODUCTIVITY

Metrics

Average teaching productivity per academic year can be measured by the total number of students taught per representative faculty member each year. Individual and program teaching productivity can be measured by the same metric. While a rising student/faculty ratio makes faculty productivity increase and costs fall, many argue that quality declines as student/faculty ratios increase, particularly if average class size increases. Those who take this position assume there is a tradeoff between this productivity measure and quality. If they are correct, then the academy made a significant investment in higher quality from 1980 to the present. As we will see in the following sections, the student/faculty ratios in public and private institutions have been declining for the past three decades as costs have risen rapidly. Unfortunately, the objective measures of quality show no improvement in quality.

Let p_f be average faculty teaching productivity, e be enrollment, f be the number of faculty, and n be the average number of courses taken per student per year. Then

$$p_f = en/f. \tag{2.1}$$

Note that e/f is the student/faculty ratio. Further, the average number of courses taken per student per year, n, depends on curriculum decisions such as the total number of credit hours required for graduation and the proportion of part time and full time students. If the college reduces the number of hours required to graduate, productivity goes down. If a larger percentage of the students are part time, productivity goes down.

Average class size is frequently employed as a proxy for "quality," since some argue quality increases as class size goes down. Let c be average class size, a be average course load per faculty member, s_d be the total student demand for class section seats, and s_s be the total number of class sections supplied. Then

$$s_d = en,$$

$$s_s = fa,$$

and

$$c = s_d/s_s = en/fa.$$

From Equation 2.1, it follows that

$$c = p_f/a. \tag{2.2}$$

Average class size increases when faculty productivity increases and when the average course load per faculty member decreases. Alternatively, average class size declines when the number of courses required for graduation declines and when the number of part time students increases. In order to keep average class size constant, the institution has to increase the number of faculty when it reduces average teaching loads.[2] Even if enrollment does not increase, costs must rise if the institution reduces teaching loads while keeping average class size the same.

One can measure nonacademic professional staff and nonprofessional staff productivity by the ratio of the total number of students per year per staff member. This metric can be applied to different staff functions within the institution, such as student services, financial administration, development, admissions, janitorial workers, and clerical workers. The argument that the quality of staff service is reduced by a rising ratio is weak. The fixed proportions argument that is part of Baumol's cost theory does not apply to the relationship between students and professional staff. Indeed, since these are overhead functions, they should be characterized by variable proportions and increasing returns to scale; an efficient, cost conscious administration should have a record of rising student/staff ratios.

Let p_s be average staff productivity and s be the number of staff members; then

$$p_s = e/s, \tag{2.3}$$

where e/s is the student/staff ratio. Staff productivity increases as the student/staff ratio increases.

Data

All of the data reported in this chapter come from the NCES's *Digest of Education Statistics* and are readily available from their website. The average number of courses taken per student per year, n, plays a part in the faculty productivity measure. Potentially, productivity can change if n changes. Since n is the average number of courses taken per student per year, it represents the impact of curriculum decisions on productivity and cost. Class size and faculty productivity go up if n goes up; however, if the administration keeps class size and teaching loads constant, then the number of faculty members must go up as n increases.

Table 2.1 contains data from 1976 to 1993 for the median number of credit hours earned by students who graduated in four years. The table also contains data for different majors. The median number of credit hours is relatively constant over that period, which suggests the number of courses taken per year by those who graduated on time was also stable.

On the other hand, Figure 2.8 reveals the proportion of students graduating within five years declined by almost 9 percent at public institutions and by over 1 percent at private institutions during the period from 1988 to 2008. The decline in graduation rates could be due to students not finishing degrees or an increase in the number of students attending on a part time basis, owing to the higher cost associated with attending college. More part time students suggest the average number of classes taken per year, n, may have declined after 1980. If this is the case, then the student/faculty and student/staff ratios may underestimate the decline in productivity.

In 1970 the student/faculty ratio in public higher education institutions

Table 2.1   Credit hours for graduation

	1976	1984	1993
Mean, all majors	124.0	123.5	126.54
Business and management	124.4	122.8	123.86
Computer science	133.3	129.3	127.55
Education	126.4	127.4	126.80
Engineering	134.8	132.3	136.91
English	117.8	114.8	127.49
Fine arts	124.9	120.5	129.57
Life sciences	122.2	121.9	128.94
Physical sciences	122.7	124.3	129.14
Psychology	119.1	120.7	125.30
Social sciences	120.6	119.2	125.48

Source: NCES, *Digest of Education Statistics*, 2008, Table 314.

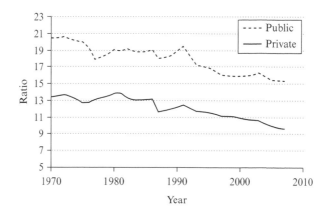

Source: NCES, *Digest of Education Statistics*, 2008, Tables 189 and 248.

Figure 2.2   Student/faculty ratios

was 20.5; by 2007 that number had fallen to 15.4, a 25 percent decline in faculty productivity. Similarly, the 1970 student/faculty ratio in private higher education was 13.5 and in 2007 it was 9.6, a 28 percent decline. Figure 2.2 contains the student/faculty ratios for both sectors over this period. The data reveal a slow decline in productivity that accelerated after 1980.

In 1976 the student/professional staff ratio in public higher education institutions was 44.8; by 2007 that number had fallen to 23.1, a 48 percent decline in productivity. Similarly, the 1976 student/staff ratio in private

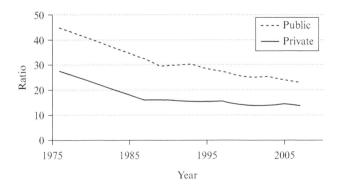

Source: NCES, *Digest of Education Statistics*, 2008, Tables 189, 243, and 244.

Figure 2.3   Student/nonacademic professional staff ratios

higher education was 27.2 and in 2007 it was 13.8, a 49 percent decline in productivity. Figure 2.3 contains the student/staff ratios for both sectors over this period. The data reveal an abrupt decline in productivity in the 1980s and that the decline in staff productivity was greater than the decline in faculty productivity.

In 1976 the student/nonprofessional staff ratio in public higher education institutions was 15.5; by 2007 that number had risen to 21.3, a 37 percent *increase* in productivity. Similarly, the 1976 student/nonprofessional staff ratio in private higher education was 10.2 and in 2007 it was 16, a 57 percent *increase* in productivity. The only higher education labor group that does not have a seat at the governance table is the one category where productivity increased during this period.

Productivity has declined in both public and private institutions and that decline is most pronounced among nonacademic professional staff categories. Productivity increased among nonprofessional staff workers. Interestingly, most of the faculty and professional staff productivity *decline* occurred after 1980, while most of the nonprofessional staff productivity *increase* also occurred after 1980.

2.5   COST PER STUDENT

Metrics

Higher education is labor intensive and faculty members are one of the more expensive labor components. A measure of faculty labor costs can be obtained by calculating the faculty wage and salary cost per student. Let w be the average salary per faculty member, W be the total expenditure for faculty wages and x_f be annual faculty wages per student. Then

$$W = wf$$

and

$$x_f = W/e = w/(e/f). \qquad (2.4)$$

The annual faculty wage cost per student increases as the student/faculty ratio declines. As expected, the faculty component of cost per student increases as faculty productivity declines. The critical policy decisions that drive faculty cost per student are average class size (c), average teaching load (a), and average faculty salary (w). When colleges/universities reduce class sizes, reduce teaching loads, and raise faculty salaries, cost per student must rise.

A similar relationship exists between cost per student net of faculty wage cost per student and professional/nonprofessional staff productivity. As staff productivity declines, other costs per student rise. If x is total cost per student, then overhead or staff cost per student, say x_s, is

$$x_s = x - x_f. \qquad (2.5)$$

We expect to find that x_s increases as p_s in Equation 2.3 declines. Given the sharp drop in professional staff productivity in the 1980s, there should be a sharp rise in non-faculty cost per student following that period.

Data

Equation 2.4 reveals that faculty wage cost per student increases as average faculty salaries increase and increases as faculty productivity declines (measured by the student/faculty ratios in Figure 2.2). Figure 2.4 contains real faculty wage rates for both public and private institutions. In both cases, real faculty wages declined during the 1970s and rose dramatically after 1980. The rise in real wages and the decline in productivity suggest faculty wage cost per student should rise sharply after 1980.

Figure 2.5 contains real faculty wage cost per student from 1971 to 2007. The real cost per student at public institutions rose from $3258 in 1971 to $4327 in 2007, a 33 percent increase. The real cost per student at private institutions rose from $4427 in 1971 to $7624 in 2007, a 72 percent increase. In Figure 2.5 note the decline in real faculty wage cost during

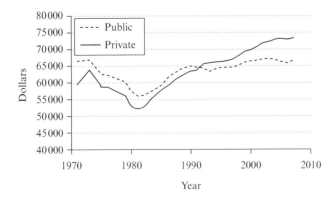

Source: NCES, *Digest of Education Statistics*, 2008, Table 257.

Figure 2.4   *Real faculty salaries*

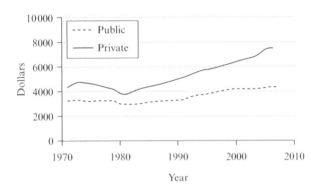

Source: NCES, *Digest of Education Statistics*, 2008, Tables 189, 257, and 248.

Figure 2.5   *Real faculty salary expense per student*

the 1970s and the steep rise after 1980 among private institutions. In both sectors, the rising real cost per student is consistent with declining productivity measured by the student/faculty ratios in Figure 2.2 and the rising real wage rates in Figure 2.4.

Equation 2.5 suggests that a substantial part of cost per student net of faculty wage costs depends on staff productivity and wages paid to staff members. Unlike the case for faculty members, there is little information available on staff salaries, even though they constitute the majority of campus employment. We know that professional staff productivity over the period under study has declined significantly, while nonprofessional staff productivity has increased. Since the number of professional staff outnumbers that of the nonprofessional staff and their salaries are higher, we expect the declining professional staff productivity to drive cost per student net of faculty wage cost higher over our study period.

During the period from 1970 to 1999, public colleges and universities increased real expenditures per student by $4253. Over the same period, faculty real wage expense per student increased by $914, or 22 percent of the total increase in expenditures per student. From 1970 to 1995, the last year expenditure data for private institutions is available, the private institutions increased real expenditures by $9577. The private institutions' real faculty wage expense per student increased by $1310, or 14 percent of the total increase in expenditures per student. Seventy-eight percent of the public sector increase in real expenditure per student came from activities other than faculty compensation, while 86 percent of the private sector increase came from activities other than faculty compensation.

2.6   STAFFING PATTERNS AND GOVERNANCE

Campus governance is shared by faculty members, administrators, and staff. Among faculty members, only full time faculty members have a seat at the governance table. Part time faculty members are "academic gypsies" who scramble between campuses, most frequently without benefits, in order to make a living. Further, full time non-tenure track faculty members (instructors) have less influence on governance than do tenure track faculty members; in 1992, 77 percent of full time faculty members were tenure track and, in 2003, 74 percent were tenure track. Among staff members, full time professional staff members share in governance. Nonprofessional staff members have little influence. Since staff members serve at the pleasure of the administration (as do instructors), they take their lead from the administration; that is, the administration has an easier time getting cooperation from staff than they do from tenure track faculty.

After the 1970s, a significant structural change took place in campus governance and that change is the result of rising non-academic employment and increasing use of both instructors and part time faculty. Figure 2.6 contains the proportion of full time faculty among all full time college and university professional employees; total professional employees include full time faculty members, administrators, and professional staff members. The data reveal that in 1976 full time faculty members represented 64 percent of total full time professional employees, and by 2007 the proportion had dropped to 47 percent. In the governance structure

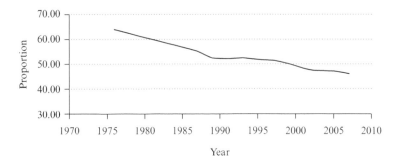

Source: NCES, *Digest of Education Statistics*, 2008, Tables 243 and 244.

Figure 2.6 Full time faculty/professional staff proportion

faculty members went from a super-majority to an administrator/staff majority. Since colleges and universities rely more heavily on full time instructors than on tenure track faculty members, the shift in governance is even more dramatic than Figure 2.6 suggests. These results help explain why most of the increase in real cost per student comes from activities other than faculty wages.

In the annual report *University Hiring in 2009*, the NCES reveals public institutions hired 33 984 new full time employees in 2008 and private institutions hired 15 429 new full time employees. Among public institutions, 52 percent of those new full time employees were administrators or non-academic professional employees, while in private institutions 54 percent were full time administrators or non-academic professional employees. Tenure track faculty members are responsible for teaching, research, and public service, while instructors are responsible for teaching only. Among public institutions, 35 percent of the full time employee increase was instructors whose sole responsibility was teaching, while the number of full time tenure track faculty members represented a *reduction* equivalent to 8.5 percent of the change. In private institutions, 18.5 percent of the increase in full time employment was in instructors and 11.5 percent of the increase was in tenure track faculty. The public institutions are replacing tenure track faculty with full time instructors, and the private institutions are hiring full time instructors at a rate greater than they are hiring tenure track faculty.

Public institutions hired another 9711 part time employees and private institutions hired 8253 part time employees. Eighty-three percent of the part time employees hired by public institutions were instructors, and 74 percent of the part time employees hired by private institutions were instructors. For every part time instructor hired by public institutions, they hired 1.5 full time instructors, and for every part time instructor hired by private institutions they hired 0.5 full time instructors.

The foregoing staffing patterns reflect a significant change in campus governance. The governance role of tenure track faculty is considerably weaker today than it was in the 1970s. The conventional wisdom among many in the higher education reform movement is that exploding costs are the result of pampered faculty with an entitlement attitude; unfortunately, faculty members have contributed to that perception. On the other hand, there is nothing pampered about part time faculty members and full time instructors; these people earn the money they are paid. As the governance role of boards, administrators, and staff members increased, costs rose rapidly. Further, governing boards and administrators set the terms of employment and determine wages paid for services rendered. Ultimate responsibility for cost rests with governing boards and administrators; therefore, it is clear administrators and board members are part of the problem.

2.7   FINANCIAL BURDENS

Since third party payers (taxpayers and private donors) subsidize higher education, the full financial burden of a college education is not borne by students and their parents. This is true even if the student receives no grants or scholarships and pays the full price of attendance. A complete discussion of the general subsidy offered students and the additional student specific subsidy available to students can be found in Winston (1999). In 1971, the full attendance price was 58 percent of total expenditures per student at public institutions and was 70 percent of total expenditures per student at private institutions. Every student who attended public institutions was subsidized an amount equal to 42 percent of the total cost, and every student who attended a private institution was subsidized an amount equal to 30 percent of the total cost. In 2001, the full attendance price was 54 percent of total expenditures per student at public institutions. In 1995, the full attendance price was 79 percent of total expenditures per student at private institutions. Private colleges and universities have always asked students to pay proportionately more of the total cost than have public institutions, and the proportion that private institutions are asking students to pay is rising.

Each student who receives an individual grant or scholarship is in fact receiving two subsidies, the general subsidy available to every student and the individual grant or scholarship (Winston, 1999). Many students receive a third subsidy in the form of federally subsidized low interest loans. This characteristic of higher education finance means there are two different burdens imposed by rising higher education cost: the direct financial burden on students and their families and the total burden imposed on society by rising higher education costs. The rising total cost of higher education represents real resources that have opportunity costs; those resources could be employed elsewhere.

Metrics for Financial Burdens

Society's total financial burden is measured by total expenditure per student divided by median household income. This total burden includes the burden on students, parents, taxpayers, and private donors. If d is total expenditure per student and m is median income, then the total burden is

$$b_t = d/m. \tag{2.6}$$

If median income increases at the same rate as expenditure per student, then the financial burden higher education institutions ask the public to bear is constant. If higher education becomes more efficient, expenditure relative to income falls over time. The burden measure may rise as a result of declining productivity or increasing quality.

The immediate financial burden imposed on students and their families is equal to the net price of attendance divided by median household income. Let the full price of attendance (tuition, fees, room, and board) be p, let g be grants and scholarships, and let p_n be the net price of attendance; then the burden on students is

$$b_s = p_n/m = (p - g)/m. \tag{2.7}$$

The direct burden on students and their families depends on how fast colleges and universities raise total attendance price, how fast taxpayers and donors raise subsidies for direct grants and scholarships, and how fast median incomes increase. Note the burden placed on students can increase significantly even though donors and taxpayers are quite generous and median incomes are rising. Gains in burden reduction can be undone by rapid increases in the attendance price. Colleges and universities have been raising the attendance price faster than the inflation rate for almost three decades. In addition, this burden can be substantial for low income students, particularly since colleges and universities are directing more scholarship money to merit aid. High achieving students come disproportionately from higher income families, so more merit aid goes to higher income families.

Public colleges and universities argue they must raise the attendance price (tuition and fees) because of declining state and local support. These institutions call themselves "quasi-public institutions," since the proportion of total revenue coming from state and local governments is declining. Let R be total revenue, T be tuition and fees, S_a be state appropriations, L_a be local appropriations, and O be all other revenue sources; then $R = T + S_a + L_a + O$ and the share of revenue provided by state appropriations is

$$R_S = S_a/R,$$

and the share of revenue provided by local appropriations is

$$R_L = L_a/R.$$

The share of total revenue provided by state and local appropriations misdirects us from the real issue. R_S and R_L must decline as a proportion of total revenues if tuition and other revenue sources grow faster than state and local appropriations. The more successful a state institution is in raising money from donors, grants, contract research, and tuition, the lower will be the proportion of total revenue derived from state and local appropriations. This would be true even if state and local appropriations grew steadily in real terms. The relevant questions are: Did real state and local appropriations per student increase and did enrollment increase, and at what rate?

From Figure 2.1, we know public enrollment grows steadily. From 1990 to 2007 public higher education enrollment grew at an average annual rate of 1.8 percent. If real state and local appropriations per student were constant, then real state and local support for public institutions increased by 1.8 percent. If real support per student is constant, one can argue state and local government commitments to higher education have also remained constant. If real support per student is increasing, state and local commitments to higher education are increasing. Should higher education expect state and local governments to increase their commitment regardless of performance? In other words, the state and local support issue for public colleges and universities depends on what happened to real state and local support per student, not its proportion of total revenue.

Data

In 1971, the total burden on society (Equation 2.6) for public colleges and universities was 21 percent and for private colleges and universities it was 38 percent. Total expenditure per student in the public institutions was 21 percent of median income and 38 percent of median income in private institutions. By 2001, the total burden on society for public colleges rose

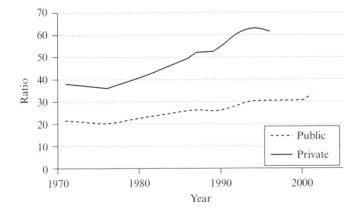

Note: The total financial burden equals total cost per student divided by median household income.

Source: NCES, *Digest of Education Statistics*, 2008, Table 346 and US Bureau of the Census.

Figure 2.7 Total financial burden

to 33 percent, a 57 percent increase in burden. By 1995, the last year the information is available, the burden for private institutions rose to 62 percent, a 63 percent increase in burden. Figure 2.7 contains the data for the intervening years. In both cases the burden began rising after 1980.

In 2002, the National Center for Public Policy and Higher Education (NCPPHE) issued a report entitled *Losing Ground: A National Status Report on the Affordability of American Higher Education*. The report highlighted five national trends: 1) increases in tuition made college less affordable for most American families; 2) government aid has been unable to keep pace with the rate of increase in tuition; 3) students are having to borrow more to go to college; 4) the largest increases in public tuition occur when the economy is slowing down; and 5) tuition increased faster than state support per student. The implications for the student burden measure in Equation 2.7 are clear: the burden increased. Item 4 is especially noteworthy. Even though student ability to pay higher tuition is lower and state government budgets are in deficit during recessionary periods, colleges and universities have enough market power to raise prices and make those price increases stick during recessions.

During the current economic crisis, colleges and universities are doing the same thing: they are raising tuition much faster than the rate of inflation (the inflation rate has actually been negative recently) (College Board,

2009). The NCPPHE's report demonstrates that since 1980 the burden imposed on families in the bottom income quintile has risen dramatically and disproportionately compared to the higher income quintiles (2002: 5).

Since 2002, the NCPPHE has issued biannual reports on the status of higher education. The most recent report is titled *Measuring Up 2008: The National Report Card on Higher Education*. The report evaluates state performance based on six criteria: preparation, participation, affordability, completion, benefits, and learning. Each state gets a letter grade for each category. Preparation depends on how well K–12 prepares students for college, participation is measured by the proportion of high school students attending college, completion is measured by graduation rates, benefits are measured by the proportion of the population holding an undergraduate degree, and learning would be measured by the value added if metrics were available. Affordability is measured by the burden measure in Equation 2.7.

For 2008, the NCPPHE gave every state in the union an F in affordability, except California.[3] The burden for lower income students had risen in every state except California. While taxpayers and donors increased their scholarship contributions, higher education institutions continued to increase the attendance price at rates that exceeded the rate of growth in median incomes and the growth rates in grants/scholarships. The NCPPHE gave every state in the union an "incomplete" in learning owing to the persistent absence of reliable metrics for value added.

The College Board reports in *Trends in Student Aid* (2008) that real debt per student borrower increased from $17 400 in 2001 to $18 800 in 2007 for students graduating from public four year institutions. The real debt per student borrower increased from $20 100 in 2001 to $23 800 in 2007 for students graduating from private four year institutions. These debt levels represent serious financial burdens for people starting their careers.

Public colleges and universities argue the increased burden on students caused by increases in tuition and fees is due to declining state and local support. They say this is evidenced by the decline in the proportion of total revenue provided by state and local appropriations. As discussed in the metrics section, this claim is misleading. Public sector enrollment increased an average annual rate of 1.8 percent from 1990 to 2007. The critical variables are real state and local appropriations per student.

It is clear states have been struggling to keep up with the growth in funding required by increased enrollment; however, the data reveal real support per student from state appropriations is roughly constant. Since enrollment rose, total real state support also rose from 1990 to 2007. Real local support per student increased during the period. One can argue the states should have increased real support per student; but one can also argue public colleges and universities are not entitled to a higher commitment from state governments if they cannot control their costs. If higher education will not control costs, any increase in state government commitment is lost to higher cost and college access does not improve. Who is responsible for the college access problem is very much an arguable point.

2.8 QUALITY

The typical college or university provides two services to each graduate: the value added to the student's personal stock of human capital and the labor market credential represented by a degree from that institution (Mas-Colell et al., 1995). The amount of human capital[4] added to each student is the primary measure of teaching quality. The quality of the labor market credential depends on the access to opportunity created by the degree. Does the degree have name recognition? Does the degree open doors not opened by other degrees? Does the attainment of the degree provide networking opportunities unavailable to others? In the review of higher education "quality" that follows, I am concerned only with teaching quality, the human capital value added by the institution. I will consider credential quality and teaching quality in more detail in Chapters 3 and 6.

The foregoing data establish a clear link between *declining* staff productivity and *rising* cost per student. Furthermore, the declining productivity in higher education contrasts sharply with increasing productivity in the rest of the economy during the same period. For example, the index for output per man hour *increased* by 76 percent from 1980 to 2007.[5] While real unit costs in other parts of the economy have been falling, real unit costs have been rising steadily since 1980 in higher education.

Apologists for higher education argue lower student to staff ratios and lower teaching loads lead to higher teaching quality. This case is made when the institution wants to increase research/grant output and it is also made when the institution says its goal is to increase teaching quality. The argument is fewer students or courses to teach give faculty more time to do research (which is assumed to be complementary to teaching) or more time to spend with individual students and to prepare for class.[6] The rising quality argument is made with respect to student/faculty ratios, not with respect to student/nonacademic staff ratios, since increasing returns to scale suggest the student/nonacademic staff ratios should increase in an efficiently managed institution. The decline in nonacademic staff productivity is hard to justify.

The real cost increases per student since 1980 might be justified if one can demonstrate a corresponding increase in teaching quality. If the declines in student/faculty ratios represent pure teaching quality increases, then we expect at least a 25 percent improvement in public institution teaching quality and a 28 percent increase in private institution teaching quality. It seems quite unlikely that nonacademic functions improved quality by 48 percent in public institutions and 49 percent in private institutions.

Unfortunately, most knowledgeable analysts express concern about declining teaching quality in higher education. For example, Derek Bok argues high academic standards are undermined by "the commercialization of higher education" (2003, 2006). David Kirp (2003, 2005) and Weisbrod (1998) make similar arguments. Bok implicitly adopts the Bowen revenue theory of costs by arguing the flow of money from the commercialization of academic research drives costs up and diverts the institution from the pursuit of its core teaching mission. Bok's research argument is most appropriate for the preeminent research universities, not the other 95 percent of the higher education community, where there has not been a flood of outside money to support research over the past 30 years. He argues the rest of the academic community has adopted the "business model" and that is responsible for high cost and lower quality. I will address this issue in more detail in Chapter 5.

William Massy in *Honoring the Trust: Quality and Cost Containment in Higher Education* (2003) argues the public's perception of higher education is declining because of quality issues and rising cost. He states: "This book argues colleges and universities are not all they can be, that they can improve the quality of education without spending more, dismantling the research enterprise, or undermining essential academic values. Its title asserts that the gap represents a breach of trust that needs to be repaired" (2003: 5). Massy expresses similar concerns about the commercialization of higher education. Many of the arguments made by such notable authors as Massy (2003), Bok (2003, 2006), and Weisbrod (1998) seem most appropriate for the elite research universities; given their institutional affiliations, it reflects their experience and is to be expected.

Overall, there is considerable concern about teaching quality in higher education. This author is unaware of any scholar who makes the case that undergraduate teaching quality has improved over the past three decades. Such quantifiable measures as exist suggest teaching quality has declined. The following subsections explore the quality related data.

GRE Scores

Objective measures of teaching quality, or value added, in higher education are notoriously few and far between. This creates serious problems for students, parents, and taxpayers who are shopping for the college experience or trying to determine what value added they will get for their tuition or taxes. Graduate Record Exam (GRE) results are one potential indicator of teaching quality. If teaching quality improves one should observe a corresponding improvement in GRE scores. Average GRE scores on the verbal and quantitative exams from 1965 through 2006 reveal verbal scores declined by 12 percent while scores on the quantitative exam increased by 10 percent. These GRE scores do not clearly indicate an improvement or a decline.

Graduation and Retention Rates

Beyond the direct cost of education (the student's net price of attendance and subsidies per student), the time it takes to complete a degree is an opportunity cost for the student and for society. In addition, if the student starts a degree program but does not complete the degree the student does not receive the full benefit, society loses the opportunity to provide support to another student who might have finished his degree, and the student may be burdened with debt for an incomplete degree.

Higher education institutions are responsible for designing and administering programs that graduate students on a timely basis. Their ability to do so depends on student preparation and motivation, as well as their diligence in graduating students. This shared responsibility for outcomes between students and the college is a source of considerable ambiguity about teaching quality in higher education. In any event, another measure of quality is the proportion of students in each freshman cohort who complete their degrees within five years of entry. If quality is improving in higher education, then completion rates should be increasing. The remarkable growth in student life services should result in improving completion rates.

Figure 2.8 contains five year graduation rates for public and private institutions from 1988 to 2008. Over that period public graduation rates declined by 8.8 percent and private graduation rates declined by 1.2 percent. Note, in public institutions less than 45 percent of the students in the freshman cohort from 2003 graduated within five years. Despite the greater selectivity in private institutions, less than 58 percent of the students in the freshman cohort from 2003 graduated in five years. Furthermore, studies reveal that the probability a student will eventually graduate declines as the length of time to graduation increases (Bound et al., 2009; Turner, 2004).

A slightly different picture arises when we consider freshman retention rates in Figure 2.9, which is the proportion of freshmen in the cohort who return to the institution for the second year. The freshman retention rate is a measure of how well students are matched with institutions through the admissions process. Admissions staffing has also increased substantially.

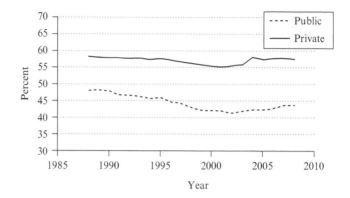

Source: ACT, 2008 Retention/Completion Summary Tables.

Figure 2.8   Graduation rates within five years

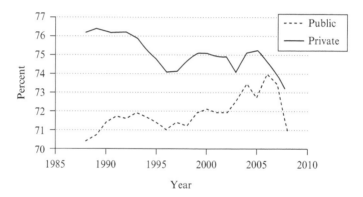

Source: ACT, 2008 Retention/Completion Summary Tables.

Figure 2.9   Retention from first to second year

The trend in the public institution freshman retention rate is increasing from 1988 to 2007, although there was a sharp decline in 2008. In contrast, the trend in the private institution retention rate is declining throughout this period. Taken together graduation rates and retention rates suggest quality is declining.

Grade Inflation

Grade inflation is said to occur when the average grade awarded rises over time. Stuart Rojstaczer and Christopher Healy report that grade point averages (GPAs) for both public and private institutions were about 2.35 in the 1930s and rose to 2.52 in the 1950s; then in the 1960s GPAs began a steep climb and GPAs at public and private institutions began to grow apart, with private GPAs growing much faster than public GPAs (2009). GPAs at both private and public institutions stabilized during the 1970s and then resumed a steady upward trend after 1980. The average for private schools was over 3.3 in 2006 and was about 2.9 at public institutions in 2006.

Harry Lewis reports strikingly similar results for the percentage of Harvard College's students who are on the Dean's List from 1920 to 2000 (2006: 110). The percentage shows a steady increase from 1920 to 1960, acceleration in the increase in the 1960s, then a contraction from 1970 to 1980, and then a resumption of the upward secular trend after 1980.

The data reveal that grade inflation is not a new phenomenon. Long term secular changes in GPAs can occur as a result of any combination of changes in student quality from one cohort to the next, changes in the quality of instruction, or changes in grading standards. In the early part of the twentieth century, a college education was not necessary for economic success, nor was it generally available to students without money. As college became more merit based, rather than due to fortunate birth, average student quality increased from one cohort to the next, and that could result in grade inflation during the move to a meritocracy in higher education. As a college degree becomes more a matter of economic necessity and society commits to college access for all, one could expect average student quality to decline from one cohort to the next. Concern over college preparation in K–12 education, the extensive offering of remedial courses,[7] and SAT scores[8] suggest that average student quality has not increased over the last three decades and may actually have declined. Therefore, with constant teaching quality and stationary grading standards, grade point averages should have declined.

A rising secular trend in GPAs for public and private institutions suggests that either grading standards are declining or the quality of instruction is increasing, if average student quality has not increased. If standards decline, quality declines and, if the quality of instruction increases, quality increases. Hence, secular grade inflation when student preparation is not improving suggests either grading standards are declining or the quality of instruction is increasing.

If the secular increase in college graduate GPAs is the product of better instruction, then the higher grades are justified and the success should be reflected by more knowledgeable college graduates. The GRE scores from 1965 to 2006 are inconclusive in this instance, while declining graduation rates do not suggest improved teaching results. The National Center for Education Statistics reports in the National Assessment of Adult Literacy (NAAL) for 2006 that scores among college graduates for "prose literacy," "document literacy," and "quantitative literacy" all declined from 1992 to 2003. In 1992 the prose literacy score was 325 and in 2003 it was 314, which is a statistically significant decline. Similarly, the document literacy score was 317 in 1992 and 303 in 2003, another statistically significant decline. Finally, the quantitative literacy score was 336 in 1992 and 332 in 2003.

The Pew Charitable Trusts sponsored the National Survey of America's College Students (NSACS) in 2006. The NSACS used the NAAL instrument to survey "a sample of 1,827 graduating students at 80 randomly selected 2-year and 4-year colleges and universities (68 public and 12 private from across the United States)" (Baer et al., 2006: 4). The survey revealed that 38 percent of the students at four-year institutions were proficient in prose literacy, 40 percent were proficient in document literacy, and 34 percent were proficient in quantitative literacy. Proficiency in these categories means the following: prose literacy – comprehend and use information from editorials, news stories, brochures, and instructional materials; document literacy – to search, comprehend, and use documents such as job applications, payroll forms, transportation schedules, maps, tables, and product labels; and quantitative literacy – perform quantitative tasks such as balance a checkbook, compute a tip, complete an order form, or compute interest (Baer et al., 2006: 4). These are clearly not high hurdles, yet 60 percent of the students from four-year institutions were not proficient.

Bok (2006), Hersh and Merrow (2005), and Kuh (1999), among others, argue that postsecondary outcomes are declining owing to a combination of student disengagement and lower academic standards. Average study time per week is one indicator of how engaged students are with their educational experience. Babcock and Marks consider average study time from four separate sources covering four different periods (2008). The time periods covered are 2003–05, 1987–89, 1981, and 1961. In 1961 students studied on average 24.43 hours per week. The average was 16.75 in 1981, 16.59 in 1988, and 14.86 in 2004. This trend represents a 39 percent decline in the average student's commitment to learning. This reduced effort is inconsistent with the notion that grade inflation is the result of improved instruction and is consistent with the proposition that grading standards have declined.

The foregoing suggests teaching quality declined over the period studied. As Stuart Rojstaczer and Christopher Healy note, "average GPAs were so high by 2006 (3.45 and above) at some schools in our cohort that it undoubtedly became increasingly difficult for graduate schools and professional schools to identify the best and brightest undergraduate students" (2009: 4). Grade point averages are supposed to be student quality signals for prospective employers and graduate admission committees. When the GPA norm becomes an "A," the information value of the signal goes to zero, forcing employers and admission officers to employ other strategies to sort good prospects from bad prospects.[9]

Academic Calendar: Contact Hours per Semester

While the number of "credit hours" required for graduation has increased slightly (Table 2.1), it is not clear the amount of classroom time spent with seats in chairs did not decline over the last several decades. The expression "three credit hours" refers to the number of hours per week the student spends in class. The academic calendar at each institution determines the number of weeks classes are in session per semester. After teaching for 17 years in public higher education, I took a position at a private liberal arts college. The first thing I noticed at the liberal arts college was the regular semesters were two weeks shorter than they were at the public institutions; three hours of college credit for the private college student represented two weeks less class time than the equivalent three hours of college credit for a public college student. As a result of the shorter semester the amount of material I covered in each class was about 12 percent less than I covered in the same classes at public institutions. The college explained the students were better, so they learned faster, and I could cover more material in a shorter time. This never seemed to work out; they may have been smarter, but I was not any smarter and could not talk any faster per class.

In a similar vein, Richard Vedder reports on his calendar experience at Ohio University:

> In 1965 when I began teaching at Ohio University, the first day of classes was September 11, and the first semester classes ended January 20, and exams on January 27. The second semester ended nearly in mid-June. There were 32 weeks of instruction per year. In 2012, the same university will offer 4 weeks less instruction, for courses. The faculty teaching loads will be 4 courses typically a year instead of 6. Whereas in 1965, the typical faculty member was in class 288 hours a year, in 2012 his counterpart will be in class 168 hours – over 40 percent less. (2010)

Another important calendar effect is the addition of short semesters between the fall and spring semesters. In the short semesters, students take one class that meets for two or more hours per day for up to four weeks. The courses taught under these conditions are less rigorous simply because students cannot master deeply analytical courses without time to do extensive homework and time to absorb complex concepts. I recall one year my son, who attended a liberal arts college, got academic credit for scuba diving in Florida with a group of other students. At my home institution, I have friends who teach short semester classes on "the sociology of coffee shops" and "the art of walking." I am sure those courses are fun and worthy topics for academic papers, but I am not sure they are worth three hours of classroom credit.

2.9   HIGHER COST AND LOWER QUALITY

Little evidence suggests higher education teaching quality has improved and considerable evidence suggests it has declined. Alternatively, the real burden on students, families, donors, and taxpayers has increased owing to rapidly rising costs; therefore society is paying more for less. Indeed, as we spend more on colleges and universities as a group, teaching quality seems to decline. In contrast, there is a growing awareness among students/parents that the credentials provided by higher education institutions are valuable and that the difference in the value of credentials from elite institutions and the value of those from lower quality institutions has increased significantly over the last three decades. We observe a secular decline in teaching quality combined with a secular rise in the relative value of elite credentials. This appears to be another anomaly. How can these two apparently contradictory trends coexist? I explore this anomaly in more detail in Chapter 3.

The similarities in GPA trends, Harvard College's Dean's List, faculty real wages, and real cost per student are striking and intriguing. Real faculty wages rose until 1970, declined for a decade, and then began to rise after 1980. Similarly, real cost per student followed the same pattern: rising until 1970, falling during the 1970s, and rising again after 1980. Now, we see the identical pattern in grade inflation data and in Harvard's Dean's List. The irony is in the apparent relationship between real faculty wages and grading standards: when real faculty wages rise, grading standards fall and, when real faculty wages fall, grading standards stabilize or rise. Better faculty pay seems to make grading standards fall.

NOTES

1. To the extent that higher family incomes are associated with higher family wealth, families with high incomes can smooth expenditures to finance college expenses out of accumulated wealth rather than current income. Low income families are more likely to

finance college expenses by their ability to borrow and current income, which are constrained during recessions.

2. If c, n, and e are constant, then $dc = -en(fa)^{-2}(adf + fda) = 0$ and $df = -da(f/a)$. For every single reduction in class load the number of new faculty required is equal to f/a. So, if the number of faculty is 100 and the teaching load was 6 sections per year, then the college must hire almost 17 new faculty members if it reduces the teaching load from 6 sections to 5 sections.

3. Public higher education in California is affordable, but the state is essentially bankrupt.

4. Human capital refers to the stock of skills and knowledge embodied in the ability to perform labor so as to produce economic value. It is the skills and knowledge gained by a worker through education and experience (Wikipedia).

5. U.S. Bureau of the Census, Table 620, Productivity and related measures.

6. In my own experience, institutions do not follow up after reducing teaching loads/ class sizes to evaluate what happened to teaching quality. An ex post appraisal of research output is easier, since one can observe publication/grant output. The problem with research release is political pressure on administrators to adopt uniform teaching loads, regardless of research productivity, quickly mounts and frequently leads to common teaching loads independent of productivity. This is the well known "academic ratchet" effect (Massy and Zemsky, 1994). There is very little public information available on teaching loads, which is a serious reporting problem among higher education institutions.

7. According to NCES, *Digest of Education Statistics*, 2008, Table 317, in 2007, 76 percent of public four year institutions offered remedial courses and 65 percent of private four year institutions offered remedial courses.

8. According to NCES, *Digest of Education Statistics*, 2008, Table 135, among college bound high school seniors the average critical reading score was 543 in 1967 and 502 in 2007, a decline of 7.6 percent. Similarly, the mathematics score among college bound high school seniors was 516 in 1967 and 515 in 2007.

9. For example, employers may rely more heavily on internships as a way to sort prospects by "test-driving" them before they are hired. The failure in GPA signal quality raises business costs and lowers employment.

3. Reputations and the Chivas Regal effect

3.1 INTRODUCTION

Simple demand theory suggests applications and enrollment should decline as tuition goes up. The opposite appears to be true among selective colleges and universities;[1] when they raise tuition their applications and enrollments increase, which implies their demand curves slope upward with respect to tuition. This phenomenon is known as the "Chivas Regal effect" among enrollment managers, after the expensive Scotch whisky of the same name.

In an article for *Money* magazine, Penelope Wang reports: "The high sticker price is actually part of many colleges' marketing strategy . . . schools have often found that raising tuition attracts more applicants because families tend to equate high price with quality. Marketers call it the Chivas Regal effect" (Wang, 2008, 89–90). Wang reports recent instances where colleges increased tuition by double digit percentages that were followed by significant increases in enrollment. There are numerous anecdotal reports concerning institutions that experimented with tuition increases and found that enrollments rose after tuition was increased (Larson, 2001).

While this anomaly is well known within higher education, economists have not considered its origin and persistence, or what it implies about higher education economics. The Chivas Regal anomaly exists because students and parents are uncertain about quality. If students and parents are well informed about quality, they have no need to use a proxy for quality, such as tuition. They would make enrollment decisions based on the institution that offers their preferred quality at the least possible cost.

3.2 EXPERIENCE GOODS AND ASYMMETRIC INFORMATION

An experience good is a product or service whose quality is unknown prior to purchase, where quality is measured by taste, durability, or efficiency of service (Nelson, 1970). Experience goods and services are quite common. One rarely knows the quality of service rendered by medical or legal specialists prior to the services being rendered. High technology products are hard to evaluate before purchase. For some of us, they may be difficult to use and their durability is always an issue. Clearly, higher education services are an experience service; one rarely knows how much value has been added until the graduate applies that knowledge.

While consumers are uncertain about quality, producers choose quality by the resources and technology they employ. Therefore, the essential feature of all experience good markets is asymmetric information between consumers and producers; producers have more information about true quality than do consumers. It is well known that asymmetric information can lead to failures in otherwise competitive markets (Holmstrom, 1999: 169). Akerlof's "market for lemons" problem is the classic example of asymmetric information induced market failures (1970).

Information based market failures are characterized by adverse selection and moral hazard effects. Akerlof's "market for lemons" problem leads to adverse selection in experience good markets. Two types of market equilibrium are possible: a pooling solution or a separating solution. In a pooling solution, the consumers do not have sufficient information to distinguish between high and low quality, so all products sell at the same price, which is a weighted average of the prices that would prevail if quality were known. In this case, low quality producers receive a premium and high quality producers sell at a discount. The pooling solution can unravel when high quality producers are driven from the market leaving only the lemons (low quality products). The pooling solution adversely selects for low quality (Akerlof, 1970).

A separating solution occurs when consumers have enough information to distinguish between low and high quality. It leads to separate prices for high quality and low quality, hence the name "separating solution." Since high quality costs more than low quality, the equilibrium price for high quality will be higher than the equilibrium price for low quality. This is why consumers associate high price with high quality. Clearly, a separating solution is preferred to a pooling solution.

A moral hazard problem arises in experience good markets when one party to the transaction has an incentive not to abide by the terms in the contract. For example, consumers consider warranties to be insurance. If the product is insured, consumers may not take preventive maintenance, which induces product failure where a failure would not occur if the consumer did not have insurance. Similarly, experience good producers always have an incentive to cheat on quality when they have a reputation for high quality. Moral hazard is an adverse incentive effect on one of the two parties to the contract.

When the market mechanism is presented with problems like this, it evolves practices that tend to mitigate that problem. Sometimes the market solution eliminates the problem and sometimes it resolves only part of the problem. In the case of experience goods, the producer reputation mechanism evolved to address the information problem. As we will discover, how well the reputation mechanism solves the information problem depends critically on the nature of the experience good. When the reputation mechanism works well, the market failure issue is minimized. When the reputation mechanism works poorly, the market failure issue is significant.

Carl Shapiro notes that a firm's reputation is a capital asset, frequently described as "goodwill," and that:

> The idea of reputation makes sense only in an imperfect information world. A firm has a good reputation if consumers believe its products to be of high quality. If product attributes were perfectly observable prior to purchase, then previous production of high quality items would not enter into consumers' evaluations of a firm's product quality. Instead, quality beliefs could be derived solely from inspection. (1983: 659)

He argues the reputation problem in these markets is inherently a dynamic problem where the producer builds reputation over time. The most important tool used to build reputation is a history of selling high quality products at less than their true cost; the reputation building firm must "exceed expectations" (1983: 660). The new firm in the industry has no history, so it has no reputation for quality. Hence, consumers assume the new entrant is a low quality producer and will not pay a premium price for his output. The new entrant must exceed consumers' expectations by selling high quality at a discount. The new entrant's cumulative loss per unit sold is the firm's investment in reputation.

In a similar manner, consumers only use price as an indicator of quality if they are uncertain about quality (Martin, 1986). If quality is determined by inspection, price cannot convey any new or useful information about quality, so consumers would inspect the quality produced by different firms and choose the price/quality combination that reflects their preferences.

Both the Chivas Regal effect and academic reputations are prominent features in higher education only because students and their parents are uncertain about the quality of the service they purchase. Students and parents have incomplete information about the value added by education. This suggests more efficient allocations of students and better use of education resources could be obtained with better quality information.

The foregoing characteristics of experience good markets suggest numerous questions about current practices in higher education. Do higher education institutions provide sufficient information about value added? Is there uncertainty about value added because it is difficult to measure, or is there uncertainty about value added because institutions have an incentive to withhold information? If institutions reveal all the information they have about value added and they are as uncertain as students/parents, what does that suggest about the way higher education is managed? It is common knowledge among insiders that colleges and universities rarely examine the relationship between the manner in which they use resources and educational outcomes (Bok, 2003: 160; Kirp, 2005: 122). If they do not try to measure value added, how do they know it cannot be measured?

The hostility demonstrated by some members of the academy towards third party quality rankings is cause for some alarm with respect to these important public policy questions. The existence of third party quality rankings reveals students/parents are willing to pay for the information. Why have colleges and universities not developed the information sources themselves if they are dissatisfied with the product produced by outsiders?[2] There are plenty of for-profit providers of quality information about products produced by the for-profit sector. Why is the relationship between the for-profit firms and their quality evaluators so different than the relationship between higher education institutions and their quality evaluators?

Following the incentives created by experience good markets does not mean members of the academy are colluding against the public interest. Many members of the academy sincerely believe value added cannot be measured and that third party ranking systems are flawed. The academy-wide bias against measuring value added and ranking systems is due to the financial incentives.

3.3 PRICE AS AN INDICATOR OF QUALITY

Consumers associate high price with high quality and this association is reflected by expressions such as "You get what you pay for." The association is a rational response since high quality generally means high costs of production and producers have to charge a higher price to recover those costs. Therefore it is not surprising that consumers would use price as an indicator of quality prior to purchasing an experience good.

Martin (1986) demonstrates that, when quality expectations depend on product price, the consumer's demand curve is more price inelastic than when quality expectations are independent of price. He also finds that, with a sufficiently strong expectations effect, the demand curve can appear to be upward sloped with respect to price; in other words, a normal experience good can appear to be a Giffen good.[3]

Suppose the firm is a monopoly, the firm's product is an experience good, and consumers use price as an indicator of quality. If the firm produces a physical product, it can significantly reduce quality uncertainty by offering consumers a money back guarantee. Why might the firm choose not to reveal product quality?

If the monopolist reveals true quality prior to purchase, he faces a demand curve with quality expectations that are independent of price. Martin's results (1986) reveal that the demand curve with expectations that are independent of price is downward sloped and is more price elastic than the price dependent expectations demand curve. Other things being equal, the monopolist can sell the same output at a higher price when quality expectations depend on price than he can when quality expectations are independent of price. The monopolist has a financial incentive not to reveal quality (Grossman, 1981: 462; Lutz, 1989: 253). Potential monopoly profits will be higher at each output level and changes in price will cause smaller changes in quantity demanded.

When consumers use price as an indicator of quality, they have a higher reservation price for the product, which allows the monopolist to earn higher rents at each output level. As with the effect of price discrimination, the monopolist always has an incentive to limit information about product quality. Individual firms have a financial incentive not to fully disclose product quality.

Competition among producers leads to more information about product quality. Experience good competitors compete by quality differentiation and that competition requires firms to reveal more information about quality. Increasing competition leads to more information about product quality, while a monopolist has an incentive not to share that information.

3.4   THE ECONOMICS OF REPUTATION

Consider a market with two quality states: high and low. Consumers cannot differentiate between the two states prior to purchase. After purchase, consumers easily determine quality and consumers purchase the product frequently.

The new high quality firm must suffer a period of losses as it sells below cost. The cumulative losses determine the firm's investment in reputation. In turn, the cumulative losses depend on the frequency of repeat purchases. If consumers buy the product frequently and can quickly determine quality after purchase, the firm can build reputation quickly. If consumers purchase the product infrequently and/or it takes a long time to evaluate quality after purchase (for example, product durability is only revealed by time), the time required to build reputation and the cost of reputation increase.

The firm can also employ quality signals as it builds reputation, such as warranties, referrals, and testimonials. Unlike exceeding consumer expectations through providing a high quality product at a low price, quality signals are not an indispensable part of reputation building. The firm can only build and maintain a quality reputation by continuing to produce a high quality product.

The moral hazard problem created by asymmetric information in reputation markets is the incentive producers have to cheat on quality. Producers with an established quality reputation can increase profits in the short run by cheating on quality. Another puzzle in reputation markets is what prevents quality cheating in equilibrium? Since consumers are uncertain about quality prior to purchase, the producer can "milk" quality reputation by cheating on quality. Quality cheating is a persistent issue in reputation markets.

The firm's ability to cheat on quality depends on the probability of detection. A low probability means more quality cheating and a high probability means less quality cheating. If detection is certain, there would be no quality cheating. Suppose consumers cannot communicate with each other and the determination of quality is difficult after purchase. Perhaps the quality issue is durability, which takes time to be resolved. In this scenario, the firm can cheat on quality for an extended period before a sufficient number of consumers become aware that the firm is producing a low quality output, so the expected return on cheating will be high and the firm is more likely to engage in quality cheating. Note, however, that, if consumers can communicate with each other about their quality experience, the probability of detection increases and the likelihood of cheating declines. More information about individual quality experiences across consumers is better.

Long run equilibrium in competitive reputation models is characterized by a premium of price over cost (Shapiro, 1983). The premium has two components. The first part of the premium represents the normal return on the firm's investment in reputation. The second part of the premium is an incentive to continue to produce a high quality product in equilibrium. In other words, this second part of the premium is a normal opportunity return to compensate the firm for forgoing the profits it could earn by cheating on quality in the short run.

Since the premium over cost is composed of normal returns, the firm earns no economic profit in long run equilibrium. Therefore, if the premium over cost exceeds the sum of these two values, new firms enter the industry. If the premium is less than the sum of these two values, firms cheat on quality and no entry takes place. If price falls below long run average cost, firms exit the industry.

Since part of the premium is an incentive to continue to produce a high quality product, minimum quality regulation has an unexpected effect on market price. An increase in the minimum quality standard has an information externality effect that causes the premium to decline (Shapiro, 1983: 661). Increasing the minimum quality standard reduces the profit incentive for the firm to "milk" its reputation and cheat on quality. Suppose the regulator sets the minimum standard[4] at the firm's current quality choice; then the firm cannot earn positive profits by cutting quality and selling the product as if it was high quality. Hence, the incentive part of the premium disappears. Shapiro concludes that improvements in the consumer's quality information lead to welfare gains (1983: 678).

In a related article, Asher Wolinsky considers an experience good market with reputations where price is an indicator of quality (1983). Wolinsky finds that the price signal exceeds the marginal cost of production and the premium of price over marginal cost increases as the information about quality decreases: less information leads to higher prices.

Holmstrom (1999) considers a monopoly reputation model, where monopoly causes moral hazard problems. He concludes that no long run equilibrium exists where a firm continues to produce high quality. The solution unravels because consumers cannot abandon the firm by buying the product from another producer. In the end, the financial incentives to cheat lead to a lower quality output and high quality monopoly equilibrium does not exist.

Hörner takes a closer look at equilibrium in reputation markets when consumers use price as an indicator of quality (2002). A stable separating solution requires that firms do not cheat on quality, alternative qualities are produced, and prices reflect the quality produced. He has several intriguing findings.

First, quality discipline among producers is maintained by the willingness of consumers to abandon producers in favor of a higher quality alternative. If consumers move quickly after observing low quality outputs, this enforces greater quality discipline among producers. Hence, stable equilibrium requires competitive alternative suppliers.

Second, this "crucial outside option" will exist as long as other firms produce variable qualities and price those outputs according to their quality, i.e. quality must be accurately reflected by price (2003: 645).

Third, consumers make decisions based on relative quality levels rather than absolute quality levels. In other words, consumers are most concerned about the quality of one producer relative to another rather than the absolute quality level of each. Consumers consider quality rankings among producers.

Finally, the correlation between price and quality is maintained by the consumer's ability to observe each producer's customer base. Being able to observe the customer base prevents a low quality producer from mimicking a high quality producer by charging a higher price. Since consumers observe the customer base, they observe the producer's existing customers abandoning the low quality producer trying to raise price and know the producer is in fact not a high quality producer. If the customer base does not abandon the firm after it raises price, the consumer knows the firm is a high quality producer. Stable competitive equilibriums require that consumers must be able to observe the behavior of each producer's customers.

A corollary implication here is that a firm trying to increase sales by lowering price would find that tactic interpreted as an attempt to lower quality; price cuts may be interpreted as an attempt to lower quality and price increases may be interpreted as an attempt to raise quality.

In summary, the formal theory of reputations and quality in experience good markets reveals:

1. a potential for information based market failure exists;
2. the firm has a financial incentive not to reveal quality information;
3. quality cheating is a persistent issue; and
4. high quality monopoly equilibrium does not exist.

In competitive experience good market equilibrium:

1. the premium of equilibrium price over average cost is composed of a normal return on reputation investment and a normal profit incentive not to cheat on quality;
2. the size of the premium increases as information about quality decreases;
3. quality regulation lowers the premium;
4. quality discipline among producers is enforced by consumers' willingness to abandon producers who do not maintain quality;
5. the correlation between price and quality is driven by the consumer's ability to observe the producer's customer base;
6. consumers make decisions based on relative quality rankings
7. price reductions may be interpreted as attempts to lower quality and price increases may be interpreted as attempts to raise quality; and
8. more competition leads to more quality information.

The competitive equilibrium results are obtained assuming there are two parties to each transaction, consumers purchase the product repeatedly, the consumer evaluates quality immediately after purchasing the product, and the consumer abandons quality cheaters. As the frequency of purchase declines, as quality becomes more difficult to evaluate, if consumers are hesitant to abandon quality cheaters, and with third party payers the formal theory suggests the premium of price over average cost will increase and quality discipline will be harder to maintain.

3.5 THE THEORY OF REPUTATION AND HIGHER EDUCATION

What does this formal theory tell us about higher education? Prestige or reputation maximization is the primary motivation of higher education institutions (H.R. Bowen, 1980; Brewer, Gates, and Goldman, 2002; James, 1990; Martin, 2005). The public's interest in and focus on college rankings is consistent with the proposition that reputations are extremely important in higher education. Similarly, parents and students tend to associate high tuition with high quality. Parents and students would not value reputations, nor would they associate tuition with quality, if they were not uncertain about value added at each institution. There is significant quality uncertainty in higher education. Theory suggests more information will lower costs and improve quality discipline.

Under the current circumstances, quality reputation competition becomes a race to spend as much as possible per student and that race has no end. This is clearly H.R. Bowen's revenue theory of cost discussed in Chapter 1. As will be demonstrated in Chapter 4, this is a situation that is tailor made for agency abuse and it explains why every increase in higher education expenditures is justified as a project that will improve quality.

The positive relationship between spending and reputation is demonstrated by Andrew Gillen in Figure 3.1 (2009). Expenditures per student are measured on the vertical axis and *U.S. News and World Report*'s reputation rating (peer assessment rating[5]) is measured on the horizontal axis. The relationship is clear: the more the institution spends per student, the higher is its reputation for quality. Under this regime, any institution that tries to reduce cost per student would be endangering its quality reputation. Responsible behavior in terms of controlling cost does not benefit the individual higher education institution, which is clearly a perverse incentive. The only institutions with enough credibility to act responsibly and perhaps change the linear thinking about expenditure and quality are the elite institutions. Unfortunately, the elite

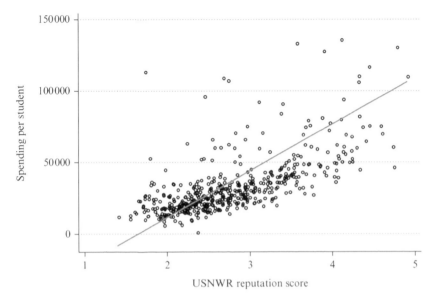

Spending per student

USNWR reputation score

Note: This is a reproduction of Figure 9 in Gillen, 2009. *USNWR* refers to this as the peer assessment rating. Note that observations were perturbed to prevent overlap and schools spending more than $150000 per student were excluded.

Source: IPEDS, *USNWR*.

Figure 3.1   Spending per student and U.S. News and World Report *"reputation" score*

institutions are just as susceptible to the principal/agent problem as are all others.

While Andrew Gillen plots a linear regression line in Figure 3.1, the data suggest the relationship might be nonlinear. In the reputation scores below 3.0 the relationship between expenditure per student and reputation appears to be horizontal, while the relationship is positive for reputation scores above 3.0. The horizontal section suggests quality reputation is independent of expenditure per student. The theory of reputation competition suggests successful high quality contenders must exceed expectations by providing high quality at the low quality price in order to establish a quality reputation. Once the institution has a reputation for high quality, then higher price is a credible signal of higher quality. If an institution with a quality rank below 3.0 tried to mimic the behavior of high quality institutions by raising its tuition, it would not be credible; students and parents would not believe higher price is an indicator of quality.

The perverse incentive not to control cost arises because the public is uncertain about quality. Reducing quality uncertainty reduces the power of this adverse incentive. Developing metrics for teaching quality (value added) would help the information problem. The public's obvious interest in third party rankings reveals it wants more information about quality. The public's willingness to look to third parties suggests the information provided by the institutions is inadequate.

The infrequency with which parents and students purchase the services provided by higher education and the difficulty associated with determining the value added by the experience mean the reputation mechanism's ability to enforce quality discipline is weak. Reputation theory implies college costs are higher than they would be if parents and students had more information about quality. It also suggests the cost of building an academic reputation is very substantial, since the time required is formidable. This explains why old institutions have particular appeal and why competition in the high quality tier tends to be segmented across institutions in the same tier and rarely by competition across tiers. There is a non-competing quality ladder in higher education. The number of institutions declines as you move up the ladder, so the force of competition declines the higher you move up the ladder. Less competition means higher monopoly rents.

Competition from New Entry

Some observers argue that increased competition from for-profit higher education providers will improve performance among nonprofit higher education institutions. This is similar to the case of primary and secondary schools, where the expectation is that increased competition through voucher systems will improve performance in public K–12 schools. The success of the University of Phoenix is cited as evidence. A careful consideration of the theory of experience goods suggests that new entry from for-profit institutions poses little threat to established colleges and universities.

For example, why does a for-profit, high quality provider not already exist, since there are no legal obstacles to entry and the wealth available to high quality institutions is significant? In other words, if a new high quality provider was feasible, why does that provider not already exist? Oddly, the University of Phoenix competes with the lower tiers in the nonprofit quality ladder, where potential rents are very low.

The absence of a high quality for-profit provider and the existence of a low quality for-profit provider may be explained by the "tyranny of present value calculations." Building a reputation for very high quality takes multiple generations. Each period the for-profit provider is building a quality reputation it experiences a loss on each student. Given the length of time before a positive return can be earned, discounting insures that positive return would have to be very significant for the firm to recover its investment in reputation. The length of that planning horizon and the size of the positive return needed explain why for-profit high quality providers do not exist. The capital market planning horizon and the higher education entry horizon are incompatible.

The higher education industry is "contestable" at the low quality step on the ladder, but it is not contestable at the high quality rung on the ladder. A "contestable" market is a market with minimum entry/exit barriers, in terms of both cost and time (Baumol et al., 1982). The power of potential entrants to enforce competitive pricing is maximized in a contestable market; therefore firm pricing still appears to be competitive in contestable markets even though there are few firms in the industry. High quality institutions do not have to worry about potential entry from outside or from lower quality institutions. Endowments at the top deter competition from lower quality institutions as long as students and parents are uncertain about quality.

In order to be successful, a new for-profit provider of high quality education services has to develop a strategy that creates a quality reputation in a short time period. A high quality new entrant would have to be extremely well funded from the beginning: as much as $1 billion would have to be committed from the beginning. Further, the high quality new entrant would have to hire world class teachers to staff the new institution and as we will see in Chapter 6 there is no way for the new entrant to find those teachers because there is currently no market for world class teachers. The reason why that market does not exist is because higher education institutions do not measure teaching value added – quality uncertainty gives the institution a financial advantage.

Therefore the institutions at the top of the quality hierarchy face little competition from the institutions below or from new entrants. This suggests undergraduate quality discipline among providers at the top is weak, which is consistent with subjective evidence. The foregoing also suggests that, once an institution establishes a reputation for high quality, that reputation will be very durable, since there are no repeat purchases in higher education and it takes a very long time to determine the quality of the education experience once it has been purchased.

Quality Cheating

The theory of reputations reveals that asymmetric information between consumers and producers creates a chronic moral hazard problem:

producers with established reputations have an incentive to "milk" those reputations by cheating on quality. The problem is so severe that monopoly equilibrium with high quality products does not exist and a competitive equilibrium without quality cheating exists only if consumers can detect quality cheating and quickly abandon producers who cheat.

The quality detection mechanism in higher education is weak. There are few real value added metrics that tell students/parents the current value added. Most value added measures reflect previous value added, as far as a generation in the past. Students are instrumental contributors to their own value added, making the institution's contribution hard to determine. Like product durability, value added reveals itself after graduation and slowly over time. Students are not sophisticated consumers of education services and they may be unwilling to abandon elite institutions that cheat on quality, because degrees from those institutions carry significant signal value in labor markets.

How could a college with a quality reputation "cheat" on value added without being caught? MacLeod and Urquiola consider an industry model where individual schools have reputations (students are uncertain about quality) and the schools use selectivity to compete on the basis of quality (2009). As a baseline case, they model the industry with entry where each entrant must take students on a first come, first served basis (they cannot be selective in their acceptance of students). The baseline case leads to efficient results,[6] which encourages entry by high productivity schools (2009: 1). When schools are allowed to select students based on ability, "competition leads to stratification by parental income, increased transmission of income inequality, and reduced student effort – in some cases lowering the accumulation of skill" (2009: 1). While MacLeod and Urquiola's primary focus is on K–12, this result has significant implications for higher education.

MacLeod and Urquiola describe these results as an "anti-lemons" effect. The results are "anti-lemon" in flavor because the firms "can influence the quality of their good by positively selecting their buyers" (2009: 2). This result follows because students are both buyers of the service and inputs in the production process that leads to education quality (Martin, 2005; Rothschild and White, 1995). The final value added per student depends on the student's native ability, her effort, externality effects from other students, the externality effect she has on her peers, and the value added by the institution. Generally, good students have positive production externality effects and poor students have negative production externality effects.

The customer as input is not unique to education; it is common in social clubs and night clubs. We are all familiar with queues of patrons waiting to be admitted to an exclusive night club. Each night the club creates a "club experience" by the mix and nature of the clients it admits. The bouncer at the head of the queue is responsible for "casting" that night's experience. The bouncer creates excess demand for the experience by admitting only the most attractive clientele. Admittance to the club is a quality signal in the market for sex. Hence, the process positively selects for higher quality customers and would be viewed as an "anti-lemon" effect.

There are traditional lemon effects (adverse selection/moral hazard incentives) in the MacLeod/Urquiola model; selectivity competition adversely selects for both lower student effort and less actual value added competition by institutions. In other words, selectivity competition enables value added cheating by institutions. The adverse effect on student effort is revealed by lower student effort levels when comparing the selectivity model with the base case. The reason why student effort goes down in the selectivity case is because selectivity reduces labor market uncertainty about student ability. Just being admitted to a selective institution is a high ability signal to the labor market. If student ability "is known, then effort cannot affect the market's perception of one's ability, reducing effort incentives" (2009: 2–3). With respect to schools, "reputation effects dilute schools' incentive to enhance productivity, since a low value added school can always enhance its reputation by being more selective" (2009: 39).

The theory of reputations literature demonstrates why each competitor's "customer base" is an important part of the quality enforcement mechanism (Hörner, 2002); if the customer base stays with the institution as it raises tuition, the students/parents assume the institution is increasing quality; if the customer base abandons the institution it is not raising quality. MacLeod and Urquiola's work reveals that, when we recognize "students as inputs to production," the customer stays with the selective provider even when value added output is low. This leads to more quality cheating and it allows elite institutions to "milk" their reputations.

Consider what this suggests about the rabid competition for admission to the elite institutions. First, a stable high quality student base at an elite institution does not mean the institution is in fact a high value added institution; it means the parents of those high quality students purchased a very expensive labor market signal. Further, the fact that the parents purchased that expensive labor market signal means the student has less incentive to excel. In contrast, parents of gifted students get more value added per dollar spent and more incentive to work hard by enrollment in a lower tier institution. Students at second and third tier institutions have more to prove than students at the bottom of the class in top tier institutions, and students at the bottom of the class at an elite institution are unlikely to be better employees than those at the top of the class at lesser institutions. It would not be surprising to learn from employers that top tier graduates have more of an entitlement attitude than graduates from lesser institutions.

Suppose in the beginning the college built its reputation over the generations by adding considerable value to good students. This process would result in a rising proportion of each class becoming very successful individuals. It is their success that establishes the college's reputation for value added. The older the institution, the more time it has had to build an impressive résumé of successful alumni, and the longer it has survived and prospered the greater is the signal that it is doing something right. Therefore old is good in higher education.

Previous alumni success makes it easier for the college to recruit better students at each point in its history. An increasing proportion of these students succeed even if the college does not improve its technology for delivering value added. Faculty members prefer good students over poor students, so they lobby for better students, since it takes less effort to teach good students and it is certainly more enjoyable.

One can also argue that it costs less to educate good students than it does poor students. It is frequently argued by the K–12 education establishment that private schools take only the "cream" of the public school students, leaving them with the high cost poor students (Biglaiser and Ma, 2003). As with the K–12 issue, educating weak students is at least as important as educating exceptional students, since there are more weak students than good students (Furchtgott-Roth et al., 2009).

Over the past three decades, the competition for good students has become more intense. The consequence is that top students are concentrated in the top institutions (Cook and Frank, 1993). This well documented competition may be evidence of "quality cheating" among institutions and evidence that colleges and universities are abandoning lower quality students where the greatest potential for adding value exists.

Stable Quality Tiers

The quality pecking order among the top 50 colleges and universities is remarkably stable. Significant movements in this pecking order are rare and when movement does take place it is usually a minor adjustment from say number 45 to number 44. Given the imprecision inherent in quality rankings such as *U.S. News and World Report*'s, among others, most movements are not statistically significant. There is more mobility within the ranks below the top 50.

Surprisingly, it is not unusual for institutions to set planning goals that promise to move the institution considerably forward in the ranks.

Frequently, major state universities announce a goal to become a "top 20 research university," when the institution is currently not in the top 50 research universities.

It is one thing to set goals to bring specific academic programs into the top 20 and it is quite another to set that goal for the entire university. This type of goal setting is almost always a public relations exercise and is inherently dishonest. The way to see this is to consider the list of top 20 research universities and ask: Which one of these institutions is University "X" going to displace and how exactly is it going to do that?

Consider the problem faced by any institution wishing to compete on the basis of quality with the quality tier immediately above it. If the institution is serious about moving up a rigid quality pecking order, it has to commit to a generation long pursuit of quality enhancement. The theory of reputations says the institution has to exceed expectations by adding more value than students expect given what they pay. That quality enhancement program will be very expensive and will have to be pursued consistently for a period longer than the tenure of the average senior administration. Few higher education institutions have a planning horizon of that length, simply because college presidents have very short tenures at each institution. This is a governance (principal/agent) problem that will be discussed more fully in Chapter 4.

Special Problems for Students/Parents

Within the class of all experience goods, a college education presents significant and unique complications. First, it is very expensive. Once the purchase is made it is irreversible; you cannot resell the service to another consumer and recover any part of the purchase price. Second, a college education is purchased once, so there is no return on sampling through subsequent purchases.

Third, the quality of the experience is not immediately known to the consumer after purchasing the service. Like product durability, it can be years after the experience before the consumer knows the true quality of the experience. Since the education experience is "bundled" with an entertainment experience, it is difficult to separate the value of the education service from the fun one has in college; do people feel nostalgic about their undergraduate days because of what they learned, or because of the entertainment value?

Fourth, the person paying for the experience is generally not the same individual consuming the service. Parents and taxpayers pay; students attend college. Parents and taxpayers may never know for sure what they paid for. Fifth, by definition students are not sophisticated consumers;

they lack the knowledge and life experiences that would enable them to judge education quality for themselves.

Sixth, a very special feature is students are active participants in producing the value added they buy (Rothschild and White, 1995). The student's talents and effort make a critical difference in the outcome. Ultimate quality is a team effort between the institution and the student, meaning accountability for value added is shared by the student and the institution. The exchange is fraught with moral hazard issues and it further confuses the determination of value added by the institution.

Finally, a college education is an investment good rather than a consumption good, although the "beer and circuses" characterization of today's higher education does ring unnervingly true (Sperber, 2001; Wolfe, 2004). The benefits one derives from a college education flow continuously over one's lifetime, rather than at the moment of purchase. The benefits are both financial and subjective. A college education provides marketable skills that contribute to lifetime income and it enhances the quality of life. It may be easy to measure the financial impact, but the valuation of the subjective benefit is difficult. Therefore it is hard to measure the return on an investment in higher education.

The size of the investment is comparable to the investment families make in housing. Homes are similar to college educations with respect to cost and frequency of purchase. They are different in the ease with which one learns about the home's quality after purchase and the ready market for used homes. In general, there is no other asset purchased by consumers that involves more uncertainty about the return on that asset and the only capital asset that does not have a secondary market. Once you buy a college education, it is yours alone and forever. It has zero resale value.

Consider the restrictions imposed on the sale of stocks and bonds. The Securities and Exchange Commission requires a detailed and audited prospectus be made available to potential investors. Those who market these securities cannot misrepresent the expected returns or risks associated with stocks and bonds without incurring a legal liability. None of this is true in higher education. Colleges and universities can make any claim they want regarding their services. That is why all promotional material in higher education is full of superlatives and why the claims vary little from one institution to another. Since the claims are the same, they provide students, their parents, and the public with little information about relative quality.

Credentials and Teaching Quality

The representative college or university sells two services: the value it adds to human capital (teaching) and/or the certification of labor market credentials. Conceptually, either of these two services could be sold independently of the other (Mas-Colell et al., 1995: 450–66); that is, an individual college might decide to offer only teaching services or it might decide to offer only "credentialing." A strategy to provide only labor market credentials entails tournament competition for admission to an elite/selective institution, followed by testing to see if the tournament competition that led to admission did in fact properly sort the students who were admitted. Credential competition requires extensive expenditures on public relations. Successful credential competition concentrates the best students in the highest ranked institutions, which is what we have observed over the past three decades (Cook and Frank, 1993).

The highly talented cohort represented by each class offers the additional opportunity for individual students to network with the most talented young people in the world. The credential and the network opportunities result in significant financial benefits over the student's professional career. Students and their parents easily identify which institutions offer the best credentials. The reputations of the elite institutions are well established, numerous rankings are available, and students/parents can review the credentials of each entering class to see if the institution continues to attract the best and the brightest.

Pure teaching quality or value added strategies are more difficult. Teaching value added is not easily measured; it requires careful entry/exit testing of each student, effort to place students on the best career path, and follow-up on how the student performs after graduation. Further, the students themselves are responsible for the process that leads to increased value. If the student is not motivated, the institution's best efforts may result in little value added. From the outside, students/parents are hard pressed to compare the price to value added ratio provided by one institution with the price to value added ratio provided by another institution. This is in sharp contrast to the price to credential ratio offered by two separate institutions; that is, students and parents are more uncertain about shopping for value added than they are about shopping for credentials.

This distinction plays a key role in the admission wars among parents. The emotion, energy, and resources parents commit to the contest to get their child admitted to a selective institution have become legendary (Douthat, 2005; Easterbrook, 2004; Fallows, 2005). Admissions professionals are horrified by the investments people make in this effort and by the distorted view they have about what happens to their child if she is not accepted by her first choice.

Parents are acutely aware that credentials are important, but they seem to discount the possibility that a student can achieve considerable professional and financial success without credentials from elite institutions (they are very uncertain about teaching value added). They hold this view despite the fact that the evidence suggests good students will succeed regardless of where they go to college. For example, Dale and Krueger find that, once we control for those student characteristics that are correlated with future income, students who attend the elite institutions have no more financial success than comparable students who attend lesser institutions (2002). A corollary conclusion from Dale and Krueger's study is that the elite institutions add no more value to these students' financial opportunities than do lesser institutions. Is this perception on the part of parents irrational, or does it represent some higher education failure?

The argument for elite credentials holds that these credentials open doors that would not otherwise be open. Clearly, a degree from a satellite state university campus will open very few doors compared to a degree from one of the Ivy schools. On the other hand, it is not obvious that that is true for institutions in the quality tier immediately below the elite institutions. However, it is true that institutions at the bottom of the quality ladder offer value added services, while the higher quality institutions offer credentials and value added.

What do experience good theory and reputation competition tell us about higher education quality and the product mix between value added and credentialing? There are two types of equilibriums in experience good markets: a separating solution and a pooling solution. The equilibrium that prevails in an individual market depends on the amount of information available to consumers. If the information is sufficient for consumers to identify high and low quality providers, a separating solution prevails where consumers pay higher prices for higher quality and price is an indicator of quality. If the information is insufficient, a pooling solution prevails where high and low quality providers receive the same price. Quality tends to unravel in the pooling solution because high quality providers receive a price that is less than they deserve, while low quality providers receive a premium.

The foregoing suggests that teaching or value added competition leads to a pooling result, while credential competition leads to a separating result. Therefore institutions prefer to compete on the basis of credentialing services. Hence, the secular decline in teaching quality (value added) documented in Chapter 2 and the secular rise in student/parent preferences for credentialing services can be explained by the fact that students/parents are well informed about credentials and poorly informed about value added.

This has significant implications at both ends of the quality hierarchy. At the top of the quality hierarchy, the emphasis on credentialing, limited competition, and limited potential entry suggest teaching quality will unravel. This is not a trivial matter. The opportunity loss due to adding less value than possible among the best and brightest the world has to offer is a serious cost. It is particularly objectionable owing to the wealth gifted to these institutions.

At the bottom of the quality hierarchy where institutions compete on the basis of value added, there are many competitors, potential entry is not restricted, and pooling solutions prevail, each institution has multiple incentives to differentiate its service by credentialing. The way out of the pooling competition is to mimic the credentialing provided by higher ranked institutions, not by improving teaching.

It is not surprising that "mission creep" among lower quality institutions is a common problem. Mission creep means two year institutions aspire to be four year institutions, four year institutions want to add graduate programs, institutions with graduate programs want to add Ph.D. programs, and institutions with Ph.D. programs want to become research universities. This leads to a costly proliferation of low quality graduate programs. The worst effect from this tendency is the opportunity loss created by not focusing on adding value to students where the potential to add value is the greatest. In other words, these institutions try very hard to be something they are not while forgoing the opportunity to add considerable value to students who are much in need of more human capital.

In Chapter 2, I discussed the secular decline in teaching quality reflected by graduation rates, retention rates, grade inflation, and student study time. During the same period, we observe a rising recognition among students/parents that credential quality in the labor market is very important; teaching quality declines and the importance of credentials increases. The foregoing shift in emphasis by students/parents is a rational response to the decline in teaching quality and to their uncertainty about what value added they are purchasing. On the other hand, students/parents can be certain about the quality of the credential they are purchasing. The problem is not with students/parents; higher education is the problem.

Quality Signaling in Higher Education

Grossman considers the experience good problem where the firm has the least incentive to fully disclose product quality, which occurs when the consumer makes only one purchase from the firm (1981: 462). Note, this situation is analogous to the student purchasing an undergraduate education. Full quality disclosure occurs when the consumer knows what full information constitutes and recognizes when the firm is not providing full information. In this case, the consumer interprets the lack of full information as a signal the firm is producing low quality. If consumers are uncertain about what full information is, the firm has the maximum incentive not to disclose quality.

There are a variety of ways firms can signal quality. Product warranties are considered a signal in experience good markets. Spence (1977) develops a competitive model with warranties, which yields a separating solution with more warranty coverage correlated to higher quality. Warranties are thought to work as signals since it is expensive for a low quality producer to mimic a high quality producer by offering the same warranty. Unfortunately, Spence's result does not correlate exactly with the empirical evidence on warranties (Lutz, 1989: 239); high quality producers frequently have less warranty coverage than low quality producers. As Lutz demonstrates, warranties are both a signal and insurance; the insurance property causes moral hazard problems (1989). Her model recognizes the moral hazard problem, where she finds that the monopolist signals through both price and warranties. The high quality monopolist may signal high quality with low warranty coverage and high price.

Warranties are rare in higher education.[7] The moral hazard issue is probably a primary obstacle to a more extensive use of warranties. If the institution guarantees an educational outcome, the student has an incentive to shirk his responsibility as a team member who produces his own outcome. It is also likely that institutions have little incentive to disclose quality since students do not repeat degree purchases and are probably unaware of what constitutes full disclosure (Grossman, 1981). Given the deficit in value added information in higher education, it is surprising that some form of conditional warranty has not evolved.

Referrals from third parties are another important quality signal. The popularity of college and university ranking systems, such as *U.S. News and World Report*, reflects the desire of parents/students to seek referrals from organizations that have invested in developing information that would allow consumers to compare one institution with another. Viewed from this perspective, attempts by colleges and universities to discredit these ranking services are inconsistent with the spirit of full disclosure (Diver, 2005; Zemsky, 2009: 72–89). Despite the widespread and specific complaints in the academy about rankings, why have colleges and universities not formulated alternative ranking procedures? Do they believe students and parents should not have this information? Alumni cannot fill the same role as ranking systems owing to conflict of interest and lack of experience with institutions other than their alma mater.

The institution's endowment per student is also a quality signal. By definition endowment per student is a costly signal to mimic. Since endowments are the cumulative capital contributions made by alumni and others, they represent bonded referrals. An alumnus can say positive things about his educational experience, but that testimonial has more weight if the alumnus posts a "bond" by contributing a million dollars to the institution. The amount alumni are willing to contribute to the institution reflects their financial success and the degree to which they attribute that success to their educational experience. It is important to remember, however, that a contribution to the endowment today reflects value added by the institution decades in the past. Therefore endowments per student are not a sufficient statistic to determine today's value added.

There are other quality cues available to consumers. Some of these indicators refer to the quality of the inputs the institution employs and other indicators refer to quality outcomes. The most important input quality series is the quality of the representative student. The actual indicators here are ACT/SAT scores, high school class rank, grade point averages, and number of National Merit Scholars. The student characteristics reflect the institution's "customer base," which is important to quality enforcement according to the theory of reputations (Hörner, 2002). Prospective students/parents observe the quality of this "base" and the institution's ability to retain that base by holding on to last year's class (retention) and then attract a similar base each year. This is important quality confirmation for prospective students.

Faculty members represent another group of quality cues. The proportion of faculty members with Ph.D.s is a quality indicator. More subjectively, the proportion of faculty members with Ph.D.s from top ranked Ph.D. granting institutions is an indicator of quality. Again the ability to attract and retain high quality faculty is part of the quality enforcement mechanism observable by the institution's customer base.

The formal theory of reputations suggests that firms can signal quality by making significant sunk cost investments in assets that reflect quality, but do not necessarily produce quality directly (Klein and Leffler, 1981; Shapiro, 1983: 662). The sunk cost investments are firm specific and non-recoverable investments whose costs can only be recovered if the firm survives and retains its customer base. They are a performance bond that says: "I am willing to put this money in an asset that represents quality even though I cannot recover the cost of the asset from any other application than its current employment."

Sunk cost investments are significant in higher education. There are four major categories: academic research, athletics, facilities, and community service. There is also evidence that investment in this form of quality signaling is excessive (Fizel and Fort, 2004; Sperber, 2001). The excess investment in sunk cost activities is the result of the principal/agent problems discussed in Chapter 4; faculty members, administrators, and trustees derive benefits from these sunk costs.

Research

Some investments in research do generate income, particularly in the sciences and engineering. The return on investment from research in the humanities and social sciences is problematic, however. Subjective evidence suggests higher education's sunk cost investment in research is inefficient. The proliferation of marginal journals across all disciplines and the publication of books with small readerships increase the number of outlets for questionable contributions (Bauerlein, 2009). Institutions raise requirements for tenure, which increases research supply, and the marginal outlets provide a demand for marginal contributions. This circumvents the quality constraint represented by space in established journals and the process of supply creating its own demand can continue without limit. The increase in research volume reflects a diversion of time from other activities, most notably teaching quality. "Mission creep" among institutions adds to the supply of marginal contributions.

Among faculty members, the discussion regarding research and teaching focuses on how research complements good teaching (Marsh and Hattie, 2002; Robertson and Bond, 2001), while parents and students tend to view time spent on research as time that could be better spent teaching students. It is clear the demand for quality teaching from parents, students, and taxpayers is the source of public and private financial support for higher education. In a for-profit environment, the demand for quality teaching would lead to a vigorous derived demand for teaching excellence, but that is not what we see in higher education. Almost all advertisements for senior faculty positions in higher education are for senior researchers. The public rarely, if ever, reads faculty research, so it is something of an anomaly why colleges and universities seem more interested in hiring gifted senior scholars rather than gifted senior teachers (Chapter 6). If colleges and universities were most interested in responding to the market's demand for high quality teaching, the emphasis on research would seem out of balance and suggest sunk cost investments in signaling quality through research were excessive.

Athletics

The cost of athletic programs, as documented by such authors as Murray Sperber, suggests sunk cost investments in athletic programs are excessive (2001). He notes that for every national champion there is a long list of losers. McCormick and Tinsley provide evidence that *successful* athletic programs provide some signal value in the form of increased enrollments and higher average ACT/SAT scores (1987). The tournament nature of athletic competition means that numerous contenders for national titles must invest considerable resources in the competition for every institution that wins a title. Further, title holders must repeat that success frequently in order to maintain any benefit they receive from the competition. Finally, those who support college athletic programs do not pay the cost of maintaining those programs. It is unclear that there is a permanent effect on enrollments and student quality.

Facilities competition

New building programs at colleges and universities are a continuous feature in higher education. Since 1980 these facilities have become more extensive and more luxurious, as well as more costly. Facilities competition is the result of reputation competition and incentives among senior administrators that adversely select for fund raising and bricks and mortar at the expense of investments in core academic programs (Chapter 6).

Community service

The newest member of the sunk cost signaling team is community service. It is fashionable for colleges and universities to claim a more active role in the development of the communities where they reside or, for that matter, the larger society as a whole. The rhetoric employed sounds laudable, but the activities themselves are frequently political, which tends to introduce more cost and partisanship on campus.

If colleges and universities safely secured their teaching value added and the cost at which it is provided, then all of these sunk cost activities might be justified. It appears, however, that the emphasis placed on athletic competition, research, facilities, and community service "wags the dog" formerly known as higher education. The diversion of resources to these activities reflects significant agency problems in higher education (Chapter 4). Sunk cost quality signaling through research, athletics, facilities, and community service creates moral hazard problems when higher education agents (faculty, administrators, and board members) draw rents from these activities. Faculty members, administrators, and board members draw personal benefits from these activities and, since it can be argued that they are of some benefit to the institution, it is not hard to see how they can convince themselves that their actions are in the institution's best interest.

3.6 CONCLUSIONS

Reputations are a dominant part of competition among higher education institutions. Reputations matter only if institutions supply experience goods or services, since consumers are uncertain about product quality.

The asymmetric information between institutions and consumers can lead to the "market for lemons" failure where high quality products/services are driven from the market. Reputations prevent this market failure only under a restrictive set of circumstances: when there are two parties to each exchange, when consumers purchase the product frequently, when consumers can easily determine quality after purchase, and when consumers quickly abandon suppliers who cheat on quality. None of these conditions exist in higher education.

The theory reveals that reputations create moral hazard problems because producers always have an incentive to "milk" the reputation in the short run: quality cheating is always an issue. A stable separating solution is possible when consumers can easily determine quality after purchase and when they quickly abandon quality cheaters. The separating solution price is higher than average cost and is composed of a normal return on the institution's investment in reputation and a normal return to reward the institution for the opportunity cost of not cheating on quality.

The separating solution in reputation markets leads to a schedule of prices and qualities, where higher price is associated with higher quality. The enforcement mechanism for this solution is the consumer's ability to observe the behavior of the institution's "customer base." If the institution raises its price relative to its competitors and its base stays with it, it means the institution is increasing quality; if the institution raises its price and its base abandons it, it means the institution is cheating on quality.

A pooling solution can prevail when there is insufficient information for consumers to differentiate between high and low quality providers. The pooling solution leads to the "market for lemons" problem because high quality providers are paid less than that quality could command under full information and low quality providers are paid more than that quality could command under full information. The pooling solution will unravel, forcing high quality providers out of the market: hence a market failure.

Higher education institutions provide two experience goods: value added through teaching and labor market credentials. Since students/parents have enough information about labor market credentials, a separating solution exists for "credentialing." In contrast, students/parents have insufficient information about teaching value added. Hence, a pooling solution prevails in the market for value added services. The foregoing explains why we observe a secular decline in teaching quality and a secular rise in the importance of credentials among students and their parents.

Institutions build reputations by exceeding consumer expectations regarding quality. This requires the institution operate at a loss while it builds its reputation. The speed with which an institution can build a reputation depends on how frequently consumers purchase the product and on how readily they can evaluate quality after purchase. The lower the frequency of purchase and the more difficult it is to evaluate quality, the more expensive it is to build reputation. The more expensive it is to build reputation, the less competition there is from potential entry.

Since students purchase a college degree only once and it takes a long time to evaluate the quality of that purchase after it is made, it takes a very long time for a college or a university to build a reputation for high quality. This is why older colleges and universities have better reputations than younger institutions. The threat from potential entry at the top of the quality hierarchy is virtually nonexistent and this is why the for-profit entry we observe in higher education occurs at the bottom of the quality hierarchy. Further, the only way to build a quality reputation is to exceed expectations by providing a higher quality than students pay for; that is, the new entrant has to invest in reputation by supplying the service at a loss. Hence, for-profit providers will not be profitable for years after entry.

Institutions always have an incentive not to practice full disclosure about quality. They have the least incentive to practice full disclosure when consumers purchase the service only once. The more uncertainty there is about quality, the higher the premium of price over cost.

Institutions can signal quality through a variety of tactics: warranties, referrals, and sunk cost investments in institution specific assets. Warranties are both a signal and insurance. Referrals are most valuable when they come from third parties. In higher education, institutions make sunk cost investments in research, athletics, facilities, and community service.

A college education is an experience good subject to all the uncertainties enumerated in the foregoing paragraphs. It is increasingly expensive, has no resale value, and is purchased only once, and it is exceedingly hard to determine quality prior to purchase. A college education is like an automobile in that considerable time must pass before you know for sure what you bought. Parents and students reveal they need more information about teaching value added and institutions reveal by their focus on inputs, reaction to rankings, and the information they provide that they are not happy about providing more information. Complaining about the inadequacies of college rankings, while providing no alternative, is not consistent with full disclosure (Diver, 2005).

The increased emphasis on college degrees as a labor market signal may come at the expense of teaching value added in college. National rankings are an accurate measure of the credential or signal value of a degree. Starting salaries for graduates from prestigious MBA programs reflect the program's national ranking (Tracy and Waldfogel, 1997). In contrast, there are very few reliable metrics for teaching value added. Therefore it is likely the separating solution we observe (a hierarchy of price and "quality") in higher education is the result of the sale of labor market signals, regardless of value added. If this is the case, the current situation (a serious value added information deficit) would not persist if it were not for the labor market signal value of college degrees.

Bryan O'Keefe and Richard Vedder (2008) argue that the growing emphasis on college degrees as labor market signals began with the Griggs v. Duke Power Supreme Court case in 1971 that made it very difficult for employers to test prospective employees before they were hired. After that decision employers turned to college degrees as a labor sorting device and that meant people who previously did not need a college degree had to make the extra investment in college to get a good job. The rising emphasis on the signal value of college and the decline in the value added contribution from college may be responsible for employers' increased emphasis on internships to sort good prospective employees from bad prospective employees. Since value added is de-emphasized in college, employers now have to "test-drive" college graduates to find the help they need.

Reputation theory reveals that quality enforcement depends on the consumer's ability to observe the behavior of each institution's "customer base." The optimal quality mix between teaching value added and labor market signaling, or "credentialing," requires more information about teaching value added per institution. Further, that information should be available to students/parents and it should be readily comparable to that of other institutions. The information should be audited and carry legal sanctions for misrepresentation. Entry and exit testing of students is a logical place to start. Better statistics on entering classes, retention rates, and graduation rates would also be useful. "Transparency" is a key objective among higher education critics and that term speaks to the teaching value added information deficit in higher education.

Finally, reputation competition creates a perverse incentive not to control cost, since the more an institution spends per student the higher the perceived quality. Reputation competition leads to an unending rise in real cost per student. From within the academy, the only institutions that might break this spiral would be the elite institutions. Unfortunately, the principal/agent problem considered in the following chapter explains why the elite institutions have no incentive to perform this valuable public service; they do not lead in this case because it is not in their interest to do so. Therefore cost control reform is not likely to come from within higher education.

NOTES

1. This relationship does not hold for institutions in the lower half of the quality hierarchy. The institution must have a reputation for higher quality before higher tuition is a credible quality signal.
2. The National Association of Independent Colleges and Universities (NAICU) and the Association of Public Land-Grant Universities (APLU) established web based accountability sites in the fall of 2007. The NAICU established the University and College Accountability Network (U-CAN) and the APLU established the Voluntary System of Accountability (VSA) site. Andrew Kelly and Chad Aldeman analyzed the information content of these two sites in a report entitled *False Fronts? Behind Higher Education's Voluntary Accountability Systems* (2010), where they found the sites did little to provide new or useful information. The intent seemed to be to merely pacify the reform movement.
3. In economic theory, a Giffen good is an inferior good (a good that consumers consume less of when their incomes rise) that takes up a very large proportion of the consumer, budget. Giffen goods are very rare and normally found among low income families in subsistence economies. If the price of a Giffen good increases it has a devastating effect on family incomes, causing families to reduce consumption of preferred normal goods and spend more on the Giffen good. The traditional example is the demand for potatoes during the Irish potato famine.
4. Note that quality regulation requires that quality can be measured after purchase.
5. The peer assessment rating contained in the USNWR rankings is based on survey results from presidents, provosts, and deans concerning the relative quality of peer institutions.
6. Since these results are efficient, MacLeod and Urquiola implicitly assume students purchase education frequently, can easily determine quality after purchase, and readily abandon quality cheaters, and there are no third party payers. This abstraction from reality is necessary in order to establish an efficient case to compare with the incremental effect of introducing selectivity.
7. Centre College has a limited warranty on specific educational opportunities, which it calls "The Centre Promise."

4. The principal/agent problem in higher education

4.1 INTRODUCTION

The productivity, cost, and quality data in Chapter 2 reveal faculty/staff productivity declined steadily while real wages increased after 1980 and, as the simple algebra of productivity/cost suggests, real cost per student rose briskly. Further, the data suggest quality has declined. These relationships are an economic anomaly, since increases in productivity are normally a prerequisite for increases in real wages in the rest of the economy.

Faculty members, administrators, and governing boards are stewards of the intergenerational social contract: adults subsidize college with the understanding students will pass that subsidy on to the next generation. Faculty members, administrators, and governing boards are obligated to insure the cost is reasonable and quality is maintained. If the costs are not reasonable or quality declines, the social contract will fail. The ultimate responsibility for preserving the higher education social contract rests on governing boards; they are the leading stewards. Administrators and governing boards set policy. Why have they failed to take the obvious steps needed to control cost?

The front runners in the contest for "highest cost sector in the U.S. economy" are higher education and health care. Both of these sectors are dependent on third party payers: insurance/taxpayers in health care and parents/donors/taxpayers in higher education. They are dramatically different with respect to the productivity issue, however. Technical innovation is continuous in health care and little innovation has taken place in higher education for the past two centuries. Except for the classroom technology, Adam Smith would be familiar with what happens in most of today's classrooms. In health care, technical change constantly pushes the service frontier forward, making new services available that were previously impossible. Since people have insurance, patients have a claim on whatever the new technology creates. In health care, rising productivity through innovation and capital deepening continuously drives costs up.

In higher education, innovation is stagnant and productivity declines while real wages increase. This makes higher education a unique case;

something very different is afoot in the academy. In this chapter, I explain how a largely unrecognized and unchecked principal/agent problem leads to rising real wages and declining productivity.

Agency problems vary from outright theft to simple shirking; theft takes financial resources from the institution and shirking takes productivity from the institution. Theft does take place in higher education, but it is mercifully rare. Conscious agency abuse is not the primary problem in higher education; faculty, administrators, and board members do not set out to serve their own self-interest at the expense of students, parents, taxpayers, and donors.

The problem is more subtle than that. First, faculty, administrators, and board members have come to think of themselves as major "stakeholders" (principals) rather than as professional agents hired to serve the interest of others. Second, sometimes the agent's and the principal's interests overlap; when the overlap occurs, no matter how small the overlap, faculty, administrators, and board members can easily convince themselves their motives are pure. Many members of the academy consider themselves the most important "principals." From this false assumption, it is a simple step to the false conclusion that whatever is in my interest is also in the students' and the institution's interest.

4.2   MANAGING CASH FLOWS

Every organization, whether it is for-profit, nonprofit, secular, religious, or government, faces the same financial imperative: it must cover its cash outflows (expenditures) with cash inflows (revenues). Although periodic deficits can occur, they cannot persist; at some point chronic deficits lead to financial reckoning. While governments have the power to tax and print currency, they are not an exception to this rule, since the power to tax and print new currency has political and economic limits.[1]

Each organization must choose a strategy to ensure revenues are sufficient to at least cover current expenditures and service the organization's debt obligations. An organization can finance periodic deficits with debt as long as that debt is retired according to contractual obligations. If persistent deficits are not accompanied by proper debt retirement, the organization is insolvent and may cease to exist.

The coordination of cash outflows with cash inflows – referred to as cash flow management – is an inescapable obligation for all organizations; like death, there is no avoiding it. Organizations differ in the cash flow strategy they adopt; their choices primarily reflect the nature of the product or service they provide. For-profit organizations and nonprofit organizations represent the two nongovernment types of cash flow strategies. For-profit firms provide private goods and nonprofit institutions provide private goods to "underserved" consumers, private goods with some public good[2] characteristics, or social services deemed inappropriate for for-profit firms.

For-profit firms sell goods and services to those who have the ability to pay. Since they have to compete with other similar providers of goods and services, for-profit firms cannot succeed unless they minimize costs and are willing to innovate. The rewards for cost minimization and innovation can be substantial.[3]

People who lack the ability to pay for private goods may be "underserved" by the market for private goods. Nonprofit food banks, the Salvation Army, and Goodwill are examples of nonprofits that provide private goods to underserved consumers. Some nonprofit organizations provide products or services that have both private and public good characteristics; education services have both private and public good characteristics.

Society grants tax exempt status to nonprofits in order to increase the supply of private goods to consumers who are "underserved" by for-profit firms. Since the social objective is to produce more of these goods, they are not taxed and they are required to be nonprofit;[4] hence, all resources available are supposed to be used to increase the supply of the under-supplied product or service. Because profits would interfere with this goal (the personal gain flowing to owners could be used to expand output), a balanced budget (expenditures equal to revenues) is the financial norm among nonprofit organizations.

The public has a financial stake in all tax exempt nonprofit institutions. The public's financial stake is the tax proceeds forgone. In other words, the public makes an investment in these institutions each year that is equal to the amount of tax receipts foregone. Therefore, even if the nonprofit accepts no government contributions, the public is entitled to nonprofit transparency and accountability. Private colleges and universities are accountable to the public interest.

4.3   THE PRINCIPAL/AGENT PROBLEM

When cash flows are managed on behalf of others, an opportunity for principal/agent abuse is present. Those who manage cash flows in for-profit firms, nonprofit institutions, and government agencies have the opportunity to abuse that trust. On the other hand, bankruptcy is a natural constraint on that abuse; the threat of bankruptcy limits agency abuse.

The principal/agent problem arises when one person hires another to act as his agent.[5] The problem is common among for-profit firms since owners (shareholders) hire professional managers to run the business. The managers make day to day decisions for absentee owners. The potential for abuse is always there because managers can pursue their own self-interest at the owner's expense.

When we vote for politicians, we "hire" them to act as our agents in the government. Agency abuse in politics is also well known and well documented. Elections are a regular check on agency abuse by politicians. An agency problem arises when we consult a medical doctor, since we are hiring the doctor to make decisions about our health. The doctor can inflate our medical expenses by practicing defensive medicine or by ordering tests that are in the doctor's financial interest but are in fact unnecessary. Lawyers may not always have their clients' interest in mind. Clergy can exploit vulnerable individuals. The principal/agent problem is common in every public, private, religious, or secular institution in our society.

No institution or group of institutions is immune to the principal/agent problem. Human weakness and self-interest insure agency problems occur wherever individuals make decisions on behalf of others. It does not depend on individual commitment, professionalism, self-sacrifice, or any other characteristic we may use to describe dedication. It is easy to rationalize one's behavior by arguing that our self-interest coincides with the interests of people we are charged with serving. After all, sometimes it is true: our interests do coincide.

The principals who claim the firm's residual profit are specific individuals with well defined and adjudicated property rights. The mechanisms by which these principals can change the agents who manage the firm are also clearly defined. This is not true for nonprofit institutions. The nonprofit principals are individuals whose claims on the institution are poorly defined and whose property rights are "held in common"[6] with a large set of other individuals. Further, the mechanism by which nonprofit principals relieve managing agents is poorly defined and, in the case of higher education, tenure means principals cannot discharge faculty members. Finally, there is no clearly defined financial residual to be claimed by principals in nonprofit institutions.

The fact that financial residuals are not clearly defined in nonprofit institutions does not mean they cannot be generated by effective cash flow management. The "commercialization" of research creates financial residuals and extension teaching programs are designed to maximize the residual they generate (Chapter 5). Since nonprofit principals have no claim on these financial residuals, they are routinely claimed by the nonprofit agents in the form of expenditures that benefit the agents. Hence, faculty real wages increase even though faculty teaching productivity declines (Chapter 2).

The anonymity of nonprofit principals and the habitual taking of financial residuals by nonprofit agents lead to confusion among those agents about who is a principal and who is an agent. For example, if one asks higher education employees who the "primary stakeholders" are, they are most likely to say students, faculty, and staff. Note that students are transients; they are only in residence for approximately four years. If you consider yourself a "primary stakeholder," then there should be nothing wrong with diverting some of any given financial residual to your own use. This is how chronic agency abuse becomes institutionalized.

The economic impact of principal/agent abuse is always higher cost than necessary. When politicians abuse their agency position, say through earmarks that further their political interests, government expenditures are higher than necessary. Defensive medicine and induced demand for medical services make medical expenses higher than necessary. "Golden parachutes," poorly designed incentive bonuses, excessive consumption of perks by executives, private jets, lavish office furnishings, or expensive junkets all raise business costs to levels that are higher than necessary to provide the goods and services for-profit firms produce.

Higher education's dismal cost control record strongly suggests the academy has serious unresolved principal/agent problems. The higher education principals are students, parents, alumni, donors, and taxpayers, while the agents are faculty members, staff, administrators, and trustees. Clearly, there are many professional, dedicated people in business, government, medicine, and the clergy, just as there are similarly motivated people in higher education. Still we have agency abuse in all those sectors.

The severity of the principal/agent problem depends on: 1) how well the principal's interests and the agent's interests are aligned (this requires an incentive compatible contract – a contract that gives the agent a financial incentive to do things that also promote the principal's interests); 2) the probability the principal will detect self-dealing by the agent; and 3) the existence of market, institutional, or regulatory constraints on agency abuse.

The alignment of the agent's interest and the principal's interest depends on compensation contracts. For example, in for-profit firms the principal's interests are served by increasing profitability and rising stock prices. If the agent receives a fixed salary as compensation, he does not share in rising profitability or a rising stock price. Hence, most managers receive incentive compensation in the form of profit sharing and stock bonuses. Unfortunately, incentive compensation among for-profit firms has been abused by boards of directors who are supposed to act as agents for shareholders. This is why executive compensation among U.S. firms is so much higher than among similar firms in other industrialized countries. This is a serious failure in corporate governance.

Detecting the agent's self-dealing depends on how well informed the principal is about the agent's activities. Clearly, if the principal is as well informed as the agent, the principal would not allow the agent to make decisions at the principal's expense. Information is essential to preventing the agency problem. This is why "transparency" is the key word in all agency issues. A lack of transparency leads to principal/agent abuse.

The discipline imposed by competition serves as a natural constraint on agency abuse. Competition among for-profit firms for consumer patronage and competition for permanent financing in the capital markets introduce numerous constraints on agency abuse among for-profit firms; nevertheless agency abuse is still a serious problem. Competition from competing political parties limits agency abuse in politics; nevertheless agency abuse is still a serious problem. For-profit firms are subject to extensive government regulation and elaborate disclosure rules; still agency abuse is a problem. The institutional structure of capital markets creates incentives for numerous private individuals and organizations to closely follow the for-profit firm's activities. Media organizations have a strong taste for agency stories involving for-profit firms and politicians. Despite all of this oversight, agency abuse occurs routinely.

4.4   CONSTRAINTS: MARKETS, REGULATION, OVERSIGHT, PERFORMANCE, AND WHO PAYS

The Market for Control

When a higher education institution performs poorly, there is no established procedure by which its management team (administrators and governing boards) can be replaced.[7] This is in sharp contrast to either politics or the well defined "market for control" among for-profit firms. The market for political control is a regularly scheduled event: politicians must stand for re-election regardless of their performance and in extreme cases they can be recalled or impeached. These "markets for control" are a serious constraint on agency abuse; nevertheless agency abuse is common among for-profit firms and in politics.

In for-profit firms and in nonprofit institutions, agents are tasked with the day to day management of cash flows. Having responsibility for cash flow management offers the agent an opportunity to take decisions that benefit the agent; after all the agent is managing expenditures. On the other hand, the imperative to manage those cash flows such that the institution does not become insolvent acts as a natural constraint on agency abuse. The existential threat to an individual institution is significantly different for for-profit firms than it is for higher education institutions. In other words, capital markets can be a very important natural constraint on agency abuse.

A critical difference between nonprofits and for-profit organizations is that businesses have complete access to capital markets – both debt and equity markets.[8] Businesses can balance short term cash flows by issuing commercial paper and they can raise permanent capital by borrowing in the bond market or issuing stock in the equity market. Treasury T bills and commercial paper issued by for-profit firms are the primary debt instruments traded in what is popularly known as the "money market." Having access to capital markets places for-profit firms in competition with other firms also seeking capital and thus subjects them to the discipline imposed by market competition for these financial resources.

Nonprofit institutions have limited access to debt markets, but not equity markets. Nonprofits cannot issue commercial paper to finance short term cash flows, but they can get permanent debt capitalization for real assets. Nonprofit "equity capital" comes from the market for charitable giving (Martin, 2005: 89–113). Regular equity capital markets generate considerable for-profit oversight, while the market for charitable giving leads to very little nonprofit oversight.

Debt markets lead to some oversight of both for-profit and nonprofit institutions. Financial institutions that lend directly to these institutions write restrictions into the loan agreement that are designed to protect the lender from subsequent changes in the borrower's financial condition. The lenders also monitor the borrower's behavior. In the bond market, bond rating agencies evaluate the borrower's financial condition and may change the bond rating in response. These practices put some constraints on agency abuse in both for-profit and nonprofit institutions that borrow.

Investors hold financial assets issued by for-profit firms, nonprofit institutions, and governments in a portfolio of assets. They manage the risk in the portfolio by diversifying the type and number of assets held in the portfolio. The combination of assets yields an expected portfolio return and a portfolio risk. The investor's objective is to maximize the expected return given the systemic[9] risk he is willing to accept. The optimal portfolio is composed of risk free assets (like Treasury T bills) and risky assets. Each asset is evaluated on the basis of its expected return and the systemic risk it represents; each characteristic is measured by explicit metrics.[10] Any other asset that has the same expected return and systemic risk combination is a perfect substitute for the assets held in the investor's portfolio. Therefore the investor will not hesitate to substitute these other assets for any asset in his portfolio that does not meet market expectations. When investors shed an asset that does not meet expectations, the asset's price declines and the organization that issues the asset sees its capital costs increase.

Shareholders and bondholders continue to hold their stake in for-profit firms as long as the firm at least meets market expectations.[11] If the organization exceeds expectations, measured by what the market expects its rate of return to be adjusted for the risk, the firm creates new wealth and it attracts more investors. If it does not meet expectations, stakeholder wealth declines, and eventually the organization's existence will be at risk.

The for-profit firm's performance is measured by profitability, which determines return on investment in the firm's stock and bonds. Their performance is measured quarterly, as well as annually. An individual firm's performance is easily compared with that of other firms. Since agency costs reduce profitability, the constant demand to meet or exceed market expectations is an important constraint on agency abuse.

The extra cost from agency abuse represents management's extraction of a surplus from the firm. That surplus comes directly from the surplus that the firm is supposed to maximize (that is, the profit). The more surplus captured by management for its own benefit, the lower the firm's rate of return. The fact that agency abuse in for-profit firms directly reduces the metric by which these firms are evaluated in a competitive market suggests it is easier to detect agency abuse in for-profit firms. Nevertheless, agency abuse is common.

The firm cannot maximize return without minimizing cost, so market discipline leads to effective cost control in the firms that survive. Financial analysts, individual investors, financial intermediaries, investment bankers, traditional bankers, regulators, takeover firms, and customers constantly survey, compare, and inspect the performance of the for-profit firm. Private oversight helps to control agency abuse; this is particularly true when the outsiders have a financial incentive to pay close attention. There are no private oversight groups with a financial incentive to pay close attention in higher education.

A for-profit firm can go out of business even if it succeeds in covering all cash outflows with cash inflows. Higher education institutions do not go out of business unless they have chronic unfunded deficits. Earning a surplus is not sufficient to prevent liquidation among for-profit firms. The firm must meet market expectations or its existence is in peril. The process by which this happens is the mechanism that reallocates capital in our system to a higher end use.

In order to understand this, consider the firm's "economic balance sheet" in contrast to the firm's accounting balance sheet. The accounting balance sheet is a historical document; it records the historical values of assets and liabilities. An "economic balance sheet" records the current market values of the firm's assets and liabilities. The entry that "closes" the economic balance sheet is the wealth[12] created by the firm.

Let the current market value of the firm's assets be A^m. This is the value the firm would receive if it sold all its assets today. Similarly, let D^m be the current market value of the firm's debt, the value the debt holder would receive if he sold the debt today, and let E^m be the current market value of the firm's equity. The current market values of the firm's debt and equity are relatively easily computed since they represent bond prices and share prices. The market value of the assets is harder to determine if most of the assets are real assets not sold in auction markets like the bond market or stock market. If W is the wealth created by the firm then the economic balance sheet is:

Economic balance sheet

Assets	Liabilities
A^m	D^m
W	E^m
$A^m + W$	$D^m + E^m$.

Since this is a balance sheet,

$$W = D^m + E^m - A^m.$$

Suppose the market value of the firm's debt and equity exceeds the market value of its assets, then $W > 0$ and the wealth created by the firm is positive; the firm creates value that is greater than the value represented by the market value of the assets it employs.

Alternatively, suppose the market value of its assets exceeds the market value of its debt and equity; then $W < 0$, wealth is negative and the firm is worth more dead than it is alive. It says an outsider could buy all the equity, sell all the assets, pay off all the debt, and walk away with a profit. Further, let W^{max} be the maximum wealth that could be created with the firm's assets and assume $W > 0$, but $W^{max} > W$. Even though the firm creates positive wealth, it is not living up to its potential. Arbitragers, takeover firms, or "sharks" constantly look for firms where these situations exist and they are providing a useful social service because the assets employed by a firm with negative wealth creation or where the firm is not meeting its potential should be employed in some other application or be managed by other managers. Note that the firm can be taken over even though it is profitable and creates positive wealth. The threat of takeover and liquidation or reorganization is a powerful deterrent to agency abuse.

The foregoing describes the "market for control" among for-profit firms; there is no market for control among higher education institutions. When assets are not used efficiently in higher education there is no mechanism that directs those assets to a higher end use. Once "charitable equity" is invested in a higher education institution, it stays under the control of that institution no matter how poorly it is applied. Further, higher education agents do not have to stand for re-election or face a competing team in an election on a regular basis as do our politicians.

Since nonprofits do not have access to equity markets, they do not face the competition found in those markets. Nonprofit institutions raise "equity capital" in the unregulated and ad hoc market for charitable giving. They compete with other nonprofits for the subsidies or donations provided by third party payers, which can be taxpayers or private donors. This competition tends to be segmented, however, and therefore less "competitive." Third party contributors (donors and government agencies) have strong preferences concerning their contributions and do not easily shift their funds. A person prepared to donate $1 million to Princeton is not likely to be willing to donate that money to any other institution, even if another institution could put the funds to better use. Nor do charitable donors seek out the highest end use for their funds, as do investors in for-profit equity markets. From society's perspective, the private charitable flow is "inefficient" from the outset.[13]

Competition from Potential Entry

The threat of competition from new entrants is a constraint on for-profit firms. The capital necessary to compete with existing firms is readily available from efficient capital markets. Since agency abuse artificially raises the firm's cost, it creates an opportunity for new entrants to provide similar products and services at a lower cost. This threat puts a limit on agency abuse among for-profit firms.

As we learned in Chapter 3, successful entry is expensive and takes a very long time in higher education. Even though the potential rents are significant for a high quality provider, there has been no new entry in the past half-century in the market for high quality higher education. Since the new entrant has no reputation prior to entry, the entrant would have to provide high quality at a price less than cost for a very long time in order to build that reputation. It could take the new entrant a couple of generations to establish a reputation for high quality. The equity capital markets are not that patient, so high quality higher education institutions face no threat from potential entrants. Therefore new competition is not a constraint on agency abuse in higher education.

Regulation

Businesses are highly regulated by the federal government, state governments, and the stock exchanges where they are listed. The federal agencies with direct regulatory responsibility are the Securities and Exchange Commission, the Treasury Department, the Justice Department, the Federal Trade Commission, the Food and Drug Administration, the Environmental Protection Agency, and in the case of the banking system the Federal Reserve System. This is a prodigious amount of regulation. The goal of this regulation is to protect consumers and investors. Regulation reduces the ability of for-profit firms to take advantage of investors (principals) who do not have as much information as the firm's managers. The regulations require full financial disclosure and set standards for the information required. Avoiding the costs of defective products, avoiding environmental damage, and avoiding the cost of misleading financial information are the primary reasons why for-profit firms are subject to regulation. The existence of regulation confirms that society knows there are serious agency problems among for-profit firms.

The nonprofit sector is remarkable for its absence of any meaningful regulation. The absence of regulation suggests society is unaware there are agency problems in the nonprofit sector. Marion Fremont-Smith observes:

> A distinguishing feature of the nonprofit sector is the freedom within which its component entities are allowed to operate. The vast number of organizations that comprise the sector . . . are under no duty to account to any governmental agency on a regular basis. The rest operate largely without supervision by any state official and with minimal oversight by the federal government, oversight, moreover, that is generally limited to assuring that they meet the conditions for exemption from federal taxes. Governments require no accountings of the methods by which nonprofit organizations pursue their missions, nor make any attempt to assure that charitable assets are used effectively or efficiently.
>
> In part this failure to provide meaningful regulation has been justified on the grounds that, because they are formed to "do good," the people who run nonprofit organizations will likewise "do good"; they will not profit at the organization's expense nor be reckless in their management of its assets. (2004: 1–2)

The primary federal regulation of nonprofits is through the IRS. The exempt organizations section at the IRS is responsible for nonprofit oversight; in 1975 that section employed 2075 people and in 1997 they employed 2100, even though the number of nonprofits had grown by 57 percent (Fremont-Smith, 2004: 460).

Oversight by Private Groups

The profit motive insures that numerous private individuals and groups practice continuous oversight of for-profit firms. Security analysts devote themselves to the analysis of select firms and industries, arbitragers do detailed analyses of prospective takeover targets, investment bankers do complete "due diligence" analyses of all clients who want to issue new bonds or stock, and individual investors conduct their own analysis of information mandated by government regulation.

Aprill and others note that a large number of private groups act on information concerning for-profit firms and that there is a virtual absence of such groups with an interest in nonprofit organizations (Aprill, 2007). There is no corresponding financial incentive for private groups to engage in nonprofit oversight. There is no market for control of nonprofits, so there is no personal benefit to be derived from oversight. Furthermore, the absence of government regulation means little information about the non-profits' financial activities is available to the public. Despite the allegations of voter fraud, violation of its bipartisan tax exempt status, and receipt of federal money, the public knows nothing about ACORN's financial practices. Since nonprofits are established to "do good," their situation is like the "tragedy of the commons"; they are available to the public and nobody owns them, so they can be abused by the people who work there.

Media Oversight

The media vigorously pursues agency problems in the government and in the for-profit sector. Politicians and CEOs in handcuffs make excellent copy. This media oversight is a useful public service. The media shows little interest in nonprofit agency problems, unless they deal with wayward televangelists or priests who are pedophiles. Fremont-Smith claims the lack of media reporting on wrongdoing in nonprofits is

> attributable to the nature of the regulatory process, which provides privacy during the investigatory stages and relies in many instances on threat of litiga-tion to force settlement of disputes, the terms of which are rarely disclosed to the public. Finally, the press seldom reports the outcomes of litigation, so the terms of most of the cases that are settled subsequent to the filing of a suit are similarly not made available to the public. (2004: 13)

Nonprofits tend to get a pass from the media.

Gene Maeroff notes that media education coverage focuses on K–12 and is limited to three higher education stories: college sports, tuition, and admission to elite institutions (2005: 11–22). He states:

Journalists could ask similar questions (as they do about K–12) about higher education, but they usually do not. They act as if it were an article of faith that America's higher education is the best in the world – almost beyond criticism – while considering pre-collegiate education seriously flawed and, therefore, ripe for scrutiny. The image of a supposedly high-quality system of higher education, operating with the precision of a fine engine, seems to awe journalists. Like most Americans, journalists do not see past the ivy. (2005: 12)

Performance Measures

Among for-profit firms, performance is measured by profitability on a quarterly and an annual basis; further, agency abuse raises cost and lowers profit; thus agency abuse lowers the for-profit performance measure. Unfortunately, a dollar's worth of profit in one company may not be the same as a dollar's worth of profit in another company. Profit is a financial or accounting metric and the path to reported profit can be long and tortuous. Accounting conventions are not applied uniformly by all firms, which leaves the window open for management to "manage their earnings" by adopting different legal (sometimes illegal) accounting practices. For this reason, financial analysts are very concerned about the "quality" of reported earnings; this is why they spend a great deal of time analyzing the notes to the financial statements reported by the firms. The firm can conceal agency abuse by manipulating the quality and timing of earnings reports.

The firm's reported earnings may not reflect the firm's true financial condition. For example, the use of stock options for compensation overstates a firm's profits. Options are not recorded as an expense. They are a substitute for salary, which would have to be recorded as an expense. The firm may also take other actions that make its earnings look better than they really are, some of them reaching the level of actual fraud. A firm may accelerate the recognition of sales (recording items as sold after they have been sent to a distributor or retailer even though they are unlikely to be sold). It may capitalize items that should be expensed (capitalized items can be depreciated over time, reducing their reported cost). It may understate the reserves it needs for bad debts (this was a critical component in the sub-prime mortgage crisis). As in the Enron case, firms can also use elaborate off-balance sheet partnerships to hide liabilities. Such abuses led to the 2002 passage of the Sarbanes–Oxley Act, which attempts to reduce the principal/agent problem in for-profit firms by increasing financial transparency.

It is difficult to measure a nonprofit organization's performance, and it is difficult to make comparisons between nonprofit organizations. A misbehaving nonprofit manager extracts surplus from the organization in the same manner as do misbehaving managers in businesses: by not minimizing costs. There is an important difference, however. The surplus taken by the nonprofit manager does not reduce profit, because there is no profit. In for-profit firms, the surplus that is taken reduces profit, making the abuse more easily detected. The extra costs stemming from principal/ agent problems in nonprofits are difficult to see.

Nonprofits are often evaluated on the basis of their "activity ratio." That is the proportion of every dollar contributed to a nonprofit that actually goes to the designated beneficiaries of the nonprofit – to carrying out its mission. The higher the activity ratio the better, since this normally means the amount used to benefit clients or students increases. While this is a good metric, it is not perfect. The proportion depends on accounting values rather than real values and, as we know from our experience with for-profit firms, accounting values can be manipulated.[14] Accounting conventions give nonprofit managers considerable latitude in assigning expenditures to different cost accounts, so the activity ratio can be "managed" by administrators (Lederman, 2009; Stecklow, 1995).

Whether the activity ratio actually measures efficiency depends on the transparency of the organization's accounting practices and since nonprofits are virtually unregulated and are not required to release audited financial results to the public no one can determine the "quality" of their activity ratios. It does not seem to matter a lot, anyway. In a recent study of donor contributions to nonprofits, Frumkin and Kim (2001: 273) found that donor contributions are independent of the organization's "activity ratio." It may not matter because the reported activity ratios are meaningless. Since agency abuse in nonprofits results in higher cost, the nonprofit managers can apply those higher costs to the beneficial part of the activity ratio, making the institution appear more efficient when the opposite is true.

The Role of Third Party Payers

The people who consume private goods are the same people who pay for those goods; hence, a for-profit firm's customers are able to judge whether or not they received value for what they purchased. As a consequence, for-profit firms have a strong incentive to make their customers happy if they expect repeat purchases or referrals from their current customers to other customers.

In nonprofits and in particular in higher education, the people receiving the service and those paying for the service are frequently not the same people. Clearly, charitable donors and taxpayers pay a substantial part of the higher education burden. Further, parents frequently pay tuition and fees for children who actually receive the services. Hence, parents, donors, and taxpayers frequently do not know what they are paying for. We see similar problems introduced by third party payers in the high cost of health care. If you consider the true higher education customers as those who pay for education, then those customers are relatively uninformed about the value they have received. That lack of information leaves considerable room for agency abuse.

The only source of ex post information about value available to parents, donors, and taxpayers comes from students and students may have a strategic incentive to misrepresent their experience or lack the maturity to render a good judgment. The "beer and circus" atmosphere on many campuses suggests students are interested in entertainment and are less engaged in education than they used to be (Sperber, 2001). Tom Wolfe's *I Am Charlotte Simmons* is a compelling story about current campus culture (2004).

4.5   NONPROFITS, AGENCY PROBLEMS, AND REPUTATIONS: A TOXIC MIX

A school's most valuable asset is its reputation. Indeed, academic discussions often consider maximizing reputation as the chief objective of a college or university.[15] As an institution's reputation increases, it becomes more selective in admissions, alumni contribute more, donors make larger contributions, and it has more access to grants.[16] All of this causes the institution's revenues to rise. Furthermore, revenue sources become more diversified as reputation increases, so the school is less dependent on tuition. In contrast, institutions at the bottom of the reputation ladder are tuition driven and must be concerned with filling each freshman class. Increasingly diverse revenue sources reduce financial risk, just as increasing revenues make the institution wealthier.

In Chapter 3, we learned why higher education reputations are durable, why institutions have an incentive to maintain quality uncertainty, and how quality reputation limits current and potential competition. We also learned in Chapter 3 that any institution that tries to control cost runs the risk of reducing its quality reputation and creating controversies that damage reputations. As long as the public perceives a positive relationship between cost and quality, reputation competition is a race to see who can spend the most, which creates fertile ground for agency abuse. Combining these results with what we learn about the principal/agent problem in this chapter explains why higher education refuses to reform and why it is the least innovative sector outside government (Getz et al., 1997). Reputation maximization leads to a bias against reform and against innovation.

Higher education institutions are biased against reform and biased toward ever increasing revenues. Consider an organization that produces multiple products or services. Suppose there is a shift in consumer preferences away from one type of service and toward another service. In higher education this might be, say, a shift away from pre-law majors towards engineering or computer science. There are two ways the organization can respond to this change in preferences: It can shift resources from the less favored service toward the more favored service, or it can leave existing resources in place and acquire new resources to increase the output of the service that consumers now want.

Owing to profit maximization/cost minimization, the for-profit firm shifts resources from the failing services toward the preferred services before it seeks new resources. If the firm does not do this, it will not minimize costs and maximize profits. Its risk adjusted rate of return will be lower, and it is likely to become a takeover target.

There is no such market discipline in higher education. By and large, higher education institutions finance shifts in preferences with new revenue sources rather than by reallocating existing resources. As long as the college or university can raise additional revenue, there is no market imperative that requires it to reallocate existing resources.

Closing down obsolete or duplicate programs and using the resources freed by that kind of internal reform will be controversial. Faculty members fiercely resist attempts to end programs with small enrollments, even though they may be costly to the school. This resistance causes controversy, and administrators and trustees avoid controversies because of their impact on that critically important commodity, reputation. In other words, reputation maximization leads to a bias against reform and a preference for seeking more revenue.

If an institution's problems go unaddressed, education suffers. The students may not realize they got less than they paid for until some years in the future. It may take a generation or more before the institution's problems show up as less successful alumni. The negative effect on reputation from unresolved problems is delayed for a long time; hence, to the present generation of administrators, faculty, and trustees, the cost of a diminished future reputation is small, while the cost of a diminished current reputation is high.

Suppose you are a faculty member, an administrator, or a trustee. Fixing a serious problem will take years, and it will involve considerable controversy. Alternatively, the problem and the controversy can be avoided by applying more cash to the institution. The faculty members, administrators, and the board members ask themselves: Do I want my tenure to be known for controversy or to be known for an increasing flow of new funds into the institution? The answer is obvious. More funds trump controversies. Thus board members hire presidents for their fund raising abilities and pay lip service to cost control.

These incentives adversely select for the wrong kind of campus leadership. The leadership problem extends from top administrators through deans and department chairs, who are hired for their ability to bring more resources into the college, not how well they use current resources. Indeed, using the current resources efficiently will get the administrator fired. Any change in the existing distribution of resources must adversely impact some group who will actively resist that change and that resistance will be controversial.

In addition, most administrative staff members have de facto tenure. That is due to the presence of tenure among faculty members and a strong preference for "equity" on most campuses. The resulting rigidities convert campus expenditures into fixed costs that cannot be changed without considerable controversy. The things that need to be done do not get done.

Attempts to raise quality run into the same rigidities. The typical faculty member is an average teacher or researcher who will have trouble achieving higher quality and thus is resistant, at least passively, to the demands for higher quality. Indeed, the typical faculty member views campus resources as a fixed pie, such that more rewards going to exceptional teachers or researchers must come from their share of those resources.[17] The faculty members who benefit from higher standards are the exceptional teachers and researchers. Unfortunately, faculty decisions are made by majority vote and, since the direct beneficiaries of an efficient quality enhancement proposal are in the minority, the proposal is unlikely to pass muster under shared governance.

4.6   AGENCY PROBLEMS AND COST

Despite strong constraints on agency abuse in for-profit firms, agency problems are common in those firms. Since the constraints on agency abuse are weak in higher education, the probability of agency abuse in higher education is higher than the probability of agency abuse in for-profit firms. From numerous studies and the evidence in Chapter 2, we know higher education has a dismal cost control record and a disappointing quality record. Agency abuse always leads to higher cost than necessary; therefore agency abuse is a primary cause of high cost in colleges and universities. The role played by agency abuse is not well known owing to the absence of regulation, little private oversight, and scant media coverage.

In Chapter 1, we explored the four traditional explanations for rising costs: 1) the bundling of additional services; 2) unfunded government mandates;[18] 3) Baumol's cost disease; and 4) Bowen's revenue theory of cost. From the discussion of agency problems in this chapter and the review of Bowen's revenue theory of cost in Chapter 1, it is clear that the revenue theory of cost is driven by unresolved principal/agent problems.

The principal/agent problem also increases costs through the bundling of additional services and Baumol's cost disease. Faculty, administrators, and trustees derive personal benefits from the additional services provided by colleges and universities. The necessity to pay some faculty higher real wages owing to rising opportunity wages (Baumol's cost disease) tends to elevate all faculty salaries because the faculty insists on "salary equity" among faculty members. Administrators and trustees comply with salary equity (which eliminates pay for productivity) in order to avoid controversy and preserve the institution's reputation. Faculty members resist the adoption of new technology and administrators/trustees comply for similar reasons; this causes the rate of innovation in higher education to be much slower than in other sectors of the economy (Getz et al., 1997). In addition, the principal/agent problem leads to excessive investment in quality signaling through research, athletics, facilities, and community service, as discussed in Chapter 3. Therefore the bundling of additional services, Baumol's cost disease, and Bowen's revenue theory are complementary causes of higher cost than necessary.

Marion Fremont-Smith argues that performance problems in non-profit institutions are always "governance failures" (2004: 15). Clearly, agency abuse is governance failure. Governance is "a method or system of management."[19] Good governance implies the management methods or systems serve the principal's objectives, not the agent's private objectives. Governance fails when the principal's objectives are not served. Since higher education cannot control costs and its quality has declined, its governance has failed and the governance has failed because of the principal/agent problem. A close inspection of that governance structure and the conflicting incentives in play reveals why governance has failed.

Governance

Higher education institutions have a unique structure: governance is shared among boards of trustees, administrators, and the faculty. This structure is not an accident. Shared governance minimizes transactions costs in higher education, reflects the distinctive technology of teaching/research, and recognizes faculty ownership of the human capital assets that are the central productive assets in higher education.

Faculty human capital produces the knowledge and skills that every student needs to become educated (Martin, 2005: 42–57). Faculty human capital is the only indispensable input in higher education; without the faculty's human capital there is no college or university. Further, teaching value added is only as good as the faculty's knowledge of their own discipline and their ability to communicate that knowledge to others. Faculty members contribute capital assets to the enterprise and that is why they have a seat at the governance table and are not just employees.

In a perfect world, shared governance would be a natural constraint on the higher education agency problem, just as the market for control constrains the agency problem in for-profit firms. Board members, administrators, and faculty members would monitor each other. Each group has considerable inside information; faculty members have more information about day to day operations than do board members and they have considerably more knowledge about what constitutes academic quality than do either administrators or trustees. Each inside group has more information than students, taxpayers, parents, alumni, and donors, and they are in a better position to act as a check on each other.

Unfortunately we do not live in a perfect world and the internal monitoring does not take place. Administrators artfully play the two groups off each other. They stand between faculty members and trustees, cutting off the communication required for real shared governance. Administrators tell faculty they cannot involve themselves in issues the board considers its prerogative because the board will resent the intrusion. They tell the board it cannot intrude on faculty prerogatives for the same reason. Some administrators prohibit communication between faculty and board members. They do this because it prevents the board from getting complete information about campus activities.[20]

Board members agree to these arrangements because they do not understand shared governance and typically come from organizations (such as for-profit firms) where a strict hierarchy prevails. To most board members, talking to faculty about campus issues appears to be a violation of "the chain of command," when in fact it is an essential part of shared governance. Board members don't realize this and have little faith in the arrangement anyway.

Some faculty members shirk governance responsibilities in order to pursue research or consulting opportunities; others invest excessively in governance responsibilities in order to advance their personal financial situation; and still others invest in governance because they have a grievance. There are too few faculty members who invest in governance in order to improve the institution.

The popular public conception is governance fails because pampered, eccentric, and temperamental faculty members are derelict in their duty.[21]

As with all popular conceptions, there is some truth to the notion: faculty members are part of the problem. On the other hand, recall from Chapter 2 that two-thirds of the increase in cost per student comes from costs other than faculty wage and salary cost per student, and in 1976 faculty members represented 58 percent of campus employment in public institutions and 42 percent of campus employment in private institutions; by 2005 those percentage had fallen to 37 percent and 34 percent respectively. Further, enrollment at public institutions increased by 50 percent and 89 percent at private institutions from 1976 to 2005. The real growth in campus employment has not been among faculty members, even though enrollment growth has been significant. Furthermore, it is important to remember that faculty wages and teaching loads are set by administrators and board members; if wages go up while productivity goes down, that is policy made by administrators and boards.

There were also some important trends in faculty composition during the period from 1976 to 2005 that are at odds with the notion that the primary problem is powerful faculties who demand something for nothing. First, from 1970 to 2005 the proportion of the faculty employed full time fell from 77 percent to 52 percent. Almost half today's faculty members are part time instructors: people who have no seat at the governance table, are paid very low wages, and have few benefits. Another trend among public universities is the replacement of tenure track faculty with non-tenure track instructors with no seat at the governance table.

Stephen Bowen (2009) reports that over two-thirds of the staff members in the Maine University System are non-instructional staff and that the system spends $2 on non-instructional staff for every $1 it spends on instructional staff. Across institutions, the higher non-instructional to instructional staff ratio is associated with higher costs per degree in Maine.

For the past three decades the faculty's power within colleges and universities has declined steadily, while at the same time the college cost problem has accelerated and teaching value added has declined. Campus power shifted to administrators as costs accelerated after their moderation in the 1970s.

If the cost problem is due exclusively to pampered faculty, costs should have stabilized and declined over the last three decades, since the faculty's governance share declined sharply over that period. There is an agency problem with faculty members, but there is also an agency problem with administrators and board members. It is important to remember that the faculty does not set its own salary and teaching loads; the authority to set those policies rests with administrators and board members.

The mix of agency problems among faculty, administrators, and board members varies considerably from one institution to the other. In some instances, the primary problem is with faculty members and in other instances the problem is with administrators or governing boards, while at others it is with all three. On the other hand, there are still other institutions that get it right and are good shepherds of both cost and quality. However, since real cost is rising at unacceptable rates at both private and public institutions and quality is declining, it is clear that the average, or representative, institution has not controlled its cost and maintained its quality.

A single agency template for higher education does not exist. For example, as you move up the quality hierarchy the governance power held by faculty increases. The reason for this is that faculty at the most elite institutions are very mobile; they can readily move to other institutions. In a recent article describing Harvard's financial problems, Richard Bradley describes the impact of an $11 billion drop in Harvard's endowment on its faculty (2009). He reports that some faculty members threaten to leave if the university does not find a way to close the financial gap. Despite what this threat might say about loyalty, it is not an idle threat; most of Harvard's faculty members have the credentials to move if they choose to. This is not true among faculty members near the bottom of the quality tier; they tend to be very immobile. This significantly weakens their position in the governance structure. Therefore we expect to find the core agency problem may be among faculty at one institution, administrators at another institution, and board members at still another institution.

Agency Issues with Administrators and Board Members

For the sake of discussion, I classify senior administrators into three types: the public relations administrator, the professional manager, and the public intellectual. All three of these classifications are stereotypes; their purpose is to facilitate discussion. Real senior administrators have elements of all three types in varying proportions. My purpose is to demonstrate why nonprofit status and reputation competition lead to a bias among board members against two types of senior administrator and a preference for the third type.

The public relations administrator focuses on image and fund raising (Chapters 3 and 5). The administrator may come from a career in higher education development, politics, or nonprofit development. The professional manager is focused on the efficient use of resources and the smooth administration of the university. The manager may come from higher education financial management or a managerial position in the for-profit sector, government, or the military. The public intellectual is focused on academic quality and invariably comes from a faculty position within higher education. She will be an established scholar who may have spent time in government service. Larry Summers, the former president of Harvard, is an example, as is the current president of Harvard, Drew Gilpin Faust.

Given the choice, faculty members prefer to be led by scholars, since the public intellectual is well aware of the issues that are most important to faculty members. It is not surprising then to find that most public intellectual presidents are found among the elite institutions where faculty members have the strongest governance role. Governing boards at the elite institutions know their reputations draw considerable financial support regardless of the president's fund raising skills. The downside is reflected by Harvard's current experience, where Bradley reports President Faust is not prepared for the budget downsizing required by the shrinkage in the university's endowment (2009).

Dennis M. Barden of Witt/Kieffer, an executive search firm specializing in higher education, reports in The *Chronicle of Higher Education* that the candidates' "Rolodex" of potential donors is the principle qualification for the job (2009). He admits to being uneasy about this as the primary qualification at institutions with "considerable intellectual renown." Barden knows something is not quite right with this oversized emphasis on money when he says "a part of me simply wants hiring decisions to be based on individual accomplishment, ability, and experience – that is to say, on merit – and not on the basis of 'connections'" (2009).

Barden's report reveals board members have a strong preference for public relations administrators rather than professional managers or public intellectuals. This tilt towards the public relations administrator also suggests faculty preferences are not decisive in the selection of presidential candidates. The tilt is driven by reputation competition. Unlike the professional manager, a public relations president will not stress the efficient utilization of existing resources; he will raise more money for new initiatives and leave the existing resource allocation unchanged. This is what the board wants him to do, since any attempt to reallocate resources will be controversial and that will damage the institution's reputation.

If the public relations president is also a careerist, he knows his own career is advanced by no controversies, and a trail of new satellite activities, new buildings, and a rising endowment. Who could complain about that? This is exactly the point; new buildings and a larger endowment are not controversial. This record insures a step up in his next job. Unfortunately, all quality problems are left for the next president and the new satellite activities and new buildings ratchet the institution's cost structure up to a new permanent level that will have to be funded for the foreseeable future.

Suppose the board and the president agree they should fix the cost and quality problems before adding new satellite activities or new buildings, or raising more endowment.[22] First, this means trustees are admitting the institution has unresolved problems. In the current environment, the president knows this is a career ending strategy even if she succeeds in making progress. Her central problem is measuring progress on cost control and quality versus measuring progress in terms of new buildings and more endowment. It is no contest; new buildings and more endowment are obvious additions, while progress on cost control or quality is less tangible and the results are debatable. Further, making progress on cost control and quality inevitably makes some people on campus very angry and that anger would follow the administrator wherever she tried to move.

The foregoing scenario illustrates the primary agency problem with governing boards: they are entrusted with the preservation of the higher education social contract and they are failing in that duty. The governing boards are the stewards of this social contract; it is their responsibility to maintain quality and to insure costs are reasonable (Martin, 2005: 1–41). The costs are not reasonable and quality is declining.

Trustee Incentives

Serving on college and university boards signals wealth and status to one's peers (Martin, 2005: 89–113). In general, the larger the institution's endowment or the more successful its athletic programs, the greater is the social status associated with serving on the board. An ideal tenure as a college trustee is a period of sharply rising endowment and no controversies.

The status signal is a double edged sword, however. If the institution experiences public controversies, the reputations of individual board members will be damaged. Therefore board members avoid controversies; if there are financial improprieties, faculty/staff misbehavior, or any number of potentially embarrassing events, the board's first impulse will be to keep it quiet. Few people are willing to serve on the board of a troubled institution, while many would like to serve on the board of a well-regarded and stable institution.

The foregoing reveals the personal interests of administrators and board members are not served by reform, while their interests are served by a growing reputation for quality. This leads to a studious avoidance of difficult questions concerning the connection between expenditures and outcomes. It is better not to ask these questions. If you know expenditures did not result in positive outcomes, you would be obligated to fix the problem, so it is better not to know.

A prohibition on asking uncomfortable questions is a natural consequence of these incentives. The prohibition is enforced by "collegiality codes." If a board member suspects there is a problem in a specific program and questions the benefits from that program, the broad member risks being disruptive. This has a significant chilling effect on anyone who may be tempted to raise similar questions. Boards can be effective stewards of the social contract only if they are willing to ask the hard questions and then follow up on the answers they get.

Faculty Agency Issues

Research generates significant financial reward, status, and mobility in higher education. Indeed, research and administrative jobs are the only career tracks that lead to national prominence in higher education. Chapter 3 reveals why colleges and universities are willing to invest in research as a quality signal. Faculty members are only too willing to accept this task since it fits our personal preferences for study and writing and our career aspirations. It is more interesting than preparing undergraduate lectures.

Strangely, exceptional teaching is not a career track to national prominence; this is strange because parents, donors, and taxpayers are clearly willing to pay for exceptional teaching and are indifferent to research. Considerable insight can be obtained by considering why a robust market for senior scholars exists but a market for senior teachers does not exist. I explore the absence of a market for gifted senior teachers in Chapter 6.

Mark Bauerlein considers the dramatic imbalance in research and teaching incentives where he finds the increased research volume comes at the expense of both research quality and teaching quality (2009). Bauerlein suggests colleges and universities need to reconsider how they compensate and promote faculty members (change the incentive structure). He also suggests Ph.D. programs offer separate program tracks, one for research and another for teaching.

The research rewards induce gifted faculty to spend considerable time and effort pursuing research; the absence of rewards for exceptional teaching lead to neglect of that activity. Research success shifts faculty members' loyalty to their profession rather than the institution where they are employed. Successful researchers tend to underinvest in campus governance.

Faculty members retain exclusive control over campus curriculum. The exclusive control leads to legendary conflicts over "core curriculum" at many institutions, both elite institutions and lesser lights. Unfortunately, radical politics are sometimes substituted for sound curriculum. This has a disastrous effect on the formulation of a dynamic curriculum that meets society's needs. As faculty members, we seek to "clone ourselves" when it comes to designing curriculum, so left to our own devices we construct curriculum that prepares students to pursue Ph.D.s in our discipline. Since only a handful of students go on to Ph.D. programs, this distorts the curriculum. We also tend to introduce our own biases and identity politics into curriculum. Other voices need to be heard when it comes to curriculum design; trustees and alumni should participate.

Destructuring Curriculum and the Academic Ratchet

"Destructuring" is the unwinding of traditional curriculum, where departments require fewer courses, place less emphasis on course sequence, substitute specialty courses for core courses, and choose less faculty responsibility for student course selection (Zemsky, 1989). Following Zemsky's confirmation that curriculum "destructuring" was widespread, the issue attracted considerable interest. Zemsky expected higher education to correct the problem. Unfortunately, he found:

> The faculty had learned only too well the pleasure of allowing each other to do his or her own thing. Reinstituting requirements would have made faculty responsible for what their students took with them into the next set of courses in an ordered and sequenced curriculum.
>   And that turned out to be the most important lesson of all. Presenting evidence of a problem – no matter how compelling – is not sufficient to change academic practices. Faculty freedom and autonomy trump evidence every time. Those who argue that greater transparency, that is, more evidence as to the academy's problems and failings, will either compel faculty to change or force public entities and accrediting agencies to change always underestimate the inertia in the system. (2009: 120–21)

This is an egregious governance failure and represents serious agency abuse on the part of faculty. Faculty members are able to ignore facts because administrators and board members will not risk controversies; administrators and board members avoid controversies because reputations are essential to higher education competition.

Massy and Zemsky consider the "academic ratchet," which is the tendency of productivity rewards to be propagated to all faculty, resulting in a permanent increase in costs (1994: 2). Hence, lower teaching loads for productive research faculty get propagated to all faculty because faculty insist on equality of treatment,[23] not just "fairness" (1994: 2). The net effect of this trend is to increase the number of faculty members required to provide the same level of undergraduate teaching. Therefore costs must be higher.

Further, the emphasis on equality of treatment that propagates lower teaching loads for all faculty members necessitates a pooling solution

(Chapter 3) for teaching and research. Good teachers and bad teachers receive the same compensation and good researchers and bad researchers receive the same compensation. The pooling solution adversely selects for lower quality teaching and lower quality research. These practices not only raise cost, but also lower quality. Massy and Zemsky call this process the academic ratchet because it ratchets teaching productivity down and cost up to a new and permanent level.

Massy and Zemsky's analysis models department level behavior, so the curriculum and teaching load decisions are made at that level (1994). They punctuate the seriousness of these trends with former Dean Henry Rosovsky's farewell address to the faculty of Harvard's College of Arts and Sciences, where he said:

> I suspect teaching loads have declined significantly. Indeed, it has become extremely difficult to say what constitutes standard teaching loads. . . . From the point of view of a dean two observations are in order. First, the dean has only the vaguest notion concerning what individual professors teach. Second, the changes that have occurred were never authorized at the decanal level. (1994: 21).

Dean Rosovsky's statement is remarkable for what it reveals about governance and the principal/agent problem in higher education. The dean of Harvard's College of Arts and Sciences does not know what teaching loads are in individual departments and does not have control over those teaching loads! This is a clear governance breakdown and obvious agency abuse on the part of the faculty.

Curriculum Packing

Academic programs need students to insure their continued existence. If the program's student/faculty ratio is in a secular decline, the program could face slow administrative liquidation when faculty positions are lost due to retirements. Also, faculty members are well aware their role in campus governance declines as their numbers decline. Therefore faculty members in these programs have a personal financial stake in recruiting students. There are three ways to recruit students: raise the benefits to each student (better teaching and improved job prospects), lower the cost to each student by giving high grades (part of the motivation behind grade inflation) and persuade the rest of the faculty to make your courses part of the required curriculum. This is a political process, not an academic process: faculty in low enrollment programs form coalitions that support each other's courses for inclusion in the "core curriculum." Faculty members in programs with growing enrollments have little incentive to oppose "curriculum packing"; it is much easier to avoid the conflict that would inevitably follow if they oppose these additions.

On the other hand, if curriculum is driven exclusively by enrollment some programs would disappear owing to a lack of employment opportunities and others might disappear simply because they are difficult. One could end up with a university that does not have humanities programs or a physics program. There are core programs that each university must have in order to call itself a university. The balance between faculty self-interest and the legitimate needs of the university can be difficult to find. It is worth noting that institutions rarely consult the student body, parents, alumni, or the governing board about curriculum content; generally, faculty are quite prickly about curriculum.

The curriculum packing process can lead to peculiar outcomes. Undergraduate students may be required to take humanities courses, multiculturalism courses, or identity politics, while students graduate from college without ever taking an economics course or a math course. For example, in 2007 the Intercollegiate Studies Institute (ISI) administered "a basic sixty-question multiple-choice exam on American history, government, foreign affairs, and economics to over 7,000 freshmen and 7,000 seniors from fifty colleges and universities nationwide" (2010). The average senior's score on this exam was 54 percent, which is a failing grade. They found that the average senior had taken only four courses in history, political science, or economics. The ISI reports that the differences between freshmen and seniors reveal that colleges tend to "stall" the student's progress on civil literacy while altering opinions about "polarizing social issues."

The inability of Ph.D. programs in the humanities to respond to the chronic excess supply of humanities faculty is further evidence of faculty agency abuse that perpetuates the high cost effects owing to the academic ratchet. Darcy O'Brien reported in 1979 that:

> It may be difficult for anyone not actually involved in graduate education to appreciate the gravity of the situation or even to sympathize with its most obvious victims, those students who spend years working for a doctorate only to find it of no practical use. Perhaps the plight of the unemployed PhD deserves little attention compared to far more critical unemployment problems in America today. But these jobless PhD's are merely the visible detritus, the inescapable reality, of a system of higher education that – unsure of its priorities and inclined, like government, to self-perpetuation – no longer can be said to be performing its job well. (1979)

O'Brien makes the case that graduate programs in the humanities were not telling students about real job prospects (1979). He quotes some faculty members who admit the misdirection is necessary in order to keep their graduate programs and he explains how universities benefit financially from having graduate students to teach undergraduate classes. He also notes how institutions benefit from a ready supply of part time faculty members and how they benefit from turning over tenure track faculty without granting tenure. The story reminds one of Marx's evil capitalists who maintain a "reserve army of the unemployed" for exactly the same reasons.

More recently, William Pannapacker (using the pen name Thomas H. Benton) wrote three articles for the *Chronicle of Higher Education* entitled "So You Want to Go to Graduate School?" (2003), "Graduate School in the Humanities: Just Don't Go" (2009), and "The Big Lie About the 'Life of the Mind'" (2010). Thirty years later, Pannapacker is covering the same ground as O'Brien and reports that less than half the humanities Ph.D.s minted each year find tenure track jobs. Pannapacker concludes that "graduate school in the humanities is a trap" and what is worse it is designed to be a trap.

Steve Malanga finds the most troubling part of Pannapacker's articles is he

> repeats an accusation that O'Brien made in 1979, which is that graduate programs and humanities professional organizations cook their employment statistics intentionally to mislead would-be graduate students. They do this by counting as employed every graduate who is working in the field – including low-paying adjunct teaching positions and non-tenure jobs that are dead ends – without making distinctions. Pannapacker sums up the deception by observing that, "there is still almost no way . . . for students to gather some of the most crucial information about graduate programs: the rate of attrition, the average amount of debt at graduation, and, most important, the placement of graduates (differentiating between adjunct, lecturer, visiting, tenure-track positions, and nonacademic positions)." Were he still writing on the subject, O'Brien might observe that thirty years is a long time to be keeping this vital information from students. (2010)

Pannapacker concludes:

> It's hard to tell young people that universities recognize that their idealism and energy – and lack of information – are an exploitable resource. For universities, the impact of graduate programs on the lives of those students is an acceptable externality, like dumping toxins into a river. If you cannot find a tenure-track position, your university will no longer court you; it will pretend you do not exist and will act as if your unemployability is entirely your fault. It will make you feel ashamed, and you will probably just disappear, convinced it's right rather than that the game was rigged from the beginning. (Benton, 2009)

It is worth noting the information withheld from graduate students is information about the program's value added and we learned in Chapter

3 the institution always has an incentive to withhold that information. In contrast, consider what would happen to any for-profit organization that sold an investment opportunity with misleading information. The university's attitude is a primitive form of caveat emptor. Note also the motivation on the part of faculty is to preserve their humanities graduate programs; since students are principals, this is clear agency abuse. Despite the foregoing, what is remarkable about this situation is how multiple generations of humanities graduate students could remain so uninformed. This persistent misinformation could not exist if humanities faculty members were honest with their students; however, honesty would reduce enrollment and adversely impact the faculty's financial situation.

Specialty courses and programs based on identity politics are another form of curriculum based principal/agent abuse. Like Ph.D. programs in the humanities, courses and programs based on ideology lead to few employment opportunities. Steering students to these courses and programs does the students a disservice by both radicalizing the students and leaving them with no means of earning a living. That mixture of radicalization and few employment opportunities can also be costly to society; educated and disaffected young people with little to do and a lot of debt cannot be in our collective interest.

Overview of Agency Issues

In the interest of perspective, there are colleges and universities that do a professional job of controlling cost and guarding quality. Any sensible reform program would identify these institutions, document how they address cost and quality issues, and then explain to the public why it takes exceptional courage to do what they do in a market dominated by reputation competition. The public needs to be made aware of the fact that not all campus controversies are bad; some very constructive things can come from controversy. For example, in a recent article about financial crises, Kent John Chabotar, president of Guilford College, offers a pragmatic program for working through a financial crisis (2009). He raises questions that should be asked before the institution finds itself in difficulties.

4.7   SUMMARY AND CONCLUSION

Every institution must manage cash inflows/outflows in order to prevent insolvency. The management of cash flows leads to the principal/agent problem whenever agents are hired to take decisions on behalf of principals. The two primary nongovernment strategies for managing cash flows are for-profit firms and nonprofit organizations. Since principal/ agent abuse always leads to abnormally high cost, bankruptcy is a natural constraint on principal/agent abuse. A rapacious agency problem leads to financial collapse, while a chronic agency problem leads to a persistent history of high cost.

The principal/agent problem is universal; it is found among for-profit firms, politicians, the medical profession, the legal profession, and non-profit organizations. The public is well aware of the agency problem in for-profit firms and politics. The severity of the agency problem depends on how well the principal's interests and the agent's interests are aligned through compensation contracts, how well informed the principal is, and the number and variety of institutional constraints on agency abuse. The principal's and the agent's interest can be aligned by incentive compensation contracts; incentive compensation contracts are rare in higher education. Principals are well informed when the organization's financial records and operations are "transparent"; there is a serious lack of transparency among higher education institutions, as their financial records and operations are opaque.

Institutional constraints on agency abuse include such things as: markets for control; competition from new entrants; regulation; oversight by private groups; media oversight; performance measures; and the significance of third party payers. For-profit firms are subject to intense capital market competition. The market for control acts as a direct constraint on agency abuse among for-profit firms; there is no market for control for higher education institutions. New entry among high quality colleges and universities is very costly and takes a very long time. Competition from new entry is not a practical constraint on agency abuse in higher education. For-profit firms are subject to extensive regulation by the federal government; there is very little regulation of higher education institutions. Numerous private groups have a personal financial interest in the oversight of for-profit firms; no private groups have a personal financial interest in the oversight of higher education institutions. The media has a demonstrated preference for scandals among for-profit firms and politicians; the media gives higher education a pass. A for-profit firm's performance is measured by profits, and agency abuse directly reduces profits; a nonprofit institution's performance is measured by the "activity ratio," which is unaffected by agency abuse. The person who pays for products and services provided by for-profit firms is the same person who consumes those products and services; the people who pay for services provided by higher education are not the same people who consume those services.

Despite the widespread use of incentive contracts, more transparency, and extensive institutional constraints on agency problems in for-profit firms, agency problems among for-profit firms are common. In sharp contrast, the factors that would limit agency problems in higher education are quite weak. Agency abuse always results in higher costs than necessary. Higher education has an established record of rapidly increasing real costs per student and declining quality. The foregoing suggests there are chronic and unresolved agency problems in higher education. This conclusion is consistent with H.R. Bowen's revenue theory of higher education cost (1980).

Owing to nonprofit status, Bowen's revenue theory of cost leads to a revenue to cost spiral in higher education. Any increase in the student's ability to pay for higher education will be captured by higher tuition. Therefore the college access problem cannot be solved until the higher education cost disease is cured.

In Chapter 3, we learned why reputation competition is so dominant in higher education. The combination of reputation competition, nonprofit status, and unresolved agency problems leads to a bias against reform and a preference for ever increasing revenues and a fixed allocation of existing resources. This bias leads to the foregoing revenue to cost spiral.

Agency problems are always a governance failure. Higher education has a peculiar governance structure where the agents, faculty members, administrators, and board members share governance. In a perfect world, shared governance would be a natural constraint on agency abuse in higher education, as the market for control is among for-profit firms. The popular conception holds that pampered faculty members are responsible for the chronic agency problem in higher education. The facts suggest something different.

Most of the increase in cost per student from 1980 to the present comes from overhead expenses. Most of the growth in college/university employment comes from growth in non-instructional professional staff. Almost 50 percent of faculty members today are part time faculty with no seat at the governance table and many tenure track faculty have been replaced by full time instructors who also have no seat at the governance table. Clearly, the faculty's governance role has been weakened over the last three decades. It is important to remember that it is administrators and board members who have the authority to approve teaching loads and salaries, not faculty members. If faculty members were the primary problem, costs per student should have stabilized or fallen from 1980 to the present. Therefore there are significant agency issues with administrators and board members.

The primary problem with administrators and board members is their preference for public relations presidents who are singularly focused on raising more endowment or extracting more support from state governments. They avoid the tough decisions about the use of existing resources because those problems are controversial and reveal the institution has unresolved problems that damage the institution's reputation.

NOTES

1. Governments face market constraints on their ability to finance deficits. As the deficit rises as a percentage of GDP, the interest rate the government must pay increases, and interest payments on debt climb as a percentage of total expenditures, driving the deficits higher until the government is forced to default on its sovereign debt. The current sovereign debt crisis in Greece is a classic example.
2. A pure public good is said to be "non-excludable and non-rivalrous," meaning once the good is supplied the producer cannot prevent everyone from using the good without paying for it and one person's consumption does not diminish another's. The classic example is a lighthouse. If the producer cannot prevent people from using the good without paying for the service, he will stop providing the good. The conventional solution is for the government to tax people and use the proceeds to support the public good.
3. A comprehensive discussion of the theory of for-profit firms can be found in Varian (2006).
4. Profit is a surplus that is retained and since it is retained it is not used to benefit those who are the targeted beneficiaries of the nonprofit. Hence, in order to benefit the maximum number of recipients, profit must be zero.
5. See Holmstrom and Milgrom (1991) and Mas-Colell et al. (1995: 471–510) for a more detailed discussion of the principal/agent problem.
6. In one sense, the agency problem in nonprofit institutions is like the "tragedy of the commons" that led to the enclosure movement in England. When pasture land was owned in common, individuals had an incentive to overgraze the land. This adverse incentive led to lower agricultural productivity for all who owned the land in common and that finally led to the enclosure movement.
7. This is a common problem among all nonprofit institutions and it contributes to agency abuse.
8. The terms "firm," "corporation," and "business" will be used as equivalent expressions in this chapter. Further, all of these terms are meant to represent publicly held organizations whose shares are traded on organized stock exchanges. Privately held firms and corporations do not have separation of ownership and control.
9. There are two types of risk: firm specific risk and systemic risk. Firm specific risk is risk peculiar to the individual firm. All of that risk can be diversified away at little cost, so the market does not compensate investors for bearing firm specific risk. The only risk they can expect compensation for is systemic risk.
10. By the capital asset pricing model, the expected return is equal to the risk free rate of return plus the firm's beta times the reward the market pays for bearing one unit of systemic market risk. The firm's beta is the correlation coefficient for the firm's rate of return regressed against the market's rate of return.
11. The firm's debt and equity have value to individual investors according to how they contribute to the investor's portfolio of assets. The contribution made to the portfolio depends on risk and return. Investor wealth is created when the firm achieves a risk adjusted rate of return in excess of the expected risk adjusted rate of return. Capital is withdrawn from the firm when it fails to meet expectations. Persistent failure to meet expectations leads to bankruptcy or takeover by outsiders.
12. Wealth is the "plug" for the balance sheet, the entry that makes the balance sheet footings equal.
13. The term "inefficient" is used cautiously at this point. It refers only to the public good

character of the donations, since they are not allocated on the basis of productivity. If the donations were not tax deductible, then the public would have no stake in the allocation and the donations would be a private expenditure representing individual preferences. It is the tax shelter that gives the public a seat at the table.

14. One college president I know argued "managing campus resources" meant deciding which account the expenditure should be charged to.

15. The traditional objective for higher education institutions found in the literature is to maximize reputation (see James, 1990). A more complete discussion of objectives in higher education can be found in Martin (2005) and Brewer et al. (2002).

16. Brewer et al. (2002) offer a complete and very accessible discussion of structure and strategy in the higher education hierarchy.

17. This is a common perception among faculty members, although it can be argued that everyone benefits from improved quality since this drives all wages higher in the program. Unfortunately, for too many faculty members, it is relative wages that matter.

18. Unfunded government mandates such as Title IX do increase higher education costs as they do in every other sector of the economy. However, it is not obvious that the cost burden from this source is higher in education than it is in other sectors. Therefore the much higher relative rate of cost increase in higher education is unlikely to be the result of government mandates.

19. Dictionary.com.

20. I have seen a college president remove administrative staffing data from a committee report on cost control at the college because he did not want to explain why overhead staffing had grown so much over the past ten years.

21. The faculty members are the students' most important advocates on campus, not administrators who have little contact with students.

22. Trustees would never agree to this unless the cost control and quality problems were a serious and public threat to the institution's reputation.

23. Note the relationship between "equality of treatment" and the separation of pay and productivity discussed in Chapter 1.

5. Commercialization: The devil made me do it!

5.1 INTRODUCTION

Derek Bok (2003), David Kirp (2003, 2005), Gaye Tuchman (2009), and Jennifer Washburn (2005) among others (Engell and Dangerfield, 2005; Gardner, 2005) argue "commercialization," "corporatization," or "commoditization" is responsible for higher education's insatiable demand for money. Derek Bok defines "commercialization" as "efforts within the university to make a *profit* [emphasis added] from teaching, research, and other campus activities" (2003: 3). These authors criticize the direction higher education took after 1980; they are troubled by the abandonment of traditional academic values for what they believe are "corporate values." The belief that higher education's unseemly pursuit of money comes from an alien corporate influence is common among faculty members (Bok, 2003: 19; Tuchman, 2009). Supposedly, the problems come from alien values such as efficiency, competition, treating students as customers, and just too much business influence on campus (Berube, 1998).

Having served for 30 years in higher education and been employed for almost a decade in publicly traded corporations, I think there is something not right with this argument. The first clue that something is wrong comes from the fact there is no "profit" in higher education. The for-profit organization is precisely defined; the principals (owners) are the residual claimants[1] in an enterprise that maximizes the surplus between revenues and costs (Alchian and Demsetz, 1972). That surplus can be maximized only if costs are minimized. No one in higher education is minimizing teaching and research costs in order to provide a surplus for students, parents, donors, and taxpayers. Indeed, we know from Chapter 4 that colleges and universities spend all the revenue they have. Research and teaching cost minimization is a non-starter in higher education. The classic profit motive does not drive higher education.

Those who argue the "pursuit of profit" motivates higher education must have a non-traditional definition of profit in mind; so what do they mean by "profit"? Colleges and universities are pursuing more revenue. Why not just call it revenue maximization? Bok et al. call it "profit" because the purpose of generating more revenue from tangential activities is to produce a surplus of revenue over cost, so the surplus can be claimed by the agents (faculty, administrators, and trustees). The captured surplus is not returned to students, parents, taxpayers, alumni, or donors. This is simply the principal/agent problem discussed in Chapter 4: more revenue is pursued not to provide relief for parents and taxpayers (principals), but to provide more resources for faculty, administrators, and trustees (agents).

The second clue the argument is misdirected comes from the documented history of corporations. The "corporate model" leads to lower cost and stunning improvements in product quality.[2] The improvements in for-profit product quality make it impossible to create price indices[3] that truly reflect how much better off we are today than we were 40 years ago. So how could a model that works so well in for-profit firms have exactly the opposite result (high cost and low quality) when adopted by higher education?

5.2   AGENCY PROBLEMS AND MARKET VALUES

The "commercialization" or "corporatization" argument is analogous to that of a child caught with his hand in the cookie jar. He explains to his mother: "It's not my fault; the devil made me do it." Members of the academy are suspicious of corporations[4] and capitalism in general (Ellis, 2010). Bok notes that market or business influences are offensive to many in the academy: "Rarely, if ever, does one read that a university's efforts to 'commercialize' its educational programs or its research activities have met with applause from its students or enthusiasm from its faculty. On the contrary, to commercialize a university is to engage in practices widely regarded in the academy as suspect, if not downright disreputable" (2003: 18). Since the corrupting influence resembles market capitalism, academics think it is market capitalism taking hold in higher education.

The reality is higher education did not surrender to the capitalist model in 1980; it surrendered to something more insidious. Higher education enthusiastically embraced the public relations model in 1980 and it is that chilling embrace that is responsible for the widespread abandonment of core academic values. Trustees, administrators, and faculty members welcomed the public relations model on campus because reputations are built by effective public relations and reputations rule in higher education. They welcomed the public relations model because it was in their financial interest to adopt the model. Higher education's problems are home grown; they are not imposed by an "outside agitator," such as capitalists, on an unwilling academy.

David Kirp, Derek Bok, Gaye Tuchman, and Jennifer Washburn (and others) made an honest mistake; they see greed in higher education and assume it represents nefarious capitalist values. This is not surprising for several reasons. First, the market mechanism depends on the pursuit of self-interest. Therefore when you see people pursuing self-interest it would not be irrational to assume they are faux capitalists. On the other hand, politicians pursue self-interest regardless of whether they reside in communist, socialist, or capitalist economies. Greed is a universal human failure. The pursuit of self-interest is not unique to capitalism.

In addition, the only business stories covered by the popular media concern agency abuse by executives. Executives in handcuffs make excellent copy. When Hollywood needs a villain, it is an investment banker or a global corporation. The public hears few positive stories about business people and fewer still positive depictions of the corporate world in the education sector, the media, or the movies. Therefore it is not surprising that many people think agency abuse is a common capitalist value.

The general public does not realize that stock markets and bond markets rest on trust and trust could not survive if agency abuse were the norm in modern capitalist firms. The recent global financial crisis clearly illustrates this point. One month the world's financial portfolio is worth trillions of dollars and the next month it is worth 30 percent less. A crisis of confidence is a partial collapse of trust. The fact that these periodic crises do not lead to a total collapse of asset values means the bedrock trust is still there. It also explains why unstable governments or socialist governments in third world countries remain underdeveloped. There is not enough trust in their capital markets to allow them to raise the investment necessary for development.

The real "alien model" adopted by higher education is the public relations model. The pernicious influence is not corporate America; a better analogy is a political campaign managed by "spin-doctors" and "money men." Political operatives are not concerned about cost minimization; they raise all the money they can, and the "product" they sell is image, rather than substance. Further, political campaigns are a black hole that cannot be filled by contributions. The behavior found in political campaigns is consistent with that in modern higher education, while the management of colleges and universities bears no resemblance to how corporations are managed. Finally, public relations values (or absence of values) are utterly at odds with traditional academic values; that is why Bok, Krip, Tuchman, Washburn *et al.* are so obviously uneasy with these trends.

The product produced by public relations is a carefully crafted reputation. We learned in Chapter 3 that reputations rule in higher education; hence, it is clear why higher education sold its soul to public relations in 1980. None of this was forced on higher education; the academy could have said no at any point. Faculty members, administrators, and trustees did not say no because it was in their personal interest to say yes.

5.3   WHO IS THE PRINCIPAL AND WHO IS THE AGENT?

In his article entitled "Why Inefficiency Is Good for Universities," Michael Berube argues waste in higher education is good (1998). If Berube means waste is good for individual members of the academy (the agents) then he is right; if he argues waste is good for society, he is demonstrably wrong. If Michael Berube is confused about who is a principal and who is an agent, then he might sincerely believe inefficiency is good for higher education. Since higher education exists for the benefit of society, Berube's argument is deeply flawed and it illustrates the core incentive problem in higher education: faculty members, administrators, and trustees assume they are the principals.

There is danger hidden in this confusion. It played a part in the August 2009 firing of former UNLV president David B. Ashley. As with other states, Nevada has serious budget problems as a result of the current recession. Governor James Gibbons announced significant budget cuts for higher education in January of 2009 and the University of Nevada System apportioned those cuts to individual institutions within the system. At an anti-budget cut rally on the UNLV campus that month President Ashley told the audience "I took a political risk and said, 'That budget doesn't make any sense. We should reject it completely.'" He then instructed students to "Go right past the Governor" (Feldberg, 2009).

President Ashley was trying to protect his university and the evidence suggests he was well regarded by the faculty and staff, since a recent evaluation described him this way: "The descriptions most often used by those interviewed when describing President Ashley were: brilliant, honest, supportive, personable, and thoughtful; a problem solver, a data driven decision maker, a quiet leader, a collaborator, an engineer, and a calm leader" (Tavares, 2009).

The governor, the legislature, and the system regents represent taxpayers. They were elected to make exactly this kind of decision. Therefore, when President Ashley defied the governor, the legislature, and the system he could be seen as defying the principals for whom he was supposed to act as agent. Practically, however, if he had not resisted the budget cuts, faculty and staff members would have considered his actions a betrayal of the university's core interest, since they assume their interests are the same as the institution's (they are the principals).

This is the double bind frequently confronting senior higher education administrators, not just during this season of budget crises. The true principals (parents, donors, alumni, and taxpayers) are abstract and remote, while faculty, staff, and trustees are personal and close. It is not a surprise that administrators regularly side with the other agents.

5.4 THE COMMERCIALIZATION CASE

Derek Bok identifies five contexts in which critics consider the "commercialization," "corporatization," or "commoditization" of higher education:

1. general economic influences on the academy such as student demand for individual majors;
2. the "influence" of corporate culture on campus;
3. the rise of "vocational programs";
4. an emphasis on controlling costs; and
5. attempts to measure outcomes (2003: 3)

In each case, the presumption is the impact is "bad." In context 1, members of the academy argue students follow "trendy" majors and neglect traditional majors that contribute more to "the life of the mind." As Bok notes, this criticism is common among humanities faculty whose programs have low enrollments and whose fields are "accused of having lost their intellectual moorings" (2003: 5). The "lost moorings" theme is explored by Victor Davis Hanson and John Heath in *Who Killed Homer? The Demise of Classical Education and the Recovery of Greek Wisdom* (2001). Hanson and Heath argue the decline in humanities majors is due to the faculty's obsession with identity politics and ideology.

The assumption in context 2 is that corporations have an agenda and that agenda is to make higher education a vassal of corporate America. No one in higher education ever bothers to ask business people about that hypothesis or, if business people speak to the accusation, listen to what they might say. The first thing a thoughtful business person[5] would say is: "We depend on very productive, highly motivated people, so we have no interest in making higher education a vassal state, since your culture would destroy our business." The second thing a business person might say would be: "As a parent, I would like to see higher education control its costs and improve its quality." The third thing would be: "I would also like to see the academy become more objective and less ideological." The public realizes what the academy does not: the greatest threat to academic freedom comes from inside, not from outside, of higher education.

In context 3, the assumption is "vocational programs" lack academic rigor. This is a curious assumption to anyone who is familiar with curriculum content in disciplines like computer science, applied mathematics, economics, finance, or engineering. These fields are not welding; they use prodigious amounts of mathematics and statistics. Further, they have well developed formal paradigms for solving complex problems and testing the proposed solution. Faculty from the humanities and some social sciences are most likely to complain about vocational or applied programs.[6] It is common among faculty at liberal arts colleges, although liberal arts colleges owe their existence to the pre-vocational training they provide for medical doctors and lawyers. Strangely, these faculty members do not think music and the arts are vocational training.

The assumption in context 4 is any reduction in cost necessarily means a reduction in quality. Since higher education rarely examines the relationship between activities and outcomes this assertion is an article of faith, not a conclusion drawn from evidence. Bok notes:

> protestations of this kind cannot hide the fact that very few universities make a serious, systematic effort to study their own teaching, let alone try to assess how much their students learn or to experiment with new methods of instruction. Instead, faculty members invoke all manner of rationalizations – academic freedom, professional autonomy, privacy – to resist efforts to subject their teaching to outside scrutiny. (2003: 26)

Finally, the assumption in context 5 is outcomes cannot be measured. Like context 4, this assertion is an article of faith; it does not rest on evidence. The assertion is also curious since faculty members measure outcomes every time they grade papers or exams; if outcomes cannot be measured then grading is a fraud. It is instructive to note that this assertion frequently comes from academic disciplines with the least knowledge of measurement techniques. As Bok suggests in the foregoing passage, faculty strongly oppose attempts to measure outcomes, since measuring outcomes makes faculty members accountable. The "lemon effect" in academic labor markets considered in Chapter 6 reveals why teaching careers self-select for people who do not want their productivity measured. Similarly, the role quality uncertainty plays in reputation competition from Chapter 3 reveals why colleges and universities have an incentive not to measure outcomes. In addition, administrators have no incentive to measure outcomes since it only reveals problems they would be responsible for correcting.

The areas where commercialization is thought to be most destructive to academic culture are research, teaching, and college sports. In each instance new external revenue can be generated by the exploitation of research, adult/executive education, and sporting events. The new money leads to corruption and corruption undermines core academic values: pursuit of truth, objectivity, and substance. Again, the notion that money leads to corruption is universal; it is not unique to capitalism.

Research

Some critics argue higher education's honor was mugged by the Bayh–Dole Act of 1980, which allowed universities to patent research results even if the research was funded with federal funds. Prior to this time, any research result funded in whole or in part by federal funds had to be in the public domain. After the Act, the rewards could be captured by private interests through patents, regardless of federal funding; Bayh–Dole privatized federally funded research. Granting the patent rights to universities was perceived to be an opportunity to supplement university funding. In essence, the Bayh–Dole Act traded open access to some research for a new source of university funding, faster commercialization of research, and the reciprocal leveraging of federal and private research funding. The federal government knew, as did the corporate sector, they were creating an opportunity for the private sector to leverage their research dollars by funding university research.

Following the economic disasters of the 1970s, this policy seemed to be a reasonable way to improve general productivity and economic growth. It is important to remember that university finances were under severe pressure throughout the 1970s; therefore the Bayh–Dole Act was a rational response to a known need. The rise in university research revenues, the U.S. economic growth that followed 1980, and the improvements in general productivity over the same period seem to be consistent with the objectives of the Bayh–Dole Act.

While the Bayh–Dole Act accomplished what it set out to do, as with all public policies it had unintended consequences. The unintended consequences are used to demonize the Act. Jennifer Washburn writes:

> Since 1980 and especially over the past fifteen years, a foul wind has blown over the campuses of our nation's universities. Its source is not the stifling atmosphere of political correctness or the influence of so-called "leftist radical professors" that have received so much attention from pundits, journalists, politicians, and gadflies, but a phenomenon that has gone comparatively ignored: the growing role that market forces and commercial values have assumed in academic life. (2005: ix)

The foregoing absolves higher education of responsibility for what happened; the problems are assumed to be an external "foul wind" invading the campus. This argument is eerily reminiscent of the civil rights era, when locals claimed racial problems were caused by "outside agitators."

In order to accept the argument that external forces are responsible, one has to believe higher education is full of silly foolish people who do not know that influence follows money. In other words, one would have to believe administrators in particular do not know that if corporations put stockholders' money in the pot they expect a return on that investment. Further, are we to believe that administrators and principal investigators think that, after they sign a contract with these firms, the firms will not expect those contracts to be honored? Does any educated adult who lives in a capitalist society not understand that? The relevant question not being asked by Washburn and others is: Knowing corporations expect return on investment, why did university administrators not negotiate the appropriate safeguards in the agreements they signed with the private sector? This was not done at gunpoint, they could have said no. There were thousands of competent lawyers available who could have helped the universities craft agreements that would protect academic values, if those values were in fact important to administrators and principal investigators. How many academics have not read *Faust*? How many cheating husbands get away with telling their wives "It's not my fault. She was just so seductive I could not resist"? An alien corporate influence is not responsible.

There were bad outcomes that were clearly not in the public interest. For example, Washburn makes the following report:

> When researchers at the University of Utah discovered an important human gene responsible for hereditary breast cancer, for example, they didn't make it freely available to other scientists, even though we – the US taxpayers – paid $4.6 million to finance the research. They raced to patent it and gave the monopoly rights to Myriad Genetics, Inc., a start-up company founded by a University of Utah professor, which proceeded to hoard the gene and restrict other scientists from using it. (2005: xii)

Washburn does not notice that no outsiders are involved in this case; it is entirely the University of Utah administration and a faculty member. If cherished academic values were threatened here, why did they go forward? What failed *inside* the campus?

Another example reported by Washburn (2005: 1–48), Kirp and Berman (2003: 207–20), and Bok (2003: 151–3) is an agreement between the drug firm Novartis and the University of California at Berkeley in 1998. In exchange for $25 million in funding, the agreement gave Novartis the exclusive right to patent the research results of one-third of the University's Plant and Microbial Biology Department (PMB). What made this agreement contentious was Novartis's exclusive access to the research and the amount of control it could[7] exercise over the PMB's research agenda. There was considerable controversy on campus about the agreement, mainly by faculty in disciplines not supported by outside private interests. The controversy spilled over to the California State Senate, where hearings were held, chaired by Tom Hayden, a well known radical in the 1960s. In 2001, Goldie Blumenstyk reported in the *Chronicle of Higher Education* that: "The deal creates a pool of money for basic, unconventional research of their [the PMB's] own choosing in a way that no grant from the government, a company, or even a foundation ever would" (Kirp and Berman, 2003: 218). Blumenstyk also reported that critics of the agreement could not "point to business intrusions." An internal Berkeley report[8] came to the same conclusion in 2003.

Kirp and Berman report that Michael Crow, Columbia University's former director of technology transfer and current president of Arizona State University, said he would never sign an agreement like the Novartis/Berkeley agreement, stating:

> One company said it could raise $400 million if we gave them a stream [of licenses] and we turned them down. No firm should have a steady stream of *anything* from the university. Giving one company that kind of control can stifle research – and it is important to decide, on a case-by-case basis, whether a technology should mainly be used for private purposes or the public interest. (2003: 217)

Universities do not have to make bad deals with industry; they just have to have the wisdom, professionalism, and personal objectivity to say no.

Corporate misbehavior does exist; there are examples where corporations inappropriately interfere with the research process and with the publication of results. In 1990, a clinical researcher, Betty Dong, at UC San Francisco found that Synthroid, a popular thyroid medication, produced by Boots/Knoll Pharmaceutical, was only as effective as readily available generics. Washburn reports Dong's "university approved contract" with Boots/Knoll required their approval before she could publish her results; the university's legal counsel approved her intention to publish her results anyway; the paper was accepted by the *Journal of the American Medical Association* (*JAMA*), but, prior to publication, the University asked Dong to withdraw the paper for fear of the lawsuit (Washburn, 2005: 19–20). After the *Wall Street Journal* exposed the company's misbehavior the paper was published in *JAMA*. Clearly, the public interest would have been served had the paper been published earlier. The real story here is not that Boots/Knoll, which had a contract with UCSF, tried to enforce that contract; the real story is why did UCSF agree to the contract in the first place and then, when the public interest was at stake, why did they back down and ask Dong to withdraw the paper? Again, what went wrong *inside* UCSF?

Another frequently cited case concerns Tyrone B. Hayes, a UC Berkeley biologist who had a research contract with Ecorisk, Inc. to study the effect of atrazine, a weedkiller, on frogs. He found considerable damage to frog populations. Hayes apparently did not know his contract with Ecorisk, and the manufacturer of atrazine gave them control over publication. Washburn reports: "Again, just as in the Betty Dong case, the UC grants office had *somehow allowed* [emphasis added] this glaring breach of academic freedom to slip into the contract" (Washburn, 2005: 21). Why did Professor Hayes not read the contract he signed? How could such an obvious contract issue be approved by the UC grants office? Again, the problem comes from within the campus.

Bok considers another case at the University of Toronto, where a pharmaceutical company sought to suppress Nancy Olivieri's research results (2003: 73–5). In summary, Bok observes:

> The Dong and Olivieri cases also raise questions about how willing medical schools and their affiliated hospitals are to resist pressure from corporate donors and how careful they are to protect their faculty from signing agreements with undue restrictions on publication. Faculty members rarely read the fine print of their research contracts, written as they are in the dense prose to which the legal profession is so famously attached. (2003: 74).

These are the right issues, but there is no excuse for not reading a contract before you sign it.

In the foregoing incidents, corporations dealt with whoever they found in authority at the university. The corporations had no role in choosing the people who made these decisions; the university administrators were chosen by the governance structure. In every case, the people who were supposed to protect the institution's interests and values did not do that. As Bok points out, no one knows how many of these instances go unreported (2003); however, the number and the intensity of the controversies suggest this is a systemic problem, not a problem due to a few "rogue" employees. In other words, there must be something in the incentive system that leads administrators and research faculty to sacrifice academic values.

The university's grants office competes with similar offices across the country. This competition is scored by the number of grant dollars it attracts each year; indeed, that number is part of the Carnegie classification for research universities. A steady increase in the dollar value builds academic reputation. The institution with the largest grant portfolio each year and/or the highest number of grant dollars per faculty member can claim its faculty produces the most valuable research. As Chapter 3 demonstrates, reputations rule in higher education.

Consider the representative administrator. The university always prefers more grant revenue to less and administrators from presidents, provosts, and deans to department chairs are rewarded according to how much outside revenue they bring to the university. Indeed, a consistent record of fund raising is a ticket to a higher paying job, either in the current university or with another. The benefits of more revenue to the administrator's career are immediate, while the negative effects are speculative and may be delayed for a considerable period. It is likely the administrator will have moved on before the consequences come home. This is the same agency problem corporations face with executives; they can pump up short run earnings at the expense of long run earnings when their compensation depends only on immediate results.

Each administrator responsible for negotiating and monitoring agreements with corporate sponsors knows his institution prefers more grants to less, that its reputation is enhanced by more grants, and that it follows a public relations model designed to preserve and increase the university's reputation. If the administrator adopts a hard-nosed negotiating stance with the corporate sponsor he risks the corporation taking the sponsorship elsewhere, he risks complaints from the principal investigator, and he risks the corporation complaining to the senior administration that he is not being cooperative (not good for reputation). If he is compliant, everyone he hears from in the short run is happy. The long run cost of being compliant can be significant, as the preceding episodes illustrate. It will take a person of considerable character to make everyone unhappy in the short run in order to avoid a worse problem in the future, particularly when the administrator gains immediately by being compliant.

Now, consider the typical faculty member who is the principal investigator in a research project. His employment prospects are enhanced by more grant money. Each contract represents a new line item in his CV and the more money involved the better. In some disciplines, the personal financial opportunity can be enormous. The money provided by the grant will make the research possible and without those resources and purchased release time from teaching it is unlikely he will be able to do the research. He also knows time is of the essence; other people are working in the same area. The principal investigator's power with respect to the university increases as his grant portfolio expands. Grants are portable, as are the overhead payments made to the university, so a large portfolio makes the principal investigator very mobile; he can easily find another university willing to hire him and his grants. Under these rules of engagement, it is remarkable that any administrator or principal investigator refuses to lie down for a corporate sponsor.

There is an exquisite irony in the commercialization story. The corporate sector wrestle with adverse incentive effects constantly. They are honest and pragmatic with themselves, however. They know the problems are internal and not imposed on them by some outside influence. As market conditions change, new incentives and new realities require that for-profit firms reorganize their activities in order to compete. Modern management professionals understand incentives and they know how to organize an "incentive compatible"[9] system. In its arrogance and bias, higher education assumes it has nothing to learn from institutions outside the academy; worse still, higher education blames its internal problems on the very people who could help it make its incentive structure compatible with the academy's objectives.

Teaching

Attempts to earn a financial surplus from teaching have a long history (Bok, 2003: 79–98); it started with correspondence courses in the late 1800s that were controversial from the beginning. The issues were the quality of the courses and the institution's policies that tended to insure they earned a surplus from the endeavor. "Eventually, critics prevailed and university-sponsored correspondence programs went in to decline" (Bok, 2003: 82). These programs were followed by campus based extension programs that offered courses in the evenings and on weekends. As more adults attended college, these programs grew. Postgraduate extension programs followed; these programs include professional continuing education for doctors and lawyers, special training for mid-career executives, and accelerated graduate degree programs. Customized courses for corporate clients are growing in popularity; these courses are focused on problems and issues specific to the corporate client. The customized courses are a blend between contract research and teaching. They are likely to continue to grow in popularity and to be extended into government services.

From the beginning, correspondence classes, extension programs, postgraduate extension programs, and specialized training were something apart from traditional teaching programs.

> On most campuses, the administration regards them as marginal. Their courses are generally created to meet a public demand and are discontinued if they cannot attract more than a few students. At private universities, in particular, officials often judge their extension school deans primarily by the size of the surplus they give to the central administration and regularly push them to increase their contributions. Even universities that do not try to make a profit

pay their extension instructors only modestly at best and rarely offer any financial aid to students. (Bok, 2003: 83)

Tenure track faculty members prefer to teach during the day; therefore they are not enthusiastic about teaching in the evening or on weekends. As a consequence, administrators tend to staff these programs with adjunct faculty or non-tenure track faculty who are much less expensive than regular faculty. Indeed, adjunct faculty members are the least cost alternative since they are part time employees.

Why do faculty members and administrators tolerate dual teaching programs with such significantly different objectives and values? Are the students who attend extension programs less worthy than the students who are enrolled in regular programs? Suppose the university reorganized regular programs so they were designed to create a surplus, what would be the faculty's first question? They would want to know who the surplus was for. Administrators and tenure track faculty members know they are the beneficiaries of the surplus created by extension programs. The adjunct faculty members who have to rush from one part time posting to another in order to make a living are clearly not the beneficiaries and the students who attend these programs are not getting the best instruction possible. Again, this is simple agency abuse. If academic values were strictly adhered to, the extension programs would be run like regular programs.

The values conflict created by extension programs has an internal origin and is not imposed by an outside or alien influence: extension programs are not staffed and administered the same way as regular programs because the academy will not allow the university to offer faculty members the financial incentives required to take on the extra work associated with these programs. First, paying faculty for the value they create in these programs would eliminate most of the surplus that is currently shared by people who do not contribute to the creation of that surplus. Second, a culture of "salary equality"[10] prevails in higher education and that leads to deep suspicion of anyone willing to do more for more compensation. If these institutions were corporations, the issue of more compensation for more work would never arise; it is the absence of corporate influence that creates the conflict.

Sports

The "college sports problem" is not universal among colleges and universities; it does not trouble Division III institutions, since they have no athletic scholarships, and it appears not to be a problem for the elite academic institutions either. The big-time sports (B-TS) problem is restricted to a few private universities and many of the flagship state universities.

Frank Deford calls college sports "America's modern peculiar institution" (2005: 145); the inference is to slavery and the analogy is the manner in which students/athletes are exploited by the system. Deford goes further by stating at the outset: "The first thing to understand about big-time sports and academia is that they simply cannot work together. Never have and never will. Big-time sports, or 'B-TS,' will always win, and they will always adversely affect education" (2005: 145).

Since 1980 the amount of money flowing into college sports has grown exponentially and the problems associated with B-TS programs have grown right along with the cash. Deford notes these problems began in earnest when universities gave up financial oversight of athletic programs: "When Johnny Wooden, the most successful college coach of the twentieth century, retired from UCLA in 1975, his salary was a mere $42,000. Yet now that athletic departments are their own fiefdoms and can easily raise money from gung-ho supporters who care nothing for real education, we are treated to incredible examples of athletic indulgence" (2005: 147). Deford's point is punctuated by the new head basketball coach at the University of Kentucky, whose contract is reported to be worth over $30 million.

The academic costs associated with B-TS programs are reduced admission standards, declining academic performance among athletes, very low graduation rates among athletes, creation of low quality athlete friendly courses/majors, a culture of academic dishonesty, corruption in recruiting, and the illusion of a career in professional sports (Bok, 2003: 41–6). The academic scandals, such as cheating and alteration of transcripts, along with the recruiting scandals compromise the institution's integrity and its reputation. From my own experience at LSU, a golf athlete was struggling in my class and came to talk to me. He explained the problem was that as golf was a minor sport they had to drive to all of their tournaments and that caused him to miss class too frequently. I asked him if he had talked to his coach about the problem and he said he had; so, I asked, what did your coach say? He replied, the coach said "Don't get confused, son. You came here to play golf, not to get an education." These are values that are completely inconsistent with higher education.

While the foregoing represents the costs, there are almost no benefits from the B-TS program. Only a handful of universities generate an accounting surplus and that surplus does not include the capital cost for playing fields and athletic facilities (Bok, 2003: 38–9; Deford, 2005: 146–7). The universities that do not consistently produce champions lose money.

So there is Deford's peculiar American institution, an institution that is all cost and no benefit to the home universities, and an institution that exploits the student athletes who make it possible. Nonetheless, the status quo persists year after year. The reason it persists, of course, is because the people who benefit from the status quo make the decisions and decision makers do not include university presidents. Any president who tries to end a B-TS program gets fired. Again, this is nothing more than the principal/agent problem and greed. For example, coaches are supposed to be agents for the students/athletes. Instead, they ruthlessly exploit those athletes and then abandon them when their eligibility expires.

The problems B-TS programs create for universities are not due to the market or the corporate model; in fact, just the opposite is the case: These problems arise because universities are not governed by the corporate model. Consider the following thought experiment.

Let the university be an enterprise governed by the corporate model. The enterprise recognizes the profit potential in its B-TS program, is aware the program cannot be truly profitable under the current structure (the rents are captured by the insiders), and realizes it is incompatible with its primary education enterprise. It knows the B-TS program is the tail and the education enterprise is the dog. The conflict with education includes values, best management practices, and objectives; in other words, if the university were a corporation it would know considerable profit can be earned by spinning off the B-TS program as a separate corporation and by so doing avoiding the damage the program does to its core activities.

The university may retain part of the ownership, or sell all its ownership; in either case it has a franchise agreement with the B-TS program where the program pays an annual fee for the use of the university's name. The fiction that athletes are students and amateurs is no longer necessary; they are professionals recruited and paid by the B-TS corporation. Since the myth that the athletes are amateurs is gone, there are no more "recruiting scandals." The NCAA becomes a league governing organization as in major league baseball, football, and basketball. Salaries paid to coaches and players are determined by the market and coaches are no longer able to exploit the players.

The university receives a capital payment for whatever part of the B-TS program it sold. If the university retains part ownership, it is also entitled to a dividend income stream and seats on the corporation's board. The B-TS program is now at arm's length from the university; it cannot corrupt admission standards, curriculum standards, or campus finances. Further, the university president no longer has to deal with athletic supporters or state politicians who insist on tampering with the athletic program.

The foregoing is a solution to the B-TS problem derived from the corporate model. Corporations spin off unprofitable activities that are not part of core activities and they recognize the capital asset value of successful activities that are unrelated to their primary business endeavor. The same cannot be said for universities; therefore the problems universities experience with sports programs have nothing to do with the market. The problems are certainly not due to too much corporate influence; indeed, the reverse is true.

5.5   FACULTY DE-PROFESSIONALIZATION

In her ethnography of "Wannabe U" Gaye Tuchman argues the "coercive accountability regime" favored by central university administrators is inspired by "neo-liberalism" (market capitalism) and the purpose is to "de-professionalize" faculty members in order to turn them into docile employees; that is, the transparency and accountability reform movement is a sneak attack on the faculty's professional status (2009). She asserts that "audit or accountability regimes" are really faculty "surveillance" systems. Tuchman does not mention higher education's dismal cost control record or its chronic quality problems; therefore she never makes the connection between those issues, the public's demand for reform, and the central administration's (presidents, provosts, and governing boards) natural response to the demand for reform. For Tuchman, the progressive introduction of accountability arises spontaneously from administrator need to control every aspect of the institution, while the facts are the chain of causation flows from cost/quality problems to the public's demand for reform to central administrator adoption of process control practices developed in the for-profit sector. The chain of causation does not run in the reverse direction, as Tuchman seems to assume.

Tuchman states:

> This book is about how being "business like" has affected today's public research universities. . . . It argues that the new emphasis on business has introduced new sorts of administrators who have different kinds of relationships with the professoriate. Increasingly, they try to govern them rather than to govern *with* them. As a result, the process of auditing has become ever more important, as administrators create situations in which faculty members must account for themselves. Indeed, these administrative actions appear to be encouraging an *accountability regime*. (2009: 21)

Following a discussion of the insidious nature of accounting and statistics, Tuchman says "This conception of an accountability regime appears to resemble Foucault's panopticon – a surveillance machine akin to a prison constructed so that a jailer can see all the prisoners, but none of them can see him" (2009: 45).

The pejorative nature of terms like "coercive regime," "surveillance," "jailer," and "prisoners" reveals more about the author's ideology than it does about the topic in question. It is another "foul wind" sweeping across the campus or a group of "outside capitalist agitators" who are responsible for the problems that concern the public (causation flows from outside agitators and interference in campus governance to high cost and low quality, rather than from problems to outside interference).

It is true; professionalism is a vanishing virtue among far too many faculty members. The secular decline in professionalism enabled the ascendency of itinerant professional administrators who climb the success ladder from one university to another. Contrary to Tuchman's hypothesis, however, the decline in faculty professionalism is not the result of a conspiracy on the part of administrators, governing boards, and scheming capitalists. Declining faculty professionalism is a self-inflicted wound and it leads to rising administrator power. The decline in professional behavior created a vacuum easily filled by administrators.

According to Dictionary.com, an "accountable" individual is obligated to "report, explain, or justify something" to another individual, while an "autonomous" person is "self-governing" and subject only to his or her own rules. Also, a "professional" is someone who is "expert at his or her own work" and professionals are normally granted limited autonomy.

When spending someone else's money, we are never autonomous even if we are professionals; this is clearly true for the most autonomous among us, the President of the United States. No member of a free society is ever autonomous; we are all accountable. Therefore faculty members are now and always have been accountable to students, parents, taxpayers, and donors (the principals). Whatever limited autonomy faculty members enjoyed in the past they enjoyed by the good graces of the principals and that limited autonomy was always conditional on performance. The fact that some faculty members, perhaps Tuchman, assume their autonomy is a divine right is further evidence higher education has a serious principal/agent problem.

Advanced education and technical training are necessary conditions for professional status; however, they are not sufficient. To be professional one must also require little supervision, maintain high standards/ethics, and be worthy of the trust given to professionals. Further, the professional must put the client's interest ahead of his own interest.

Being a member of a profession carries with it the responsibility to maintain standards throughout the profession. For example, the legal profession maintains procedures for disbarring lawyers who do not serve their client's interest; similarly, medical doctors can lose their license to practice medicine for similar offenses. Those who rule on disbarment and medical licenses are third parties unassociated with the professional whose behavior is in question. There are no such safeguards for students who are cheated by a college professor. A professional cannot expect to remain unsupervised if he allows his colleagues to run amuck; that is, professions have codes of conduct that must be enforced, since the bad behavior by some endangers the livelihood and autonomy of all professionals. In the interest of "collegiality" (live and let live), the professoriate abandoned responsibility for faculty conduct.

Faculty members as a group will not discipline shirking faculty. Individual faculty who miss more classes than the students, are rampant grade inflators, do not hold office hours, teach subjects in class that are outside their own training, spend more time on outside employment than they do at the university, do not prepare for class, do not return assignments in a timely fashion, are abusive to students, and take their personal grievances to the media are not subject to faculty censure and are not professionals. Terrible teachers who punish and short-change students for decades are ignored by the faculty. Faculty members expect administrators to deal with these problems and, when administrators do something about the problem, the faculty frequently sides with the miscreant.

Rather than encourage bored faculty members to choose another career, they say nothing. This is a serious problem in many lower quality institutions because too many people chose academic careers for the wrong reasons; it was not intellectual curiosity or a passion for teaching that drove them so much as it was risk aversion (the security provided by tenure) and the separation of wages from productivity. For example, I was told by a department chair (whose faculty and students complained about her frequent absences) that the reason she decided to become an academic was so she would not have to come to work every day.

The decline in professionalism leads to abuse of tenure, particularly among the research "wannabes." When a university is in "transition," as Tuchman calls it, it creates significant agency opportunities for tenured faculty. Tenured faculty members control department resources. The "old guard" got tenure with little publishing, so they cannot compete when the university shifts its emphasis to research. A too typical model unfolds when this happens. Since the old guard cannot, or will not, publish and they control department resources they set very high publication stand-ards for assistant professors, deny tenure to most assistant professors, and recruit a new crop of assistant professors who produce a steady stream of publications claimed by the department. The tenured faculty members divide the spoils among themselves, all in the name of high research standards. Tuchman reports:

Echoing complaints heard in university communities for decades, one Ashton psychologist, who was not employed at the university, described assistant professors in his neighborhood: "At cocktail parties the assistant professors complain that the tenured members of their departments demand that we publish a lot . . . [to receive] tenure, but they're not willing to work any harder than they've ever done and that hasn't been very hard." (2009: 26)

While Tuchman is wrong about why administrators continue to introduce accountability measures, she is right about the impact of declining faculty professionalism and administrator ascendency on shared governance. The weak governance role now played by faculty is the proximate cause of exploding nonacademic professional employment and rising cost per student. The thing to bear in mind is, as the faculty's governance role declined and the power of administrators and governing boards grew, costs rose dramatically and quality declined. It is not the "business model" that is responsible for this perverse result; it is the public relations model. The clash of values is between public relations values and academic values. The business model would place much more emphasis on cost and product quality. Further, the business model would happily reward both professionalism and increased productivity.

Tuchman repeatedly notes administrator obsession with reputation and image but does not make the connection between compulsive image building and public relations. "Chasing a sterling reputation, central administrators seemed to ask what they needed to say to garner approval. To some faculty, they seemed more concerned with the 'image' used to market their product (a university education) to customers (students and their parents) and clients (the firms that would hire the university's graduates) than with the product itself" (2009: 11).

5.6 TYING CONTRACTS AND BUNDLING

It is argued in higher education that diverse services give students more choice. In reality, when colleges and universities bundle services they increase the cost and *reduce* student choice. The services bundled by the institution are offered, frequently at lower cost, by other nonprofits and by for-profit firms. In other words, students have as many choices and more freedom to choose if the services are *not bundled* by the college or university.

When for-profit firms bundle services in one price, such as cable/satellite television, consumers pay for services they do not want. Bundling prevents consumers from buying only the services they want and from finding the least cost provider for each service. This is particularly disadvantageous for students when colleges tie housing, food, and entertainment with education by requiring students to purchase the entire bundle as a condition of enrollment.

Over the past three decades, colleges and universities have added new nonacademic services and raised the quality of those services provided to students. Most of these products and services are indirectly related to education at best. More services and higher quality services mean more people are employed at the institution and that means higher costs. In the past, student housing was basic, food was institutional, students provided their own entertainment, medical care was provided by parents, and foreign travel was paid for by students and parents. Today, institutions provide luxury living accommodations, gourmet food, elaborate entertainment, first class athletic facilities, foreign travel, health insurance, and extensive counseling services.

The academy argues new and higher quality services are forced on them by competition from other institutions. This is curious; why do higher education institutions compete via the quality of auxiliary activities and not compete on the basis of teaching quality? Given the secular decline in the quality of undergraduate education in America, why not seek world class teachers and fix grade inflation before taking on new products and services?

Faculty members, administrators, and board members draw personal benefits from luxury accommodations, good food, entertainment, athletic facilities, and foreign travel. Similarly, bundling additional services is part of facilities competition designed to demonstrate quality by making investments in sunk costs. As with research, the principal/agent problem leads to excessive investment in sunk costs. In other words, bundling is further evidence of principal/agent issues in higher education. There is a conflict of interest in the decision to incorporate these expensive new services into the institution. Chapters 3 and 4 reveal why institutions bundle other services and do not compete on the basis of teaching quality. Quality uncertainty conveys economic advantage in the tying good, fixed cost investments in other services signal quality, and principal/agent abuse leads to excessive investment in quality signals.

Colleges and universities could outsource these new services and let students pick and choose what services they wanted to use on a fee per service basis. Instead, they bring the services under their direct control and bundle their cost into the total price of attendance. In some instances, they go further than that; for example, a liberal arts college builds luxurious new dormitories and dining facilities and then requires all students to live on campus and eat at the new dining hall. The administration explains that living on campus and eating in the dining hall are an "essential part of the college experience"; the effect, however, is to limit the students' choice and prevent competition from local providers of food and shelter. Or the institution automatically enrolls every student in its health insurance plan, even though the student may be covered by her parents' health insurance. If she does not opt out of the enrollment, she pays twice for health insurance (Holbrook, 2010).

This type of contractual relationship has a long and somewhat notorious history in antitrust prosecutions. Generically, they are known as "tying contracts" and are one of the "anticompetitive practices" listed in the Clayton Act (1914). They are illegal when the effect is to limit competition. Tying contracts provided the basis for the Microsoft antitrust case, where Microsoft was accused of tying or "bundling" the sale of its operating system with Word, Excel, PowerPoint, and Explorer. The tying good in the Microsoft case is the operating system and the tied goods are Word, Excel, PowerPoint, and Explorer. Since Microsoft has a virtual monopoly in operating systems, tying the sale of its operating system to components tended to extend its monopoly into word processing, spreadsheets, presentation software, and web browsers. In higher education the tying good is education and the tied goods are room, board, entertainment, travel, athletic facilities, and the campus bookstore.

Bundling can be justified when there are complementarities in production or in consumer preferences[11] (Fang and Norman, 2006: 946). If there are complementarities in production, the production cost of the package is less than the sum of the production costs for the two goods produced separately. Hence, a lower price for the bundled pair than the sum of the two prices separately reflects complementarities in production. Similarly, if there are complementarities in preferences, the consumer's reservation price for the two goods is higher than the sum of the two reservation prices if the two products are purchased and consumed separately. Bundling creates more consumer surplus in this instance and, therefore, is preferred from society's standpoint. For example, there are complementarities between fine food, good wine, and elegant dining accommodations that explain the appeal of four star restaurants.

The modern term for tying contracts is "product bundling." Pure bundling occurs when the provider offers a single package composed of multiple products. Mixed bundling occurs when the provider offers multiple packages. Cable/satellite television providers follow mixed bundling strategies. Most consumers would prefer to construct their own bundles from the channels offered; however, that option is rarely, if ever, available. Since providers do not allow consumers to construct their own bundles, bundling must provide institutions with some economic advantage.

Economic theory reveals that product bundling facilitates price discrimination and acts as a barrier to entry (Adams and Yellen, 1976; Carbajo et al., 1990; Dansby and Conrad, 1984; Fang and Norman, 2006; Nalebuff, 2004; Schmalensee, 1982). The effectiveness of price discrimination and entry deterrence with product bundling depends on the correlation of consumer reservation prices for the two goods in question. If the reservation prices are perfectly negatively correlated, price discrimination is very profitable and, if the reservation prices are perfectly positively correlated, entry deterrence with product bundling is most effective.

An explanation of positive and negative correlation among reservation prices helps explain how this works. A consumer's reservation price is the maximum amount the consumer would pay for this product; it represents his highest valuation of the product and means he will purchase the product at any price equal to or less than the reservation price. Consider two goods, A and B. Each consumer has a reservation price for each good. Suppose consumer 1 has high reservation prices for both A and B, consumer 2 has low reservation prices for both A and B, and all other consumers have similar pairings of reservation prices. Each consumer is an observation; then regress reservation prices for good A against reservation prices for good B. Given the foregoing reservation price pairings among consumers, the regression yields a strong positive correlation.

Now assume consumer 1 has a high reservation price for A and a low reservation price for B, consumer 2 has a low reservation price for A and a high reservation price for B, and all other consumers have similar pairings. Regressing reservation prices for A against reservation prices for B will yield a strong negative correlation. This is the scenario where price discrimination by bundling works best. The reason is when products A and B are bundled they are sold as a package with a single price. Since each consumer's pairing of the two goods is far apart, the provider can in effect sell the low valued good at a higher price than the consumer would normally pay since it is tied to the product the consumer really values. The essence of this situation is there is considerable disagreement among consumers about the value of goods A and B.

When the reservation prices are strongly positively correlated, consumers are in agreement about the relative values of the two goods (they are relatively equal in value, even though some think the pair are high value and others think the pair are low value). Since the relative values from each consumer are about the same, the provider cannot gain an advantage by bundling the two goods (tying one to the other) and charging one price for the bundle; the provider is better off selling the two goods separately from a price discrimination perspective. However, the bundle may serve as a very effective entry deterrent when reservation prices are positively correlated.

As a barrier to entry strategy, bundling products works by raising the incumbent firm's profit and lowering the expected profits after entry for the single product potential entrant. Since the potential entrant's expected profits are lower, he is less likely to enter the market. When reservation prices are positively correlated, bundling is an ineffective barrier to entry strategy. As Nalebuff explains,

> The reason is that a one-product entrant has everything its customers want when the valuations for A and B are negatively correlated. The markets for A and B are essentially different groups of consumers. In contrast, when A and B are positively correlated, the same group of consumers is buying both A and B and, thus, a one-product entrant cannot satisfy its customers. (2004: 160–61)

The extended cost of reputation building in higher education means for-profit potential entry at higher quality levels is not credible. Credible potential entry for any given quality tier comes from institutions in quality tiers below the incumbent institution's tier. As one moves up the quality tiers, the revenue stream per student increases and it is less dependent on tuition and fees. Diversified revenue streams lower the institution's financial risk. Larger and more diversified revenue streams per student make entry from below more attractive, but they also make it more difficult for lower tier institutions to move up. Improvements in perceived quality are expensive, so lower tier institutions need more revenue per student before they can demonstrate higher quality. It is no surprise that higher education institutions are constantly pursuing "transformational gifts," gifts that allow them to demonstrate higher quality.

When incumbent institutions bundle additional services, they complicate the entry problem for institutions in lower tiers. In order to be a credible competitor, the potential entrant must provide a comparable package of bundled services that supposedly demonstrate quality. If competition was based only on teaching quality, the other bundled services would be irrelevant, the cost of entry would be lower, and the quality tiers would be contestable. Hence, teaching quality uncertainty is a competitive advantage for institutions in the higher quality rankings and that barrier to entry increases their market power.

The effectiveness of bundling as an entry barrier depends on whether or not reservation prices for the services offered are positively correlated. The tying good is undergraduate education and the tied goods are room, board, entertainment, facilities, travel, and student services. As one moves up the quality tier, the quality of the students rises steadily. Indeed parents and students consider average student quality at each institution as one of the most important quality signals. Student preparation for college is positively correlated with family income; hence, family incomes tend to rise as student quality increases. Higher family incomes mean the student's ability to pay for bundled services increases. It also suggests student preferences with respect to the tying good (education) and the tied goods (room, board, entertainment, facilities, travel, and student services) are positively correlated. High income families place high value on education, comfortable accommodation, good food, facilities, travel, and abundant student services. Bundling should be an effective barrier to entry in higher education.

Some service bundling may be justified by complementarities in production and consumer preferences. There should be few production complementarities between education and room, board, and textbook sales. There may be some production complementarities between education and entertainment (drama departments), travel (education benefits from travel), and student services (student mental health). On the other hand, it is not obvious where the production externality ends, the agency benefits start, and the barriers to entry kick in. The same can be said for complementarities in consumer preferences. The educational experience is enhanced by travel and some forms of entertainment.

5.7   CENTRIFUGAL RANDOMNESS AND STRATEGIC DECISIONS

H.R. Bowen's conclusion, considered in Chapter 1, that higher education programs and activities are distributed as if by "centrifugal randomness" suggests they are not following a common "best practices" technology for producing core academic services (1980: 228). As a result, colleges and universities provide diverse services and activities; the "border" of each institution in activity space (see Figure 1.2) differs considerably from one institution to the next. In contrast, the "borders" of for-profit firms in the same industry are very similar.

The centrifugal randomness in higher education services sharply contrasts with specialization among for-profit firms; the contrast reflects core differences in how senior managements make strategic decisions. Higher education institutions make strategic decisions based on an informal political process unique to each institution, while for-profit firms make strategic decisions based on a thoroughly vetted analytical process common to each firm. For-profit firms use the capital budgeting process to make strategic decisions. The local political process applied by higher education means that each institution is a historical accident; it looks the way it does at the present because in the past there was a unique set of personalities among faculty members, administrators, and trustees that determined where the institution invested its resources. Nonsystematic choice rarely leads to efficient results.

Consider the strategic decisions faced by each institution (higher education and for-profit firms) at any point in time. Each institution chooses from a portfolio of "investment" opportunities. The opportunities have different costs and benefits that flow to the institution over time. The costs and benefits have both quantifiable and non-quantifiable components. The quantifiable components can be measured in dollar terms and converted into present values. The non-quantifiable components require seasoned managerial judgment. In order to make the right judgment call concerning the non-quantifiable components, the manager must have considerable industry specific experience.[12]

In a deliberate goal oriented process, the first step would be to classify the opportunities on the basis of whether they represent independent opportunities, substitute opportunities (you cannot do one if you do the other), or complementary opportunities (doing one enhances the other opportunity). The next step is to rank-order the projects on the basis of the present value of their quantifiable costs and benefits. The present value of the quantifiable costs and benefits allows the management to see what the opportunity costs will be if it chooses one project over another based on the non-quantifiable components. The foregoing is a summary of the capital budgeting process common to for-profit firms.

There is no corresponding model for making strategic decisions in higher education. First, many in the academy argue higher education decisions cannot be quantified. Without quantification it is impossible to compare one "opportunity" with another, so the opportunity with the most powerful political support is the opportunity chosen. Second, among higher education insiders there is a studied lack of curiosity about the relationship between actions and outcomes. We spend our time critiquing every aspect of the rest of society, but when it comes to our own activities we are suddenly disinterested. Worse still, many members of the academy consider it rude to ask questions about how resources are allocated and what outcomes they might achieve.

Periodically, higher education institutions throw their institutions into frenetic "long range planning" (Tuchman, 2009: 152–72). Frequently, these activities are managed by public relations people. Since public relations managers are hired to manage image and many of their target donors are among the board of trustees, they want a document free of controversy, full of superlatives, and short on deliverables; this can lead to the worst case scenario. The administration empanels scores of committees, trying to include as much of the faculty and staff as can be accommodated. These committees are notorious among faculty members as a waste of time; they are too large to be functional and the culture of having everyone express their opinion on every issue makes the meetings endless.

The manner in which higher education uses and organizes committees differs considerably from the way corporations use committees. Corporations do not empanel "committees of the whole" when they have a task to accomplish. When corporations bring large numbers together, they do so in order to communicate; when they have a task to accomplish, they form small working groups who act as a team. They expect the team to keep management posted and once a course of action is identified and approved the team is frequently tasked with implementing the project. Real action comes from small working groups; "committees of the whole" are formed for public relations purposes. Teamwork is not a common value in higher education, as the "herding cats" expression will attest.

In the worst case scenario, the final strategic plan is a public relations document. It is full of soaring rhetoric designed to offend no one. The purpose is to provide a fund raising document. There will be few, if any, "deliverables" and no detailed tasking of individuals with responsibility for outcomes. The stated objective is an across the board increase in "quality" and national standing, without any specifics for how that might be achieved. Vague objectives leave the administration in the position to go wherever the wind blows; this means the single biggest cost associated with higher education planning is an opportunity cost, what might have been rather than what is.

The outcome of this planning process is a bias towards bricks and mortar and against substantial development of real academic programs. "Facilities competition" is the natural consequence.

On the other hand, developing real academic programs takes a decade or more of persistent teamwork. The benefits from those programs are apparent after the administrator moves on to his next job. Therefore the president's choice is: I spend my time, effort, and the college's money on new construction or reforming existing programs and new academic programs that take a long time to mature. It is no surprise a career minded president would prefer new facilities.

Strategic decisions put institutions on different paths. What lies at the end of each path takes decades to be revealed. These decisions are the most important decisions senior management can make, or fail to make. In for-profit firms, choosing the wrong path can lead to bankruptcy. The mortality rate among higher education institutions, particularly the elite institutions, is not high, so choosing the wrong path in higher education is measured by the opportunity cost of not making the right decision. Given the political nature of higher education's strategic decisions, opportunity costs are at least as important as the well documented direct costs.

5.8 CONCLUSIONS

The corrupting influence attributed to "commercialization" in higher education does not come from outside the campus; the problems discussed in
the commercialization literature are evidence of agency problems in higher
education. As explored in Chapter 4, there are few constraints on the
agency problem in higher education, while the opportunity for self-serving
behavior is as abundant as it is in for-profit firms, politics, medicine, or the
law. The academy's insistence that misbehavior is due to "outside agitators," a "foul wind" blowing on campus, or "market thinking" does not
survive close scrutiny. An examination of the incidents in question reveals
the problems are home grown and are due to the current incentive structure in higher education. Agency problems are always due to a governance
failure and agency problems are revealed by costs that are higher than
necessary.

The data in Chapter 2 and the analyses in subsequent chapters suggest
significant changes in higher education began around 1980, following a
decade of severe financial stress in the 1970s. The significant changes were
declining faculty professionalism and the adoption of modern public relations techniques that replaced traditional academic values. The change
was introduced by the governing boards, who hired senior administrators
whose primary skills were fund raising. The professoriate did not resist the
takeover because it was in our personal financial interest not to resist. The
change had nothing to do with market thinking or the corporate model.

NOTES

1. The internal structure of the for-profit firm evolved as the efficient solution to incentive issues created by "inseparable team production," the technology that created the
   industrial revolution (Alchian and Demsetz, 1972). The for-profit firm exists because of
   the creation of a centralized power source and the factory system.
2. Derek Bok discusses this history of reduced cost and higher quality among for-profit
   firms (2003: 20–29), but fails to note the incongruity that the model could produce the
   opposite results in higher education.
3. Consider the representative automobile built in 1950 versus the representative automobile built in 2009. We can easily calculate the change in the real cost of producing these
   cars over the period in question. The problem is the 2009 model is vastly superior to the
   1950 model in terms of speed, safety, reliability, and comfort. So a simple calculation
   of the constant dollar cost of each is not the whole story; today's consumer experiences
   much higher quality per real dollar spent on an automobile.
4. For a clear expression of this bias against business methods see Waugh (2003), who
   describes the outcome as "administrative evil."
5. The existence of a thoughtful business person will be news to many academics because
   they stereotype all business people as ignorant, unrefined, mercenary brutes.
6. One of my favorite stories in regard to the bias against "vocational training" is the

associate dean (a historian) at a liberal arts college who told two economics/math majors working as interns in actuarial departments at separate national insurance companies they could not get academic credit for those internships because they "lacked sufficient academic content." This decision was upheld by the dean, an English professor. The same associate dean got academic credit for her students who dug trash out of a sinkhole on campus and the dean's daughter got academic credit for spending two weeks on an Indian reservation.

7.   As it turned out Novartis declined to exercise control over the research agenda.

8.   Robert Saunders, "Closing the Book on the Novartis Deal?," *Berkeleyan*, January 30, 2003, 1.

9.   Within an organization, the incentive system is said to be "incentive compatible" when it induces the agents to take decisions that are consistent with the principals' interests.

10. The salary "equity/equality" debate is another instance of principal/agent problems. The campus discussion about salary is usually conducted in terms of "equity," rather than "equality"; the intent among a significant portion of the faculty, however, is to create salary equality. Among those disciplines where there are chronic faculty surpluses, the argument is everyone should be paid the same since we all have Ph.D.s and we all work for the same institution doing essentially the same thing. In those disciplines where there are persistent faculty shortages, the attitude is quite different; they want the college to recognize the market realities. Beyond the self-interest of these two groups, there is the institution's or the principals' interest. Salary equality is a pooling solution where faculty members in disciplines with excess supply receive premiums and faculty in disciplines with shortages receive less than market wages. Clearly, this adversely selects for weakness in disciplines of most value to students, parents, and alumni. The principals' interests are served best by a separating solution, a salary policy based on market realities.

11. Note there are complementarities in both production and preferences in the Microsoft case.

12. We know this is true among for-profit firms from the historical performance of conglomerate firms and the economy-wide restructuring that took place in the 1980s and 1990s, when firms shed activities in order to get back to their "core competencies."

6. The Gresham effect, lemons, and teaching

> If universities truly compete with one another, why do they neglect their teaching so? At least part of the explanation is that rewards for excellent research far exceed those available for excellent teaching. Successful scientists gain worldwide reputations. They receive abundant recognition, awards and prizes, opportunities to consult, offers from other institutions, and salary increases to counter these offers. In contrast, the successful teacher is often unknown beyond her own campus. Her rewards are limited to the satisfaction of a job well done and the gratitude and approbation of her students – all pleasures well worth having but seldom comparable to the fame and other, more tangible benefits given to the accomplished researcher. Small wonder that so many professors concentrate more on research than on teaching.
>
> Derek Bok (2003: 160)

> Although superb teaching can bring popularity on the campus, no one becomes a superstar because of classroom prowess; no one makes a reputation, either in a discipline or as a media sage, by introducing twenty-year-olds to Wittgenstein or Einstein.
>
> David Kirp (2005: 122)

6.1 INTRODUCTION

Anecdotal evidence suggests that research productivity drives job mobility among senior faculty; mobility is, at best, only coincidentally influenced by teaching.[1] Indeed, an accomplished scholar who is also a poor teacher can retain considerable mobility, while an accomplished teacher who is a poor scholar has little mobility. A casual review of the employment ads in the *Chronicle of Higher Education* or *Job Opportunities for Economists* reveals that teaching institutions rarely seek to fill vacancies with anyone other than entry level candidates, while research institutions routinely seek to recruit senior scholars. Given the public's abiding interest in superior teaching and its general indifference to superior scholarship, this characteristic of academic labor markets is an anomaly.[2] There should be a vigorous derived demand for superior teaching at all ranks.

The central hypothesis in this chapter is the market for superior senior teachers is missing and that has adverse consequences for quality, cost control, and the nature of competition in higher education.[3] The absence of a market for superior teachers contributes directly to grade inflation, the misdirection of faculty effort away from teaching and towards research, a shift in faculty loyalties, the decline in the core curriculum, "mission creep" among institutions, and less value added competition and more credential competition among institutions.

The nature of this problem is revealed by Gresham's law and the "market for lemons." The classic lemons problem describes a market failure based on asymmetric information (Akerlof, 1970). If buyers cannot tell high quality used cars from low quality used cars, the good used cars may disappear from the market. When quality cannot be observed, the market must price used cars according to an average price weighted by the proportions of good and bad used cars. The sellers of bad used cars earn a premium and the sellers of good used cars receive a discounted price. The pooling solution creates adverse incentives that increase the number of bad used cars in the market and decrease the number of good used cars in the market. Again, bad used cars drive good used cars out of the market (no pun intended) and the market for good used cars fails. The market is said to fail in the sense that Pareto preferred transactions between sellers and buyers of good used cars do not take place.

The lemon problem is related to an older concept known as Gresham's law. The observation that "Bad money drives out good money" comes from Sir Thomas Gresham, who was a financial advisor to Queen Elizabeth I (Schwartz, 2004). In an economy with circulating gold and silver coins, the coins have both a face value and a commodity value as gold and silver. Gresham's law also depends on the existence of a market failure. The market must be unable to establish an exchange rate between circulating gold and silver coins that differs from their face value (Rolnick and Weber, 1986). The market failure here is the result of government policy which insists on exchanging the gold and silver coins at their official exchange rate (the government enforces a pooling solution) when that differs from their true commodity exchange rate. Citizens exchange low value coins for high value coins at the official exchange rate, melt the high value coins and sell them as a commodity; hence, "Bad money drives out good money." Thus the Gresham effect and the lemon problem both rest on pooling solutions and a market failure. The market failure drives the superior product out of the market.

6.2 THE SENIORITY/WAGE PROFILE

Wage rates that are increasing functions of both experience and seniority are empirical regularities among normal labor markets. Typically, experience is measured by the total number of years of professional employment and seniority is measured by the number of years of service with the current employer. In academic labor markets, this regularity does not hold; real faculty wages decline with increasing seniority. The longer one serves with the same institution, the lower is one's real wage, everything else held constant. The result is known as the negative seniority/wage profile in faculty labor markets among economists and is known to faculty in general as the "salary compression" problem. Since the faculty labor market contradicts the empirical regularity, it is an anomaly.

The seniority premium in normal labor markets is thought to be due to the accumulation of employer specific human capital (Mincer, 1974; Oi, 1962), a form of deferred compensation for high productivity workers (Becker and Stigler, 1974; Lazear, 1981), a screening device when the quality of workers is unknown (Salop and Salop, 1976), or the result of the cross-sectional effect of matching workers with employers (Jovanovic, 1979). Ransom and others demonstrate that the seniority premium is robust across most labor markets (Ransom, 1993: 221–3).

The Negative Seniority/Wage Profile in Higher Education

By contrast, Ransom reports that seniority is a liability for college and university faculty:

> Durable employment relationships at universities are associated with low salaries! This result is astonishing in the face of the current economic theories of the seniority–pay relation. The human-capital model, for example, suggests no reason why pay would fall with higher seniority, even in cases where there is no "specific" human capital. Likewise, the well-known matching and deferred-compensation models predict that durable employment relationships will be high-paying. (1993: 229)

The anomaly among college faculty suggests academic labor markets are different in a very peculiar manner from more traditional labor markets.

Not all of the empirical evidence suggests the seniority/wage profile in higher education is negative. Barbezat (2003) reviews 12 empirical studies beginning in 1974 and finds that, while most of these studies do find a negative seniority/wage profile, there are some exceptions. The most notable exceptions occur where faculty are represented by unions (Hoffman, 1997). Clearly, faculty members are most likely to unionize where they have the least job mobility, and, when negative seniority/wage profiles exist, a primary purpose of unions would be to eliminate negative seniority/wage profiles. The causality is more likely to flow from the negative seniority/wage profile and low faculty mobility to unionization and a positive seniority/wage profile. It is important to note that faculty unions are rarely, if ever, observed at research universities; when you find a faculty union it is in a teaching institution. Faculty members see no need for a union at research institutions, but may find unions appealing at teaching institutions.

Some of the other studies surveyed by Barbezat indicate the negative seniority premium in higher education is sensitive to specification and to the sample chosen. Many of the samples are drawn from research institutions where productivity is measured exclusively in terms of research output. Furthermore, all of these studies suffer from specification error since they have no, or have inadequate, controls for teaching productivity. After all, the almost universal absence of a reliable metric for teaching productivity is the primary point being made in this book. There are strong metrics for research productivity and few metrics for teaching productivity. It is exactly that asymmetry in the productivity information that leads to a vigorous market for senior scholars and no market for senior teachers.

What Causes the Negative Seniority/Wage Profile?

The observed negative correlation between seniority and wages in academic labor markets may be the result of wage equations that do not properly control for faculty productivity or it may be evidence of market failures peculiar to higher education. The fact that the profile is negative (the opposite of what we normally see) and persistent suggests it is unlikely to be just the result of poorly specified wage equations.

One theory holds that seniority is negatively correlated with faculty productivity. In this case, low productivity faculty members are unable to generate job offers from other institutions and tenure prevents their home institutions from firing them. Therefore long seniority is a proxy for low productivity and the negative seniority/wage profile is efficient. The result is not as anomalous as it first appears. The elimination of tenure would eliminate the negative profile. This might be called the "dead wood" hypothesis. Once you fully control for faculty productivity, the negative seniority/wage profile would disappear and be replaced by a positive profile. The positive profile is a reward for institution specific human capital accumulated by seniority.

If you fully control for faculty productivity (both research and teaching) and the negative seniority/wage profile persists the anomaly also persists, since it suggests productive faculty receive wages lower than their skills should command in the market for productive faculty. This might be called the "monopsony power"[4] hypothesis. When an employer has market power with respect to his employees, he is able to enforce wage offers that are less than the employee's marginal productivity. The classic example here is found in "company towns" where workers are subject to geographic immobility.

The central point of this chapter is there is no market for senior teachers and the reason why it does not exist is higher education does not measure teaching value added. In Chapter 3 we learned why institutions have a financial incentive not to measure teaching value added; quality uncertainty is a useful part of reputation competition. The reason why the market does not exist is revealed by the dilemma faced by institutions recruiting senior teachers from other institutions. From the outside, the recruiting institution cannot tell the difference between good and bad teachers, but the recruiting institution knows that the home institution knows the difference between the good and bad teachers currently on its staff. Therefore, if the recruiting institution makes an offer to a good teacher, it knows the home institution will counter that offer. On the other hand, if the recruiting institution makes an offer to a bad teacher, the home institution will not counter that offer. From the recruiting institution's perspective, outside offers adversely select for bad teachers. Notice the problem this creates for for-profit providers who try to compete for high value added teaching. Alternatively, there is no information problem in the market for senior scholars. Outsiders can readily observe which faculty are good scholars and which faculty are bad scholars.

Without a market for gifted senior teachers, those faculty members do not have job mobility; if they do not have job mobility, they are subject to their home institution's monopsony power and that will result in a negative seniority/wage profile. Therefore, if we fully control for research and teaching productivity and the negative seniority/wage profile persists, we have evidence consistent with the "monopsony power" hypothesis. If we fully control for productivity and the seniority/wage profile is positive, we have evidence that is consistent with the "dead wood" hypothesis.

Empirical Wage Studies

In order to address these issues, Ransom formulates an empirical model that controls for productivity in research universities. He finds that the "strong negative correlation between salaries and seniority persists, even after controlling for each individual's publication activity" (1993: 229). Therefore Ransom concludes that the negative seniority premium is not due to lower productivity. It is important to note, however, that Ransom has no controls for teaching productivity in his empirical model and his only control for research productivity is the number of publications. Ransom concludes that the negative seniority profile is due to the university's monopsony power. He speculates that the monopsony power is due to high moving costs. I argue he is right about the monopsony power but wrong about the origin of that power. The absence of a market for high productivity teachers is what creates the monopsony power.

Following Ransom's paper, Moore et al. (1998) explore the seniority profile in an empirical model with more controls for faculty productivity. They have multiple controls for both the quantity and the quality of research among economics faculty at nine state research institutions. They also have one control for teaching productivity, a dichotomous variable for teaching awards. Their primary conclusion is that the negative seniority profile disappears as progressively more controls for productivity are included in the equation. This empirical result may be due to an increase in co-linearity[5] among the independent variables.

It is important to note that Moore et al. have multiple well specified control variables for research productivity and only one, rather weak, control for teaching productivity. This is the result of a systemic lack of teaching productivity measures in the data. What Moore et al. (among many others) cannot measure is also what any outside institution could not measure if it were searching for talented teaching faculty within other institutions.

Since Moore et al. and Ransom use the controls for productivity that are available, they restrict their samples to research institutions. If the only type of productivity that is relevant to the institution is research productivity, one would not be surprised to find that the negative seniority profile disappears when we introduce more complete controls for research productivity. This interpretation seems consistent with Moore et al.'s evidence, since they find that "teaching awards . . . appear to garner no significant salary rewards in our sample" (1998: 362).

We know there is a brisk and well functioning market for scholarship. The more interesting empirical test is one conducted at the other end of the academic hierarchy: the teaching institution. Assuming we can control for teaching productivity at these institutions, if the negative seniority profile persists in a sample restricted to teaching institutions it is consistent with the monopsony power hypothesis. If the negative seniority profile among teaching institutions disappears, the data are consistent with the dead wood hypothesis. Note, however, that, if the dead wood hypothesis holds, tenure at teaching institutions adversely selects for inferior teachers. In other words, tenure at teaching institutions is an irrational policy. Alternatively, there is no irrationality associated with teaching institutions that exploit monopsony power that arises naturally from a market failure.[6] Behavior that persists tends to be optimal, so a negative seniority/wage profile at teaching institutions is most consistent with the rational pursuit of monopsony power.

6.3 THE NEGATIVE SENIORITY PROFILE AND RATIONAL BEHAVIOR

Ransom identifies two theoretical models that yield negative seniority profiles and states that they both have a decidedly "lemon-flavor," although they require the firm to demonstrate "persistent ignorance" (1993: 229). The two models are those formulated by Harris and Holmstrom (1982) and Lazear (1986). In the Harris and Holmstrom model, worker productivity is unknown initially and then revealed to all parties over time. There is uncertainty about worker productivity, but that uncertainty is symmetrically distributed. Since workers are risk averse and the firms are risk neutral, the firms insure workers by making guaranteed initial minimum wage offers, which is a guaranteed lifetime minimum wage (tenure). As high productivity workers are identified by all parties, including outside employers,[7] they are offered wages higher than the guaranteed lifetime minimum wage. Low productivity workers do not generate outside offers. The sorting due to outside offers results in a negative seniority profile for individual workers. This is the "dead wood" hypothesis mentioned earlier. The persistent ignorance on the part of firms occurs in stationary state equilibrium where firms continue to employ new workers of unknown productivity rather than waiting for their true productivity to be revealed and hiring them away from other firms.

Lazear assumes a labor market populated by type "j" and type "k" firms, where type "k" firms make employee raids on type "j" firms, which may counter the offers made (1986). The productivity of each worker is unknown when the worker is initially hired, but the exact worker productivity is revealed with probability "p" after the worker is employed and the probability that the firm knows only the distribution of productivity is "(1 − p)." The different types of firms may have different "p" s. Hence, when "p" = 1, the firm knows the exact productivity for each worker and if "p" = 0, then the firm knows only the productivity distribution for individual workers. It is useful to think of "p" = 1 being the information condition in the senior scholar market and "p" = 0 as the information condition in the senior teacher market. As "p" approaches 1, the firm is said to be more informed about worker productivity.

In this environment, turnover is highest in those labor markets where productivity is most widely known. Hence, "turnover is a proxy for market information" about worker productivity (Lazear, 1986: 143). A further implication is that one should observe the least wage dispersion[8] in those labor markets where worker productivity is least well known. With respect to higher education specifically, one expects to see greater wage dispersion at research institutions (more information is available about productivity) than one would see at teaching institutions (less information is available about productivity). Correspondingly, we would find a separating solution in the salary structure at research institutions and a pooling solution in the salary structure at teaching institutions.

The effect of outside offers in labor markets where productivities are known is to create a negative seniority profile and to attach a "stigma" to those workers who do not generate outside offers. Again, this is the "dead wood" hypothesis. The persistent irrationality issue that arises in the Lazear model is that the type "k" firms earn rents and the type "j" firms do not, which suggests that all type "j" firms should aspire to be type "k" firms. Lazear resolves this dilemma by assuming the type "k" firms must incur a cost to observe productivity (1986: 157). There is also a potential adverse selection effect in the initial wage offers because they overvalue low productivity workers and undervalue high productivity workers.

Alternatively, note that a necessary condition for type "k" firms to make outside offers in the Lazear model is that they must be able to observe individual productivity. Therefore, if "p" = 0, firms do not make outside offers and all firms are type "j" firms. When teaching value added productivity is not measured, the market for superior senior teachers does not exist and a negative seniority/wage profile is consistent with the monopsony power hypothesis.

6.4   ASYMMETRIC INFORMATION

In each of the models discussed in the previous section, worker productivity is unknown in the beginning and subsequently the worker reveals his productivity to both the current employer and outside employers.[9] The demonstration of productivity to outside employers is a necessary condition for the existence of outside offers. Suppose only the current employer can observe worker productivity, then outside employers know that the current employer will counter offers to high productivity workers and will not counter offers made to low productivity workers.[10] Under these conditions, outside offers will adversely select for low productivity workers.

Lazear's model is the only model that allows for asymmetry in the distribution of information about worker productivity and he concludes that turnover will be a proxy for productivity information (1986: 143). We observe high turnover and greater wage dispersion in labor markets where labor productivity is easily observed and we observe low turnover and less wage dispersion in labor markets where labor productivity is hard to observe. This description seems to fit the stylized facts as we understand them for the labor market for scholarship and the labor market for teaching.

Observable Productivity

Suppose there are two types of academic productivity, teaching and research, and assume both types are valued by different institutions in different proportions. Further, suppose those institutions are distributed along a continuum based on the relative emphasis they place on teaching and research. At one extreme, one observes the "teaching institution" where research is not valued and at the other end of the continuum one finds the "research institution" where teaching is not valued. Initially, the quality of individual new faculty is not observable. For the moment, assume students are homogeneous in quality.

Next, assume that academic productivity, of both types, is revealed to current employers and to potential outside employers after the new faculty is hired. Outside offers will be generated for each faculty member according to their productivity mix after their productivity is revealed. A tenure review process results in a "winner take all" solution for faculty at each point in the continuum. With non-decreasing returns to scale in teaching and research, a single institution monopolizes each point in the continuum, resulting in a "winner take all" solution among institutions as well. The academic continuum has one dimension: length based on the teaching/research mix.

Alternatively, suppose all of the foregoing holds, but students are heterogeneous such that teaching faculty who are low productivity teachers when matched with the highest quality student may be high productivity teachers when matched with a less gifted student. The inverse should also hold: faculty who are high productivity teachers when matched with high quality students are low productivity faculty when matched with less gifted students. The first effect of this assumption is the foregoing game no longer yields a "winner take all" solution for faculty. Faculty will be matched with students to find their highest teaching wage and matched with institutions to find their highest research wage. The initial "placement"[11] of each new faculty member will not be critical, since true productivity (for both teaching and research) will be revealed to outside employers and each mature faculty person will be matched with the institution in the continuum that values his skill mix most highly. The institution that values those skills most highly will be the institution that has the teaching/research mix and the student quality mix that maximizes the mature faculty's productivity.

An interesting by-product of this market structure is mature faculty are more multi-dimensional; they are typically focused on both teaching and research rather than focused only on research or only on teaching. Under these circumstances, the academic continuum has two dimensions: length based on the teaching/research mix and width based on the type of student served by the institution.

Some parts of this two-dimensional space may not be occupied. For example, a research institution that specializes in the least gifted students may not exist. A similar sorting will take place at the other end of the continuum, where workers who reveal they are low productivity researchers are distributed down and/or laterally in the teaching/research continuum. Under these assumptions, the academic hierarchy would have two prestige dimensions, one based on the quality of their teaching and the other based on the quality of their research.

Hidden Productivity

In the Harris and Holmstrom model and the Lazear model the results depend on outside employers who are able to identify high productivity workers. When productivity is hidden from outsiders, current employers have monopsony power and outside offers have adverse selection effects. Under these circumstances, the current employer has considerable monopsony power. Most importantly, however, the exercise of that monopsony power does not lead to behavior that is persistently irrational.

Assume that teaching productivity is not observed by outside employers and that research productivity is observed by outside employers. Matching of teachers with students occurs only through the tenure review process. New faculty members at teaching institutions who are mismatched with students are denied tenure and must start the tenure review process again at another institution. Subsequent mismatches may result in the candidate being driven out of academia. Those academics initially hired by research institutions and subsequently revealed to be low productivity faculty can move down the research/teaching mix and/or down the student quality ladder. The higher the new faculty's first placement on the research/teaching mix, the more options he has if he loses the initial tenure lottery. Hence, it is riskier to start an academic career at a teaching institution than it is to start an academic career at a research institution when teaching productivity cannot be observed by outsiders. Young faculty members have an incentive to start out on the research track if that is possible. Since external offers are based on research productivity, mature faculty who have focused on research productivity are going to be mobile and mature faculty who have focused on teaching are not going to be mobile.

Monopsony Power and Irrational Behavior

The problem in the Ransom model (1993) is the pursuit of monopsony power based on moving costs increases the probability that high productivity faculty will be raided by outside employers when productivity is known to those employers. The current employer exercises monopsony power when it pays a wage that is less than the faculty's marginal productivity. When outside employers can observe the faculty's marginal productivity, these monopsony wage offers result in higher turnover among the high productivity faculty. Monopsony wage offers adversely select for low productivity faculty when marginal productivity is observed by outside employers.

Alternatively, when the faculty's marginal productivity is known by the current employer and it cannot be observed by outside employers, monopsony wage offers do not adversely select for low productivity faculty. Being unable to observe faculty productivity means raiding by outsiders will result in adverse selection, since the current employer will counter offers to high productivity faculty and will not counter offers made to low productivity faculty. Furthermore, the monopsony rents earned by the current employer enable it to make more competitive counter-offers. Therefore outside offers will be rare when productivity cannot be observed by outside employers. Under these conditions, the negative seniority profile would persist even when one controls for both teaching and research productivity. The negative seniority profile is the result of monopsony power. Asymmetric information about teaching productivity can lead to monopsony exploitation of teaching faculty.

6.5   INFORMATION FAILURES IN THE MARKET FOR TEACHING

The market for superior teaching can fail at the local level or at the industry level. It fails locally when individual institutions do not establish a local market for superior teaching. The outcome at the local level is a public choice problem that depends on the strength of shared governance and the distribution of high and low productivity faculty. Persistence of a local failure depends on a failure at the industry level. If the industry successfully establishes a market for superior teaching, local failures to reward superior teaching adversely select for poor teaching and are unlikely to persist. The outcome at the industry level depends on the establishment of a reliable metric for superior teaching and the communication of that information to outsiders.

Public Choice and Local Failures

Since monopsony power leads to potential rents, the institution has an incentive to follow a pooling strategy in its salary wage offers. The strategy adopted by the institution can be described as a "salary equity" policy. A salary policy designed to preserve "collegiality" or equity in salary fixes the wage paid to good and bad teachers at the same wage rate. With no incremental reward for superior teaching, good teachers have three options: they may leave the institution if they are able, they can mimic the behavior of poor teachers, or they can accept the rent transfer from themselves to the institution.

Superior teachers who insist on high standards may run afoul of the institutions' "collegiality standards" and they may be subject to complaints from students who object to the higher cost imposed on them by superior teaching.[12] This can result in a race to the bottom in terms of teaching quality. The administrators of such policies may gain a more peaceful tenure and they may claim that equity demands that all Ph.D.s be paid the same. The cost to the students and the institution can be substantial, however. This solution can be imposed on faculty if shared governance is weak.

The local market for superior teaching may also fail even when shared governance is not weak. If the faculty is willing to impose restrictive work rules that prevent the institution from evaluating teaching, a pooling wage structure will arise. Low productivity faculty members are better off under a pooling wage structure than they are under a separating wage structure. If the median voter in faculty governance is a poor teacher, this is likely to be the outcome. Even if the institution is willing to pay a premium for superior teaching, uniform salaries will arise if the faculty will not allow teaching to be evaluated. Hence, highly restrictive practices with respect to the use of teaching evaluations may be evidence that poor teaching has driven out superior teaching at that particular institution. It is also apparent that measuring and rewarding superior teaching is not in the financial interest of researchers, since that would increase competition for the institution's resources.

The public choice equilibrium solution at the local level will be either a parallel preference for a pooling wage structure or a parallel preference for a separating wage structure by both the administration and the faculty. Parallel preferences minimize conflict, while asymmetry in preferences leads to considerable conflict between the faculty and the administration. The foregoing suggests two potential equilibrium states within each institution. Either the administration chooses a salary equity policy and the faculty chooses restrictive work rules for teaching evaluations or the administration chooses a differential salary policy and the faculty chooses aggressive evaluation of teaching. The local market for superior teaching fails in the first instance and the local market for superior teaching succeeds in the second case.

In the long run, students and the public are better off under the latter equilibrium state than in the former. In the short run, effort minimizing students are better off under the first equilibrium scenario. The second equilibrium state describes the successful "teaching institution," the institution that sees and pursues teaching as its primary mission. The liberal arts colleges may be characteristic of institutions that create local markets for superior teaching.

Unfortunately, the local market for superior teaching may fail to arise even when administrators and faculty both prefer that outcome. The students are the source of the information problem in this case. When students award superior teaching evaluations on the basis of criteria other than the value added by the teacher the additional noise introduced in the evaluations may prevent the institution from differentiating between good and bad teaching. When high teaching evaluations are driven by the professors' entertainment value, appearance, or an implicit contract to award good grades for good evaluations (evidenced by grade inflation), teaching evaluations are a poor signal for teaching productivity. This contaminates the signal value of both grades and the teaching evaluations. The natural consequence is a decline in the value of an undergraduate degree as a quality signal in the labor market.

The absence of a metric that separates good and bad teaching also results in a pooling solution, where superior and poor teachers are paid the same salary. Since superior teachers are paid less than their marginal productivity and poor teachers are paid more than their marginal productivity, the pooling solution adversely selects for poor teaching – the Gresham effect in teaching. The absence of a separating wage structure means a market for superior teaching may not exist even at the local level, despite the very best of intentions of administrators and faculty.

An Industry Level Failure

Even if a metric designed to measure teaching productivity exists, the market failure may persist. The market for superior teaching may fail at the industry level owing to information asymmetry across institutions. Under this scenario, each institution desires a separating solution and can accurately sort its faculty with respect to superior and poor teaching; however, each institution has no mechanism, nor an incentive, to share that information with others. In fact, the institution has an incentive to keep that information hidden. The faculty who are superior teachers would have an incentive to share that information with other institutions, but their behavior may be mimicked by faculty who are actually inferior teachers.

Similar information problems exist in the market for superior scholarship. The problem is overcome in the market for superior scholarship by the existence of third parties, external to the institutions, who certify the superiority of the scholarship of individual faculty members. The quality of the journals and the success of books published by faculty are the metrics by which scholarship is judged and these metrics are readily observed. These metrics are missing in the market for superior teaching. The absence of an external information source contributes to the absence of a market for superior teaching.

The market for scholars confirms that a perfect measure of faculty productivity is not a necessary condition for markets to establish a separating solution. Journal rankings, citations, grants, and the popularity of books are not perfect measures of scholarly activity, but they are sufficient to establish a market for scholars. Hence, a perfect measure of teaching productivity is not a necessary condition for the establishment of a market for senior teachers.

6.6   THE INTER-INDUSTRY GRESHAM EFFECT

The foregoing discussion concerns the adverse selection effect on teaching within and across institutions caused by the failure to reward productive senior teachers. It might be referred to as the "intra-industry Gresham effect." Good teachers will be driven out of higher education and a secular decline in quality will result. There is another broader effect that can be entitled the "inter-industry Gresham effect." The inter-industry Gresham effect is attributable to Roy (1951) and more recently to Hoxby (2004), who argues that the Gresham effect is responsible for declining productivity in public K–12 schools.

Consider an economy with multiple labor markets in multiple industries. Assume in the beginning that the cost of observing true individual productivity across workers is high and that that cost is uniform across all industries. Under these assumptions, the mix between low and high productivity workers will be similar from one labor market to the next and the wage dispersion in each labor market will be low. The uniform wages in each labor market transfers rents from high productivity workers to low productivity workers and the uniformity of wage dispersions across industries leaves the high productivity workers with little recourse.

Next, assume innovation takes place in some industries in the economy, but not in others, and, in the labor markets where innovation takes place, high individual labor productivity is revealed. Wage dispersion increases within labor markets where innovation takes place and the real incomes of high productivity workers rise and the real incomes of low productivity workers fall. High productivity workers currently employed in industries where innovation has not taken place have an incentive to migrate to industries where innovation takes place and low productivity workers in innovating industries have an incentive to migrate to industries where innovation does not take place. The sorting effect of high and low productivity workers causes rapid productivity growth in the innovating industries and a decline in productivity in the industries that do not innovate. In the industries that do not innovate, low productivity workers drive high productivity workers out of the labor market – the inter-industry Gresham effect.

Economy-wide this distribution of innovation manifests itself as a secular increase in income inequality. One would find a steady rise in GINI coefficients and increasing real returns to productivity. As Hoxby notes, the implication is "the education sector needs to have growth in the sensitivity of its rewards to performance merely to stay even with other industries and thereby avoid becoming a magnet for workers and suppliers whose productivity is poor" (2004: 219).

6.7 IMPLICATIONS

The Gresham effect and the "market for lemons" have significant implications for teaching quality in higher education. When institutions refuse to reward good teaching either because administrators hold ideological positions regarding "salary equity" or because the median faculty member wants to avoid accountability, a pooling salary solution will follow. The pooling salary solution means good and bad teachers are paid the same: Bad teachers are paid a premium and good teachers are paid less than they contribute. The pooling salary solution adversely selects for poor teaching and acts as a magnet for people who wish to avoid accountability.

The failure to measure teaching value added leads directly to the missing market for senior teachers. The absence of that market misaligns incentives and is responsible for the most costly and disturbing trends in higher education. The absence of reliable measures of value added by each faculty member is the core issue. Chapter 3 reveals why institutions have an incentive to withhold value added information and Chapter 4 reveals why it is in the median faculty member's interest to withhold value added information. Chapter 3 also reveals why governing boards are biased against reform and as a result will not insist that value added be measured and reported. Collectively, we see why the academy opposes all attempts to measure value added or to rank individual institutions. It also explains why the academy refuses to suggest alternative ways either to measure value added or to rank institutions.

Faculty

The adverse implications for individual faculty and the academy as a whole are on the allocation of time and effort, institutional loyalty, and grade inflation. Since faculty receive financial rewards and recognition only through exceptional research output, their rational response is to allocate more time towards research and less time to teaching and service. The opportunity cost of not being obsessed with research increases significantly as one progresses up the research ladder. Individual faculty members who prefer to strike a normal balance between teaching, service, and research face a serious dilemma. If they try to improve their teaching or their service, they risk losing their employment mobility and, if they maintain their employment mobility, they must shirk their teaching and service. In other words, the current system rewards faculty members who focus on a single dimension of their professional responsibilities. People with a more balanced perspective are not attracted to or will be driven out of careers as faculty members.

The recognition one receives from research is discipline specific. Prominent researchers in economics are largely unknown to prominent researchers in chemistry. The differences in the disciplines prevent chemists from being able to evaluate the work of economists or economists from being able to evaluate the work of chemists. You can do work that is well regarded by your discipline and your colleagues at your home institution who are not in your discipline will be unaware of that contribution. The financial reward comes from the ability to find another job in the same discipline at another institution. The home institution will be unaware of the significance of the faculty member's work until the faculty member draws an offer from another institution. Contrast the foregoing with local knowledge about who is a good teacher and who is a bad teacher. Under these circumstances, it is clear why the rational faculty member transfers her loyalty from her home institution to her discipline. The implications for teaching and service are obvious.

Grade inflation refers to the tendency of average grades within and across institutions to rise over time. If average student performance is getting better, this trend in grades would not be a cause for concern. Unfortunately, there is no objective evidence that suggests this is the case, as we saw in Chapter 2.

Society is concerned about grade inflation if it represents a contract between faculty members and students to lower expectations. When a faculty member lowers expectations, she is lowering standards. In exchange, she will get fewer student complaints and more time to devote to other activities, such as research. Faculty can free up a lot of time by making the class easy. The effort minimizing student prefers easier classes and is willing to compensate faculty with higher teaching evaluations.

It is appropriate to ask what behavioral model explains chronic grade inflation and lower teaching standards. Consider a faculty where half the faculty has high grading standards and the other half has low grading standards. The resulting GPA is stable as long as this balance is maintained and the faculty members follow their personal standards.

Suppose administrators rely on student evaluations to evaluate teaching quality. Further, assume real career and financial rewards to faculty come from activities other than teaching, say research, and the career or financial awards associated with high grading standards are sparse. Next, consider the problem this scenario creates for faculty members who have high standards for course content and grading. Their attempts to maintain high standards result in lower teaching evaluations, more student complaints, little support from the administration for following high grading standards, and less time to spend on those activities that actually advance their career and their financial prospects. When other professors provide easy classes, the most frequent student complaint is about how unreasonable expectations are relative to those of say Professor X, who is so much more "reasonable."

If administrators and the collective faculty do not enforce high standards by confronting faculty members with low standards, say because they want to preserve collegiality, then faculty members with high grading standards gain nothing by enforcing those standards individually. Low standards drive out high standards and we have a "lemon effect" (Akerlof, 1970). In the end, the faculty and the students arrive at a truce: faculty members do not enforce high standards and students give the faculty good teaching evaluations.[13] David Kirp's "customers" are satisfied (2003).

A similar Gresham effect unfolds owing to competition between institutions. Competition between higher education institutions exists to place their graduates on the best career tracks possible, since successful alumni lead to growing endowments and better reputation. If individual institutions allow GPAs to rise the initial effect is to make their graduates more attractive to employers and to help them get into the best graduate schools; then any institution that tries to maintain high standards puts its own graduates at a competitive disadvantage. This creates a GPA "arms race" among institutions. Again, low standards drive out high standards, another industry-wide "lemon effect." In the end, low standards are infectious within institutions and across institutions.

If institutions are not serious about measuring and rewarding superior teaching, they are also not measuring grade inflation at the individual faculty member, program, and institution level. It is clear that an incentive imbalance between teaching and research will induce rational faculty to indulge in grade inflation.

Institutions

The Gresham effect leads to "mission creep" and less value added competition among institutions. These trends result in higher real costs and lower quality. The chronic problem of "mission creep" refers to the fact that many two year institutions aspire to be four year institutions, many four year institutions aspire to be graduate institutions, and many graduate institutions aspire to be research institutions. This is a serious problem in public higher education, since it leads to the duplication of services in expensive but low quality programs. These institutions try to redefine themselves along the research track because the rewards and recognition are determined by research productivity.

There is also an expansion in the output of research with dubious value that accompanies mission creep. New journals with little social value are started to make space for this work (Bauerlein, 2009). New fields of specialization with very little scientific foundation are created and this supply of new specializations creates its own demand for faculty to staff the new specializations. All of these trends raise the cost of higher education unnecessarily. Again, mission creep is a rational response among higher education institutions when rewards are driven by research productivity.

Consider undergraduate and graduate programs at research institutions. Graduate programs in the U.S. have more than just maintained their quality in the last several decades. The reason for this is because they have strong faculty advocates in the form of highly mobile research faculty. The research faculty members have a significant influence on the institution's resource allocation and governance. At the same time undergraduate programs at research institutions may be declining. Increasingly the undergraduates are taught by graduate students, instructors, and adjunct faculty. The natural advocates for undergraduate programs are mobile senior teaching faculty and they do not exist.

Finally, the lack of innovation in the measurement of teaching productivity in higher education relative to rapid innovation in the measurement of productivity in the rest of the economy is a critical issue. The Gresham effect on teaching is a serious problem for higher education as long as the rest of the economy recognizes productivity faster than does higher education. People who would be very productive teachers choose other careers where their latent productivity will be rewarded, while some of the people who choose teaching careers prefer not to have their productivity measured.

NOTES

1. The differences in mobility cause senior scholars to have elastic labor supply functions, while senior teachers have more inelastic labor supply functions.
2. One might argue that the limited job mobility experienced by teaching faculty either is the consequence of the institution of tenure or may very well be an example of the survivor principle. In order for tenure to be a satisfactory explanation for lost job mobility, it would be necessary to explain why tenure poses no such loss of mobility for exceptional scholars. Something more than tenure is afoot here. If the lack of job mobility is due to the survivor principle, it is necessary to identify the underlying optimal process that grants mobility to scholars, but denies mobility to exceptional teachers.
3. Before proceeding any further with this point, I want to make it clear that solving the market failure problem associated with teaching in no way suggests that scholars should not have job mobility or should not be differentially compensated. Imposing a market failure on scholarship because there is a market failure in teaching would be a perverse response at best.
4. If tenured faculty cannot get an outside offer from another institution for a similar tenured position, then they must accept whatever wage offer their current employer gives them. Under these circumstances the institution has monopsony power with respect to the faculty member and can pay him a wage less than his skills should command. If he is a researcher, he can get an outside offer and escape this monopsony power. If he is a teacher, he cannot get an outside offer since the market for senior teachers does not exist.
5. The stock of publications, as well as any measure of teaching productivity, will be positively correlated with both experience and seniority. The co-linearity issue is more serious in the models where experience and seniority enter as quadratics, since co-linearity is known to cause sign reversals in otherwise correctly specified models.
6. Tenure is actually beneficial to the teaching institution in this case. Without tenure, raiding institutions would be more inclined to make offers to teaching faculty since they could then correct an error if they mistakenly hired a poor teacher. Note also that tenure protects poor teachers, so only good teachers would benefit from the elimination of tenure. Hence, the median faculty member will oppose the elimination of tenure.
7. Note that a necessary condition for this sorting effect to take place is that productivity must be revealed to outside employers. If productivity is not revealed to outside employers, the outside offers are not forthcoming and the adverse sorting effect in the Harris and Holmstrom model and in the Lazear model does not take place.
8. Low wage dispersion implies a pooling solution, while high wage dispersion implies a separating solution.
9. This is an accurate description of the market for senior scholars.
10. This describes the current market for senior teachers.

11. Oyer (2006) finds that initial placements have important long term effects on faculty research productivity and academic careers. Holding other factors constant, a new faculty member who is not initially placed in a top 50 program is unlikely to ever work in a top 50 program, while a new faculty member who is initially placed in a top 50 program is likely to be employed in a top 50 program. He also finds considerable downward mobility among those initially placed in a top 50 program.
12. I am implicitly assuming here that superior teachers demand greater effort from their students. They are more "challenging."
13. Murray Sperber describes this agreement as a non-aggression pact (2005).

7.   Inside the black box

7.1   INTRODUCTION

In 1980 H.R. Bowen derived the "revenue theory of cost" from a comprehensive empirical analysis of cost per student in private and public institutions (1980). The evidence reveals that cost per student varied considerably from one institution to another, even for similar institutions, program offerings were considerably different, and staffing patterns by program were also different. The differences were so pronounced that he suggested it was as if they had been chosen by "centrifugal randomness" (1980: 227–8). These variations mean a common higher education technology was not followed even in core academic disciplines such as basic sciences, mathematics, and the social sciences. This is significant because most of these disciplines have well established paradigms that suggest a common approach should prevail.

Bowen's general conclusions are: higher education institutions try to maximize their quality reputations, there is no limit on the amount of money they can spend on "quality," they raise all the money they can, they spend all the money they raise, and the cumulative effect is a never ending increase in expenditures (1980: 19–20). Bowen's conclusions were extracted inductively from what he observed in the data. His conclusions about college and university behavior are remarkable since they describe precisely what happened to costs after 1980. Higher education's cost history since 1980 is entirely consistent with Bowen's revenue theory of cost.

The lack of a behavioral foundation limits the usefulness of Bowen's theory of cost. Until we understand why reputations for "excellence, prestige, and influence" are so important to higher education institutions, we are unlikely to make much progress in bringing costs under control. The same thing can be said about their tendency towards unlimited spending, why they are constantly in fund raising mode, and why they spend whatever is available (rather than accumulate a surplus for hard times, an omission I am sure Harvard regrets).

This book contains a behavioral framework for Bowen's revenue theory of cost. The relentless pursuit of quality reputation is due to the nature of the services provided by higher education; education is a complex experience good. The formal theory of experience goods provides many insights into college and university behavior. The fact that revenues cap expenditures comes from the nonprofit status of higher education institutions. The constant fund raising needed to support more spending is the result of serious, unresolved principal/agent problems. Higher education's cost control record would be of less concern if these expenditures led to better undergraduate education; unfortunately, undergraduate education is not improving. The college experience is getting more expensive as its quality declines.

The problems created by experience good competition and agency abuse in higher education are due to information issues in both cases. This is why critics raise issues about "transparency" in higher education reform. Perfect information about teaching value added, finances, and operations would eliminate the agency problem and the problems associated with experience good competition. One of these information issues, the lack of information about teaching value added, is directly responsible for declining quality in undergraduate education. The market for senior teachers does not exist because of a critical information failure, too little information about teaching value added. The absence of a market for senior teachers distorts incentives away from teaching towards research and "public service" activities.

The market for scholarship works very well. It produces a high quality core and a much wider body of less significant results. The cumulative scientific and cultural value produced is evident in the health and wellbeing of our society. Whatever steps are taken to improve teaching and control costs must not sacrifice what is right with higher education and scholarship is something that is quite right with higher education. Some adjustments need to be made at the margin, since the excessive emphasis on research owing to the imbalanced incentives leads to too much investment in marginal research. If the teaching and research incentives are brought into balance, the excess investment in research is likely to disappear.

7.2   TEACHING PRODUCTIVITY, QUALITY, AND COST

Teaching productivity can be measured by student/faculty ratios and teaching loads (the number of classes taught per year). Student/faculty ratios have declined steadily over the past three decades. There is very little information available on the history of teaching loads; however, those of us who have been in the academy over this period can report that teaching loads went down even at teaching institutions. It is argued by many that lower student/faculty ratios and lower teaching loads are an investment in research productivity and better quality teaching.

The simple algebra in Chapter 2 shows the relationship between lower student/faculty ratios and lower teaching loads with higher cost per student. This connection is verified by the data in Chapter 2: as student/faculty ratios and teaching loads went down, cost per student went up. While teaching productivity went down, real wages went up (separation of pay and productivity). Apparently, this three decade investment in better quality teaching did not pay off; the data and subjective evidence indicate that teaching quality has declined since 1980. If there was a gain from these trends, it must be in research productivity.

Staff productivity can also be measured by student/staff ratios; the data in Chapter 2 reveal that student staff ratios fell substantially for the professional staff ratio and rose for the nonprofessional ratio. It is difficult to argue that lower student/staff ratios imply higher quality, since staff members do not teach or produce research. One expects these overhead functions to be characterized by increasing returns to scale. Further, the objective measures of service sector productivity outside of higher education reveal significant improvements in productivity over the last three decades (Triplett and Bosworth, 2003); while the for-profit service industries increased their productivity, higher education reduced its productivity. As the simple algebraic models in Chapter 2 suggest, the data reveal cost per student associated with these overhead activities increased sharply after 1980.

Over the period in question, student/faculty ratios decreased by about 25 percent in both public and private institutions, while student/professional staff ratios dropped by about 50 percent and student/nonprofessional staff ratios rose between 30 percent and 50 percent. Since the proportion of total employment accounted for by instructional staff declined over the period and the proportion of part time faculty and non-tenure track faculty increased, two-thirds of the real cost increase per student came from overhead expenses.

The "point of the spear" in undergraduate education is the instructor in each class. The data reveal that faculty members as a percentage of total employment declined from 58 percent in 1976 to 37 percent in 2005 among public institutions and from 42 percent in 1976 to 34 percent in 2005 among private institutions. Further, in 1970 the proportion of the faculty who were full time employees was 77.9 percent; by 2005 that proportion was 52.4 percent. Almost half of the instructors in those classrooms now are part time employees. In addition, public institutions are making greater use of full time instructors, causing the proportion of tenure track faculty to decline even further. The "point of the spear" composed of tenure track faculty is getting smaller and the spear point overall is less sharp. Beyond what happens in the classroom, the declining proportion of tenure track faculty weakens governance and the natural advocacy for better undergraduate education. This decline explains, in part, the explosion in overhead cost; smaller numbers of faculty with a seat at the governance table divert resources from instruction to bureaucracy.

7.3   REPUTATIONS AND EXPERIENCE GOODS

Reputations matter only in markets for experience goods where consumers are uncertain about product quality prior to purchase. Reputation competition leads to an efficient solution when the product is purchased frequently, it is easy to determine quality after it is purchased, and it is easy for the consumer to shift to a competitor. A college education is the most complex experience good: it is purchased once; it is very difficult to evaluate quality after it is purchased; and once purchased it is impractical to shift to a competitor. Further, it is very expensive and there is no secondary market for a college degree. Under these conditions, reputation competition in higher education is unlikely to be efficient.

The theory of experience goods reveals that price is a prior indicator of quality (the Chivas Regal effect), institutions have an incentive not to provide quality information, as market power increases quality information declines, and quality cheating is always a problem. In a monopoly situation, a stable equilibrium does not exist and quality unravels.

One of the more important implications for higher education is the impact of quality uncertainty on entry cost. Since parents/students are uncertain about quality, they assume any new entrant must be a low quality provider and they will only pay the low quality price for the service from the new entrant. If the new entrant intends to be a high quality provider, he must exceed expectations by providing high quality at the low quality price; therefore the new entrant experiences a loss on each unit of service provided. The cumulative loss per unit of service provided is the new entrant's investment in reputation. The amount the new entrant must invest increases as the frequency of purchase declines and as it takes longer to evaluate quality after purchase. For higher education, this means new entrance at the top of the quality tier (where all the rents are) is virtually impossible, since it would take multiple generations of loss per unit of service. This explains why the only new entry we see from for-profit providers is at the bottom of the quality tier. The absence of any new entry threat at the top of the quality tier increases the market power of those institutions and market power causes quality erosion.

Another important implication for higher education from the theory of experience goods is the Chivas Regal effect establishes a direct relationship between expenditures per student and reputation; the more an institution spends per student the higher is its quality reputation. Indeed, reputation competition is a race to spend as much as you can per student. This characteristic of higher education competition makes the academy ripe for agency abuse.

7.4 NONPROFITS AND AGENCY ISSUES

The purpose of a nonprofit organization is to provide more goods and services in situations where those goods are undersupplied by the for-profit sector or the goods and services have positive externalities. Since the purpose is to increase output, they are organized as nonprofit institutions[1] and they are granted tax exemption. Not spending all the current revenue the institution has is inconsistent with doing what the nonprofit is chartered to do: increase the supply of goods and services. Therefore revenues cap expenditures among nonprofits and, whenever revenues increase, expenditures increase.

Like for-profit firms, nonprofits are run by people hired to manage cash flows on behalf of other people. Managing cash flows for others always introduces the possibility of agency abuse. In higher education the agents are faculty members, staff, administrators, and trustees. The principals are students, parents, alumni, donors, and taxpayers. The principal/agent problem occurs everywhere and agency abuse results in costs that are higher than necessary. Higher education's persistent history of rising real cost per student strongly suggests there are chronic and unchecked agency problems in the academy.

Further evidence of agency problems comes from the separation of pay and productivity. The data in Chapter 2 reveal real wages increase while teaching productivity declines. Trustees and administrators set the conditions of employment and are responsible for not connecting pay to productivity, as governing groups among for-profit firms must do to avoid bankruptcy.[2]

There are many constraints on agency abuse in the for-profit sector and very few constraints on agency abuse in higher education. Despite the constraints on for-profit firms, episodes of agency abuse are relatively common. People look for agency abuse in for-profit firms. In contrast, people tend not to look for agency abuse in higher education because higher education is supposed to "do good." The constraints on for-profit agency abuse are: the market for corporate control, competition from potential entry, extensive government regulation, numerous private groups that have a financial incentive to pursue oversight, a media looking for agency abuse, a performance metric that reveals abuse (profit), and few third party payers involved in transactions.

Similarly, there are strong natural constraints among politicians and still agency abuse by politicians is common. The primary constraints on politicians are they have to stand for re-election and opposition candidates/parties are always looking for abuse. The market for "political control" is a deterrent to agency abuse.

There is no market for control of higher education institutions, little competition from potential entrants, very little government regulation, and few private groups engaged in oversight. Further, the academy has overly friendly relations with the media, has a performance measure that does not reveal agency abuse, and is heavily funded by third party payers.

Reputation competition enables agency abuse. Correcting agency abuse creates controversies and controversies damage reputations. No matter how poorly a tenured faculty member performs his duties, the university rarely tries to fire him. The process required to dismiss a tenured professor is long, lawyer intensive, and very public. During the process the faculty target can make whatever claim he wishes; the institution has to refute each charge in court, and can say nothing about the case in public. If the university targets a professor for dismissal, the target will draw public support from other marginal faculty and the process will make the productive faculty uncomfortable. The last such case was Ward Churchill at the University of Colorado and that firing was possible only because he broke strict academic rules about research.

Reputation competition also enables agency abuse by administrators. Even if the administrator's abuse is outright theft, trustees tend to settle out of court without filing charges. Neither the trustees nor the administrator wants the problem to go public.

7.5 COMMERCIALIZATION

The conviction that after 1980 "commercialization" or "corporatization" corrupted higher education is popular among insiders. This alien influence is said to be responsible for the academy's unseemly pursuit of fund raising, willingness to sell the commercial rights to its research, exploitation of extension teaching, and addiction to "big-time sports programs." It is frequently argued that "treating students like customers" leads to grade inflation and lower teaching standards. Derek Bok describes commercialization as the pursuit of "profit" from research, teaching, and sports (2003: 3).

Higher education does generate a surplus from these activities, but the principals are not the beneficiaries; the surplus is retained by the agents for their own benefit. Commercialization or corporatization of higher education is not an alien influence that corrupts the virtuous; the suspect behavior is entirely home grown. The issues considered in the "commercialization literature" (Bok, 2003; Engell and Dangerfield, 2005; Gardner, 2005; Kirp, 2003, 2005; Tuchman, 2009; Washburn, 2005) are further evidence of principal/agent problems inside higher education.

First, the people put in place to make decisions are chosen by the governance structure; they are not chosen by outsiders. The institutions are free to contract or not. The simplest among us knows that if corporations put stockholders' money into the academy they expect a return on that investment and they expect the contract to be honored. If the university does not do its own due diligence in negotiating the agreement, that is a failure inside the university. The persistent failure to protect itself in contract negotiations is due to the fact that the interests of administrators and principal investigators are not aligned with the university's interests; that is the classic principal/agent problem.

The problem in extension teaching programs is also an agency problem. Within the college or university, these programs are considered something "other" than the traditional teaching programs. They are purpose driven to create a financial surplus. That surplus is not claimed by students, parents, alumni, donors, or taxpayers. The surplus is claimed by tenure track faculty, staff, administrators, and trustees. The part time adjunct faculty, with no seat at the governance table and no benefits, are exploited by this arrangement, as are the students who attend the extension programs.

Big-time college sports programs (B-TS) are a corrupting influence on higher education. The potential financial benefits that might accrue to the university are captured by the B-TS insiders; they collect the rents that should go to the public or to the "student athletes." Again, this is an agency problem. Ironically, if universities were corporations, they would restructure the B-TS enterprise in order to eliminate the agency problems or they would spin the activity off as a separate corporation. In other words, the B-TS problem persists because universities are not corporations.

The growing tendency of colleges and universities to "bundle" new services with traditional academic services is one of the four reasons why cost per student continues to rise, discussed in Chapter 1. Bundling is also agency abuse and simple economic exploitation of students and parents. Faculty members, staff, administrators, and trustees derive benefits from activities sponsored by the college or university; bundling such things as international travel, luxury accommodation, entertainment, and food with the "college experience" provides benefits to faculty, staff, administrators, and trustees. Furthermore, bundling these services raises the student's cost and restricts his choice of provider.

A new influence did take hold of higher education after 1980. The "foul wind" blowing on campus was not commercialization; it was public relations. It was a natural accommodation because reputations are built, in part, by public relations and reputations are crucial to higher education competition. In 1980 the academy was at a crossroads: it could continue to build reputation the old fashioned way by building academic substance or it could build reputation by cultivating an image with public relations. It is to our shame that we chose image over substance and it was that choice that created the clash of values.

Building reputation by actually improving quality is a sure, but slow and tedious, process; building reputations by cultivating an image brings quick financial benefits. The quick payoff from fund raising and image building poured gasoline on H.R. Bowen's "revenue theory of cost" and it lit the match that ignited the rise in cost per student from 1980 to the present.

7.6   NO MARKET FOR TENURED SENIOR TEACHERS

The missing market for senior teachers refers specifically to a job market for tenured positions where the recruiting institution hires the faculty member because of her teaching skills. This is the teaching counterpart to the well established market for senior scholars. In response to the public's concern about teaching, colleges and universities have begun to hire non-tenure track teachers with multiple year contracts. Campus political power depends on tenure track status; command over resources depends on tenure track status. Mobile research faculty members are the most influential faculty at research universities and they are the natural advocates for graduate programs and for research. There are no mobile, tenured teaching faculty members at research universities, so there are no natural advocates for undergraduate programs at research universities.

This is also a problem at teaching institutions. Senior faculty members at teaching institutions do not have job mobility; they cannot get a tenured job offer at another comparable institution. Once they are tenured, their home institution becomes a monopsony employer. The lack of job mobility leaves them with little leverage relative to administrators. The lack of leverage makes them less effective as advocates for undergraduate education; their governance role is weak. This is part of the reason why administrative overheads have grown out of control at colleges and universities. In addition, the secular decline in undergraduate education both at research universities and at teaching institutions is in part due to the absence of strong faculty advocates for teaching.

Under the current regime, a profitable and rewarding career track exists for scholars in higher education. A successful scholar can expect rapidly rising real income, the admiration of peers in his profession, and in many cases public adulation as well. There is no corresponding career track for a successful teacher; his real income may decline over time, his students may adore him, but people outside his home institution may never know what he contributes.

Consider the implications for a young person thinking about a career in higher education. If the young person is very interested in research and thinks she can compete at that level, there is no problem; a clear route to fame is well established. Suppose our prospective professor is very interested in teaching and thinks he may have a gift for it, he knows his income prospects are not good, he is unlikely to get much recognition for what he does, and he knows his options will be significantly reduced if he starts his academic career at a teaching institution. If he starts out on the research track and fails he can fall back on the teaching track, but if he starts out teaching, he cannot move to the research track. The highly talented researcher chooses an academic career, while the highly talented teacher chooses some other career. This is adverse selection in higher education employment.

Consider the adverse incentives for graduate education. Since the real payoff in higher education is through scholarship, graduate programs train new Ph.D.s to be researchers, not teachers. There are very few, if any, quality Ph.D. programs whose primary objective is to train superior teachers.

Finally, the missing market for senior teachers leads to "mission creep." The real institutional rewards flow to research universities; therefore two year institutions want to be four year institutions, four year institutions want to have graduate programs, institutions with graduate programs want to add Ph.D. programs, and institutions with Ph.D. programs want to become research universities. At each stage, undergraduate education is diminished and it causes a costly duplication of low quality graduate programs.

7.7 RESOLVING THE INFORMATION PROBLEM

Colleges and universities have no incentive to develop reliable metrics for teaching value added; in fact, it is in their interest not to develop these metrics. Reducing quality uncertainty makes demand more price elastic and reliable metrics for teaching value added would eliminate the institution's monopsony relationship with teaching faculty. Since the faculty's governance power is driven by the "median faculty voter," the faculty as a group has nothing to gain from the development of a reliable metric for teaching value added. The median or average faculty member is not a superior teacher; superior teachers are by definition a minority among faculty members. The foregoing explains why higher education is so critical of all attempts to measure value added or rank institutions (Zemsky, 2009: 72–89).

The academy's hesitancy to reveal useful quality information is demonstrated by its reaction to the National Survey of Student Engagement (NSSE). Zemsky reports "the NSSE has been wildly successful" as an instrument to correct deficiencies in the conditions that promote positive educational outcomes (2009: 85). The NSSE is voluntary and the results remain under the control of the institutions who administer the survey. When the results are favorable in one category, these institutions boldly report them on their websites. Zemsky further reports that the people behind the NSSE "believed that colleges and universities would grow comfortable with releasing their NSSE results into the public domain as a kind of natural antidote to the U.S. News rankings. Most institutions, however, have demurred, wanting to contemplate their results in private" (2009: 85). The hesitancy is entirely consistent with the theory of reputation competition in Chapter 3; quality uncertainty creates a financial advantage.

The economics of experience goods reveals why more quality information is required for efficiency, why competitors have an incentive to withhold quality information, and why reputation competition leads to a bias against reform in those industries. This explains why colleges and universities provide little value added information and are so critical of third party ranking systems. In response to growing calls for more accountability and transparency from the higher education reform movement, the National Association of Independent Colleges and Universities (NAICU) and the Association of Public Land-Grant Universities (APLU) established web based accountability sites in the fall of 2007. The NAICU established the University and College Accountability Network (U-CAN) and the APLU established the Voluntary System of Accountability (VSA) site.

Andrew Kelly and Chad Aldeman analyzed the information content of these two sites in a report entitled *False Fronts? Behind Higher Education's Voluntary Accountability Systems* (2010). Kelly and Aldeman find:

> The site for private colleges and universities, U-CAN, is not really new at all; it is essentially a re-packaging of data that are available elsewhere, and it

provides almost no new information about costs, student experiences, or learning outcomes to parents and prospective students. In contrast, the VSA, which catalogs public schools, represents a legitimate effort to provide students with important information about how much college costs and the education students receive in return. But the VSA also suffers from numerous shortcomings. Not all institutions participate, particularly those at the top and bottom of the quality scale. The site does not allow for the easy comparison of institutions, despite the fact that the database was created to facilitate consumer choice. And many of the most crucial VSA data elements are incomplete, non-comparable, or selected in a way that often obscures differences between institutions. (2010: 1–2)

In the case of the U-CAN site, they conclude it is "a pre-emptive attempt to fend off federal or state regulators, not a sincere effort to compel institutions to focus on consumer needs" (2010: 2). While the APLU contains new information, Kelly and Aldeman find the site seems purpose driven not to allow easy comparisons between institutions (2010: 3). Kelly and Aldeman's primary policy conclusions are: 1) cost and value added transparency "must be mandatory, not voluntary"; and 2) the data collected must "clarify institutional distinctions, not blur them" (2010: 13–14).

Kelly and Aldeman's results are consistent with what we learned about the behavioral model behind Bowen's "revenue theory of cost"; more uncertainty about value added is beneficial to higher education institutions, the uncertainty leads to the association of higher cost with higher quality in a competition with no upper bound on expenditures, and the uncertainty enables acute principal/agent problems. The interaction of reputation competition and principal/agent problems creates the unbounded revenue to cost spiral that plagues higher education. The spiral endangers our global competitiveness, it contributes to an ever widening income distribution, and it means the access problem cannot be solved without reform.

Any higher education reform effort designed to correct the incentive imbalance and place more emphasis on quality improvement has to have a system of metrics to evaluate teaching value added. The measurement of value added will be resisted by insiders for the reasons enumerated in this book. A flaw will be found in every metric proposed and it will be claimed the flaw is sufficient to rule out the use of that metric. Higher education insiders will argue perfection is the standard by which all metrics should be judged.

In an imperfect world, perfection is inefficient. George Stigler carefully explained the difference between perfection, imperfection, and efficiency (1967). The lessons he provides are appropriate for the debate about metrics designed to evaluate teaching. Stigler was explaining the difference between market perfection and market efficiency when he said that market imperfection "is a terminal concept. Once this phrase has been written or spoken," the conversation stops (1967: 287). The same thing happens when insiders find fault with a particular measure of teaching quality: the conversation is over and that metric is rejected.

Stigler carefully explains why something that is imperfect may in fact be efficient, while something that is perfect may be inefficient. Information costs explain this puzzle. In the imperfect world we live in, information, like any other commodity, has a cost. Indeed, the marginal cost of information increases as more information is accumulated; as Stigler says, "information costs are the costs of transportation from ignorance to omniscience, and seldom can a trader afford to take the entire trip" (1967: 291). The efficient solution is found where the marginal cost of more information is equal to the marginal benefit of more information. In other words, this leads to a "rational level of ignorance." In a world where information is costly, perfect information is inefficient.

How do we apply this to the development of information about teaching value added? The first lesson is to reject categorically the argument that if a measure of value added is imperfect it cannot be used; perfection cannot be allowed to defeat the common good. We should recall that higher education institutions have an incentive not to develop this information or make it public.[3] Further, the separation of pay and productivity in higher education teaching causes a self-selection bias among faculty for individuals who do not want their productivity measured and the average college teacher (who is the median voter in faculty meetings) has nothing to gain, and may lose,[4] if high quality teachers are recognized.

The second lesson to be learned from Stigler's analysis of information cost is there are imperfect, but efficient, measures of teaching value added. Indeed, the efficient measures are those that are sufficient to establish a market for master senior teachers. When colleges and universities have enough information to avoid the adverse selection caused by making tenured teaching offers to faculty members at other institutions, the quality problems in undergraduate teaching will begin to turn around. Master senior teachers with national reputations are the natural advocates for undergraduate instruction, just as senior scholars with national reputations are the natural advocates for graduate programs and research.

The third lesson is a single measure of teaching value added is not sufficient to establish a market for senior teachers. Teaching evaluations alone will never be sufficient; they have too many moral hazard problems and the "mutual non-aggression pact" between students and faculty members is too well established. On the other hand, teaching evaluations, properly formatted and analyzed, should be part of the process.

The thriving market for senior scholars gives us clues about what information is needed and where it should come from. The information we have about scholarship is certainly not perfect. We know where each article is published, the number of pages, the number of co-authors, and, eventually, the number of citations. We know similar things about books. Unfortunately, there is no obvious metric for weighing level one versus level two journals,[5] how to weigh multiple co-authors, or how to determine whether all citations are the same. There are numerous anecdotal stories about extraordinarily important articles being turned down by the "best journals." The classic example in economics is Akerlof's "lemons" paper (1970). What is "influential" is also not obvious.

Another thing to notice about the information set that supports the market for scholars is that it comes from third parties. It does not come from the institution where the scholar is employed. The scholar submits her work for blind refereeing, the work is made available to the international community of scholars in her own discipline, and the influence is determined by how many other scholars build on her work.

The market for senior scholars clearly demonstrates that productivity measures do not have to be perfect in order to be efficient. There are also numerous examples outside of higher education where productivity measures are sufficient to establish a vigorous market for products or services where productivity or quality is highly subjective. The arts are a perfect example; value in the arts depends on tastes and preferences that cannot be quantified other than by the amount individuals are willing to spend. There are individual versus team productivity issues in professional sports, yet a vigorous market for individual athletes exists.

7.8   TECHNOLOGY AND REFORM

The rate of innovation in higher education is slow (Getz et al., 1997); Adam Smith would find the delivery of lectures to students taking notes very familiar. This could change and it could be an opportunity for higher education reform. First, new technology could significantly alter higher education delivery technology. Baumol's cost disease hypothesis assumes education delivery requires fixed proportions, which is the assumption that one professor is required for each class. Interactive learning technologies will continue to replace instructors in learning laboratories. Mixtures of lecture classes and learning laboratory classes allow individual professors to teach more classes in the same amount of time. In the past productivity gains were not captured by the institutions, however; the productivity gains were taken as more release time for faculty members.

Second, new technology can provide the information required to establish a market for world class teachers. Derek Bok reports: "Larry Ellison, CEO of Oracle, looks forward to a future in which e-learning will overcome the 'wild inefficiencies of American higher education' by offering 'million dollar salaries for a few star professors and access to the best teaching for millions and millions of students all over the world'" (2003: 87). Bok believes this threat is overstated since similar claims were made when movies, radio, and television were introduced. The critical difference here is the new technology is interactive in an extraordinary and facile way.

In the previous section we drew insights from the vigorous market for senior scholars. The scholarly output produced by U.S. colleges and universities makes the research universities the world class institutions they are. That output is directly attributable to the healthy labor market for senior scholars. In turn, the scholars' labor market works well because the information needed to differentiate between scholars comes from third parties who are independent of both the scholars and the institutions that employ them. What Larry Ellison is suggesting in the previous passage is e-learning will provide the critical third party platform needed to identify master teachers and that will be sufficient to solve the problem of the missing market for senior teachers discussed in Chapter 6. This development would substantially alter the incentive structure in higher education.

One can see the initial development of this information platform in websites such as RateMyProfessors.com, where students go to give objective and subjective course evaluations. These evaluations can benefit or hurt individual teachers. They can also be used to obtain some sense of the differences in teaching cultures at different institutions. I have done this by reading all of the evaluations for several liberal arts colleges with which I am familiar. I recommend that exercise to any student trying to decide between two institutions.

The development of independent teaching information could be "nudged" into existence by e-competitions. The competitors would be reviewed the same way publications are reviewed. Since content is as important as a dynamic delivery, each contestant's presentation would be peer reviewed by faculty in her own discipline. The review process is the ticket to the competition. There are a variety of ways to organize the actual competition. One possibility is by intercollegiate teaching tournaments where teachers compete with colleagues at other institutions. After a candidate passes the review process and enters the intercollegiate competition, the league picks a topic and each competitor prepares a presentation. League judges then pick the best presentation. Winning records lead to a final championship competition. It would then be easy to provide a ranking of institutions on the basis of the number of their faculty members who make it to the finals and the number who become champions in different disciplines.

Electronic courses produced by textbook publishers are another way to nudge the necessary information sources. The mechanism would be modeled after textbook publishing. The professor creates a course proposal (similar to a book proposal); the publisher reviews the proposal, contracts with the professor to produce the material, and then markets the course through online virtual universities.

The conventional wisdom within higher education is that measuring teaching value added is very difficult, if not impossible. On the other hand, we know faculty members do not want their productivity measured and higher education institutions have a financial incentive not to measure teaching value added. Hence, whether an efficient system for measuring teaching value added does not exist or it does not exist because no one has sufficient incentive to develop a system is unknown. The fact that efficient systems in related activities exist suggests the problem is a lack of incentive to develop a system. If the public offered a $100 million prize for the development of a system to measure teaching value added, it would stimulate considerable effort within and outside of higher education. Indeed, such a prize is likely to attract private venture capital. In any event, there has been little incentive to measure teaching value added to date and there is little probability we will find one if the incentives remain the same. If we find an efficient system, it will be resisted by the higher education establishment.

7.9 REFORM AND THE ELITE INSTITUTIONS

Owing to the importance of reputations in higher education, competition is oriented up the quality ladder; colleges and universities mimic institutions on the quality rung immediately above them. The goal is to move out of the teaching value added pooling solution and into the labor market credentialing separating solution.

The institutions in the ladder's lowest quartile offer only teaching value added. Since there is insufficient information to separate high and low quality value added, the price is the same for high and low quality providers. Among these institutions, price is not an indicator of quality and one does not observe the Chivas Regal effect. Further, these institutions have undiversified revenue sources, since they are tuition driven.

If an institution can move up the quality ladder, its credential value increases and that is the ticket into the separating solution that prevails among high quality institutions. The separating solution means price is an indicator of quality; the institution's demand curve is more price inelastic;

they benefit from the Chivas Regal effect in the high quality ranks; and revenue sources are more diversified. The number of competing institutions declines and the institution's market power increases as the institution moves up the ladder.

The foregoing suggests the competitive "rules of engagement" in higher education flow from the top down. The nature of competition in higher education cannot be changed by the institutions at the bottom of the quality ladder. Since for-profit entrants are concentrated in the lower quality quartile, it is unlikely that for-profit providers are going to have a significant impact on higher education.

It is more likely that reform will succeed if it starts with the elite institutions. First, there are fewer institutions at the top, so agreement on reforms becomes more likely. Second, their quality is not in question, so if they agreed to reorganize their undergraduate programs, increase productivity, and cut cost they would escape the perverse incentive created by reputation competition (reductions in cost are interpreted as reductions in quality). Third, the risk of experimentation at elite institutions is less than the risk of experimentation in the lower ranks. Fourth, the elite institutions have better intellectual capital than the lower ranks and are better prepared to find creative solutions to quality and productivity problems. Finally, since the elite institutions are the wealthiest institutions, they have a social obligation to provide solutions to these problems.

7.10 FINAL REFLECTIONS

By this point, the reader is well aware the book is critical of higher education. The analysis is most critical of the incentive system that leads to the cost and quality issues discussed; the problems are not the result of any collusion against the public interest among members of the academy. While it is not news, the agents who populate higher education are human and we need to remember that being human means being subject to all the failings known to humans. For example, my own long experience in higher education and more limited experience among for-profit firms taught me there is little moral difference between those who toil in corporations and those who toil in higher education.

The major difference between people in the business community, politics, the church, the medical profession, the legal profession, and higher education is the stakes (power and money) are different. If the stakes were the same in higher education as they are in the business community or in politics, I have no doubt we would see the same type of extreme self-serving behavior we see all too frequently in corporations and in politics.

Higher education is a frequent critic of all aspects of our society, such as culture, politics, business, law enforcement, the military, and religion. Indeed, these criticisms are an essential part of our public service. They are essential because they come from an independent outside group, hopefully without conflicted interests. For example, economists analyze public policy and provide criticism where that criticism is needed. Unfortunately, we show a surprising lack of interest in the critical analysis of our own institutions and we are habitually very sensitive to any criticism of the academy, from either outside or inside our institutions. We accept the unexamined premise that we live by a higher standard than others. This assumption is a major obstacle to reform and it perpetuates our cost and quality problems.

NOTES

1. The profit surplus taken by a for-profit firm could be used to increase supply instead, so third party payers would not get the maximum output which is their objective.
2. The United Auto Workers succeeded in separating pay from productivity over the post-World War II period and that separation eventually contributed to General Motors' and Chrysler's bankruptcy.
3. If the institution publicly identifies its most gifted teachers, it is inviting them to be hired away by another institution.
4. If teaching value added is not measured, faculty compensation is homogeneous (it is a pooling solution for compensation). If teaching value added is measured and rewarded, faculty compensation is heterogeneous (it is a separating solution) and poor teachers get low pay and good teachers get high pay. The median teacher loses when the institution shifts from a pooling solution to a separating solution.
5. Furthermore, it is not obvious how one decides what a level one journal is relative to a level two journal.

Glossary

Academic ratchet – new activities in higher education add to permanently higher costs and to a commitment to fund increases in those activities in the future; the costs ratchet up and never come back down through the abandonment of obsolete activities.

Adverse selection – when information is not symmetrically distributed (asymmetric information), market prices can adversely sort for low quality; high interest rates adversely select for low quality borrowers and the buyer's lack of information about product quality results in a premium being paid to low quality providers and discounts below cost for high quality products. This drives the high quality product out of the market; it adversely selects for low quality products.

Asymmetric information – when the information available to each party in a transaction is not uniform, one or more parties in the transaction has more information than the other parties. The more informed party has an economic advantage.

Bundling – combining multiple goods or services and selling them as a package. Bundling products/services reduces customer choice, enables price discrimination, and acts as a barrier to entry for firms that cannot bundle products. Bundling can have a positive social impact when there are economies in production or consumption.

Cash flows – every institution, private, public, or government, has cash inflows and cash outflows that have to be managed in order to avoid chronic unfunded deficits. Managers must resolve differences in the timing of inflows/outflows and insure that debt obligations are met.

Centrifugal randomness – in expenditures and staffing employed among similar higher education institutions. A defined higher education technology would suggest expenditures and staffing would be similar in similar institutions.

Chivas Regal anomaly – the tendency of consumers to associate high quality with high price; occurs only in experience good markets where consumers are uncertain about product quality. Leads to competition to spend more per student among higher education institutions.

Commercialization – the notion that higher education institutions have adopted "business practices." It is a pejorative term that blames quality and cost issues on the outside influence of business interests.

Community service – the third leg on the faculty's "academic stool"; the three component parts of a faculty member's job description are teaching, research, and service.

Contestable markets – a market is said to be contestable when entry/exit costs are at a minimum; for example, an airline's passenger service between Dallas and Denver is easily contested by other airlines that can allocate planes to serve that route and withdraw them at will (entry/exit costs are negligible). The market for highly selective colleges is not contestable; it takes decades to establish a reputation for high quality. When markets are contestable, prices are low regardless of the number of competitors. Therefore, if the airline has a monopoly on the route between Dallas and Denver, the fares will still be low because of the entry threat. If markets are not contestable, prices are high.

Cost disease (generic) – the decades long history of rapidly rising real costs, declining teaching productivity, and resistance to reform in higher education.
   (Baumol) – the separation of real wages and productivity in education and the service industries that leads to chronically higher costs.

Credential competition among higher education institutions – selectivity in admissions sends a high quality signal to the labor market for college graduates. The ability to compete on the basis of credentials is empowered by reputation.

De-professionalization among faculty – a decline in professional standing and behavior among faculty members.

Destructuring curriculum – curriculum used to have an internal order to it, where courses were supposed to be taken in a particular sequence and a core body of courses was required; the internal order in curriculum was enforced by faculty advising students; as faculty quit advising students the internal order was abandoned and replaced by an unstructured mixture of courses.

Experience goods – goods whose quality cannot be determined prior to purchase and can only be determined after purchase when consumers have "experience" with the product; it means the consumer must be uncertain about quality prior to purchasing the product.

Facilities competition – the tendency of higher education institutions to invest heavily in physical assets such as classrooms, laboratories, libraries, dormitories, student unions, athletic complexes, and other entertainment facilities. These facilities have become more luxurious and expensive over the last three decades. They represent fixed cost investments in an experience good market that represent "quality" and are also part of the service bundling problem.

Financial burdens in higher education – the increase in education costs that rise as a proportion of median household incomes over the decades. These burdens can be measured by the rate of increase in expenditures per student, the net price of attendance, and the amount of debt students carry upon graduation.

Government mandates – expenditures mandated by governments such as Title IX, students with disabilities, safety, health, and nondiscrimination.

Grade inflation – the secular rise in average grades by program and by institution. As the average grade increases the quality signal conveyed by grades declines and suggests teachers and students have reached some accommodation about grades and teaching evaluations.

Gresham effect – similar to the "lemon effect" where uncertainty about quality tends to drive good quality products out of the market leaving only the low quality products; good products are replaced by "lemons." See also *Adverse selection*.

Hidden productivity – when outside employers cannot tell how productive a potential employee may actually be.

Information failures – see *Asymmetric information*. Asymmetric information can lead to market failures or situations where transactions society would prefer do not take place.

Inter-industry Gresham effect – as productivity measurement and real wages improve in one industry the industry hires more productive workers and releases low productivity workers; the low productivity workers tend to concentrate in other industries where productivity measurement is not improving, causing productivity to decline in the industries that attract the low productivity workers.

Lemon effects – when consumers cannot differentiate between high and low quality products, a common price prevails (a pooling solution); that price represents a premium for low quality and a discount for high quality. The discount on high quality drives high quality out of the market leaving only the "lemons."

Market for control – if publicly traded for-profit firms do not meet market expectations, they become vulnerable to takeover by outsiders through the market for control; the external threat is a serious constraint on principal/agent problems among for-profit firms.

Media oversight – the role of investigative journalism in preventing principal/agent problems in government, for-profit firms, and nonprofit institutions.

Monopsony power – when an employer is the only employer or the dominant employer in a labor market, the employer has market power with respect to workers in that labor market; the employer can set wage rates and the terms of employment. In legend, this is the "company town" issue.

Moral hazard – since legal agreements are not complete with respect to all possible outcomes, they can create incentives for one party to engage in behavior that is against the interest of the other party to the contract; common in insurance, where the insured person no longer has the incentive to be diligent because he is insured.

Nonprofits – institutions organized to provide public services or private goods to groups who are "underserved" by the private market; since the objective is to expand the quantity of goods/services provided they receive tax exempt status and are expected to be nonprofit.

Pooling solution – when consumers have insufficient information to differentiate between high and low quality products, high and low quality products sell at a common price. The "pooled" price is a weighted average of the proportion of high and low quality products. The pooling solution leads to adverse selection and the lemon effect.

Potential entry – when other institutions/firms are strategically positioned to enter another market they are considered "potential entrants." The threat of entry by outsiders tends to moderate the behavior of existing competitors.

Principal/agent problem – whenever one person (the principal) hires another person (the agent) to make decisions on his behalf there is a potential for a conflict of interest; the agent always has an opportunity to take decisions that benefit his self-interest over the interest of the principal; common in politics, for-profit firms, the medical profession, the legal profession, and, of course, education.

Quality signaling – when quality cannot be readily observed, high quality producers adopt tactics designed to signal quality; the signals must be costly and difficult for low quality producers to mimic. Guarantees and warranties are more costly for low quality producers than high quality producers. Investing in high fixed cost assets whose cost cannot be recovered through any other activity (facilities competition in higher education) acts as a performance bond posted by the producer.

Rents – the economic term "rent" refers to any payment above the opportunity return that would prevail in a competitive solution. When a monopolist earns a profit above the normal profit that would accrue to a competitive firm, that premium is referred to as a "monopoly rent"; when a professional athlete earns a wage greater than his second best employment opportunity, the difference between his athletic salary and his second best salary is a "rent." Rent seeking is a powerful motivating influence in economics.

Reputation competition – the reputation mechanism evolved to address the asymmetric information problems common to experience good markets. High quality providers build reputation by exceeding expectations (supplying high quality products at lower prices than would be expected). The cumulative excess of cost over price is the producer's investment in reputation; in an efficient experience good market, the producer can maintain his reputation only by providing quality commensurate with the price.

Reservation prices – a consumer's reservation price is the highest price he is willing to pay for a product. The market demand curve can be interpreted as a schedule of consumer reservation prices.

Seniority/wage profile – in most labor markets, workers receive a positive real wage differential the longer they work for the same employer; in higher education, faculty earn lower real wages the longer they work for the same employer. Among faculty members, this is known as the "salary compression problem."

Separating solution – when buyers in experience good markets have enough information to distinguish between high and low quality products the market establishes separate prices for high quality and low quality. More quality information leads to an efficient solution that eliminates the lemon problem caused by pooling solutions.

Strategic decisions – the decisions taken by management that determine the institution's ultimate future, either prosperity or bankruptcy. At any point in time, current management is either enabled or burdened by the strategic decisions taken by past management.

Third party payers – most market transactions involve two parties, a buyer and a seller. When there are only two parties, each party has the maximum incentive to extract the best possible outcome from the transaction. Third party payers arise when the buyer's purchase is partially subsidized by others. In this case, the buyer has less incentive to extract the best possible outcome from the transaction and the third party payer is not in a position to determine whether value was received for payment rendered, so the seller is subject to less oversight from the other parties in the transaction.

Bibliography

Adams, William James, and Yellen, Janet L. (1976), "Commodity Bundling and the Burden of Monopoly," *Quarterly Journal of Economics*, **90**(3), 475–98.

Akerlof, G. (1970), "The Market for Lemons: Quality Uncertainty and the Market Mechanism," *Quarterly Journal of Economics*, **89**, 488–500.

Alchian, Armen A., and Demsetz, Harold (1972), "Production, Information Costs, and Economic Organization," *American Economic Review*, **62**, 777–95.

Aprill, Ellen P. (2007), "What Critiques of Sarbanes–Oxley Can Teach about Regulation of Nonprofit Governance," *Fordham Law Review*, **76**, 765–94.

Archibald, Robert B., and Feldman, David H. (2008), "Explaining Increases in Higher Education Costs," *Journal of Higher Education*, **79**(3).

Babcock, Philip, and Marks, Mindy (2008), "Leisure College, USA," mimeo, University of California, Santa Barbara.

Baber, William R., Daniel, Patricia L., and Roberts, Andrea A. (2002), "Compensation to Managers of Charitable Organizations: An Empirical Study of the Role of Accounting Measures of Program Activities," *Accounting Review*, **77**(3), July, 679–93.

Baer, Justin D., Cook, Andrea L., and Baldi, Stephane (2006), *The Literacy of America's College Students*, Washington, DC: American Institutes for Research.

Barbezat, Debra A. (2003), "From Here to Seniority: The Effect of Experience and Job Tenure on Faculty Salaries," *New Directions for Institutional Research*, **117**, 21–47.

Barbezat, Debra A., and Hughes, James W. (2001), "The Effect of Job Mobility on Academic Salaries," *Contemporary Economic Policy*, **19**(4), 409–23.

Barden, Dennis M. (2009), *The Chronicle of Higher Education*, **55**(29), March 27, A39–A41.

Bauerlein, Mark (2009), "Professors on the Production Line, Students on their Own," AEI Future of American Education Project, working paper.

Baumol, W.J. and Batey-Blackman, S.A. (1995), "How to Think about Rising College Costs," *Planning for Higher Education*, **23**(4), 1–7.

Baumol, W.J., and Bowen, W.G. (1966), *Performing Arts: The Economic Dilemma,* New York: Twentieth Century Fund.

Baumol, W.J., Panzar, John C., and Willig, Robert D. (1982), *Contestable Markets and the Theory of Industry Structure*, New York: Houghton Mifflin Harcourt.

Becker, Gary S., and Stigler, George (1974), "Law Enforcement, Malfeasance, and Compensation of Enforcers," *Journal of Legal Studies*, **3**, 1–18.

Benton, Thomas H. (2003), "So You Want to Go to Graduate School?", *Chronicle of Higher Education*, June 6.

Benton, Thomas H. (2009), "Graduate School in the Humanities: Just Don't Go,'" *Chronicle of Higher Education*, January 30.

Benton, Thomas H. (2010), "The Big Lie about the 'Life of the Mind,'" *Chronicle of Higher Education*, February 8.

Berube, Michael (1998), "Why Inefficiency Is Good for Universities," *Chronicle of Higher Education*, March 27, B4–B5.

Biglaiser, Gary, and Ma, Ching-to Albert (2003), "Price and Quality Competition under Adverse Selection: Market Organization and Efficiency," *RAND Journal of Economics*, **34**(2), 266–86.

Boehner, Rep. John A., and McKeon, Rep. Howard P. (2003), *The College Cost Crisis*, Washington, DC: U.S. House Committee on Education and the Workforce.

Bok, Derek (2003), *Universities in the Marketplace: The Commercialization of Higher Education*, Princeton, NJ: Princeton University Press.

Bok, Derek (2006), *Our Underachieving Colleges: A Candid Look at How Much Students Learn and Why They Should Be Learning More*, Princeton, NJ: Princeton University Press.

Bound, John, Lovenheim, Michael, and Turner, Sarah (2009), "Why Have College Completion Rates Declined? An Analysis of Changing Student Preparation and Collegiate Resources," NBER Working Paper 15566.

Bowen, Howard R. (1980), *The Costs of Higher Education: How Much Do Colleges and Universities Spend per Student and How Much Should They Spend?*, Washington, DC: Jossey-Bass Publishers.

Bowen, Stephen (2009), "Measuring Maine's Public Colleges: Non-Instructional Staffing and Cost-Per-Degree," February 5, Maine Heritage Policy Center.

Bradley, Richard (2009), "Drew Gilpin Faust and the Incredible Shrinking Harvard," *Boston Magazine*, June.

Breneman, David W. (2001), "An Essay on College Costs", in National Center for Education Statistics, *Study of College Costs and Prices, 1988–89 to 1997–98*, vol. 2: *Commissioned Papers*, Washington, DC: U.S. Department of Education.

Brewer, Dominic J., Eide, Eric R., and Ehrenberg, Ronald G. (1999), "Does It Pay to Attend an Elite Private College?" *Journal of Human Resources*, **34**, 123.

Brewer, Dominic J., Gates, Susan M., and Goldman, Charles A. (2002), *In Pursuit of Prestige: Strategy and Competition in U.S. Higher Education*, New Brunswick, NJ: Transaction Publishers.

Brinkman, Paul T. (1990), "Higher Education Cost Functions," in Stephen A. Hoenack and Eileen L. Collins (eds.), *The Economics of American Universities*, Albany: State University of New York Press.

Carbajo, José, de Meza, David, and Seidmann, Daniel J. (1990), "A Strategic Motivation for Commodity Bundling," *Journal of Industrial Economics*, **38**(3), 283–98.

Chabotar, Kent John (2009), "The Mistakes to Avoid," *Inside Higher Ed*, June 5.

Clotfelter, Charles T., Ehrenberg, Ronald G., Getz, Malcolm, and Siegfried, John J. (1991), *Economic Challenges in Higher Education*, Chicago: University of Chicago Press.

Cohn, Elchanan, Rhine, Sherrie L.W., and Santos, Maria C. (1989), "Institutions of Higher Education as Multi-Product Firms: Economies of Scale and Scope," *Review of Economics and Statistics*, **71**, 283–90.

College Board (2008), *Trends in Student Aid*, College Board, New York.

College Board (2009), Trends in Higher Education Series.

Commission on National Investment in Higher Education, Council for Aid to Education (1997), *Breaking the Social Contract: The Fiscal Crisis in Higher Education*, Santa Monica, CA: RAND.

Cook, Phillip J., and Frank, Robert H. (1993), "The Growing Concentration of Top Students at Elite Institutions," in Charles Clotfelter and Michael Rothschild (eds.), *Studies of Supply and Demand in Higher Education*, Chicago: University of Chicago Press.

Crawford, Elizabeth (2003), "Americans Give Higher Education High Marks in All Areas except Cost, Survey Finds," *Chronicle of Higher Education*, June 19.

Dale, Stacy Berg, and Krueger, Alan B. (2002), "Estimating the Payoff to Attending a More Selective College: An Application of Selection on Observables and Unobservables," *Quarterly Journal of Economics*, **117**(4), 1491–527.

Dansby, Robert E., and Conrad, Cecilia (1984), "Commodity Bundling," *American Economic Review*, **74**(2), Papers and Proceedings of the Ninety-Sixth Annual Meeting of the American Economic Association, 377–81.

Deford, Frank (2005), "America's Modern Peculiar Institution," in Richard Hersch and John Merrow (eds.), *Declining By Degrees: Higher Education at Risk*, Palgrave Macmillan.

De Navas-Wall, Carmen, Proctor, Bernadette D., and Smith, Jessica C. (2009), *Income, Poverty, and Health Insurance Coverage in the United States: 2008*, September, Washington, DC: U.S. Census Bureau.

Diver, Colin (2005), "Is There Life after Rankings?," *Atlantic Monthly*, November, 136–9.

Douthat, Ross (2005), "Does Meritocracy Work?," *Atlantic Monthly*, November.

Easterbrook, Gregg (2004), "Who Needs Harvard?," *Atlantic Monthly*, October.

Ehrenberg, Ronald G. (1989), "An Economic Analysis of the Market for Law School Graduates," *Journal of Legal Education*, **39**, 627–54.

Ehrenberg, Ronald G., (2000), *Tuition Rising: Why College Costs So Much*, Cambridge, MA: Harvard University Press.

Ehrenberg, Ronald G. (2002), "Studying Ourselves: The Academic Labor Market: Presidential Address to the Society of Labor Economists, Baltimore, May 3, 2002," *Journal of Labor Economics*, **21**(2), 267–87.

Ehrenberg, Ronald G. (2004), "Prospects in the Academic Labor Market for Economists," *Journal of Economic Perspectives*, **18**(2), 227–38.

Ehrenberg, Ronald G., Cheslock, John, and Epifantseva, Julia (2001), "Paying our Presidents: What Do Trustees Value?," *Review of Higher Education*, **25**, 15–37.

Ellis, John (2010), "How the Campuses Helped Ruin California's Economy," *Minding the Campus*, March 11.

Engell, James, and Dangerfield, Anthony (2005), *Saving Higher Education in the Age of Money*, Charlottesville: University of Virginia Press.

Fallows, James (2005), "College Admissions: A Substitute for Quality?," in Richard Hersch and John Merrow (eds.), *Declining by Degrees: Higher Education at Risk*, New York: Palgrave Macmillan.

Fang, Hanming, and Norman, Peter (2006), "To Bundle or Not to Bundle," *RAND Journal of Economics*, **37**(4), 946–63.

Feldberg, Sarah (2009), "Let the Protests Begin: College Students and Teachers Rally against Budget Cuts," *Las Vegas Weekly Blogs*, January 23.

Fizel, John, and Fort, Rodney (eds), (2004), *Economics of College Sports*, Westport, CT and London: Greenwood, Praeger.

Fremont-Smith, Marion R. (2004), *Governing Nonprofit Organizations: Federal and State Law and Regulation*, Cambridge, MA: Belknap Press of Harvard University Press.

Fried, Vance H. (2008), "Better-than-Ivy-Education: $7,376 a year," *Inside Higher Ed*, Views.

Frumkin, Peter, and Kim, Mark T. (2001), "Positioning and the Financing of Nonprofit Organizations: Is Efficiency Rewarded in the Contributions Marketplace?," *Public Administration Review*, **61**(3), May/June, 266–75.

Furchtgott-Roth, Diana, Jacobson, Louis, and Mokher, Christine (2009), "Strengthening Community College's Influence on Economic Mobility," Economic Mobility Project.

Gal-Or, Esther (1989), "Warranties as a Signal of Quality," *Canadian Journal of Economics*, **22**(1), 50–61.

Gardner, Howard (2005), "Beyond Markets and Individuals: A Focus on Educational Goals," in Richard Hersch and John Merrow (eds.), *Declining by Degrees: Higher Education at Risk*, New York: Palgrave Macmillan.

Getz, Malcolm, and Siegfried, John J. (1991), "Costs and Productivity in American Colleges and Universities," in Charles T. Clotfelter, Ronald G. Ehrenberg, Malcolm Getz, and John J. Siegfried, *Economic Challenges in Higher Education*, Chicago: University of Chicago Press.

Getz, Malcolm, Siegfried, John J., and Anderson, Kathryn H. (1997), "Adoption of Innovations in Higher Education," *Quarterly Review of Economics and Finance*, **37**(3), 605–31.

Gillen, Andrew (2009), *Financial Aid in Theory and Practice: Why It Is Ineffective and What Can Be Done about It*, April, Washington, DC: Center for College Affordability and Productivity.

Grossman, Sanford J. (1981), "The Informational Role of Warranties and Private Disclosure about Product Quality," *Journal of Law and Economics*, **24**(3), 461–83.

Hanson, Victor Davis, and Heath, John (2001), *Who Killed Homer? The Demise of Classical Education and the Recovery of Greek Wisdom*, New York: Encounter Books.

Harris, Milton, and Holmstrom, Bengt (1982), "Theory of Wage Dynamics," *Review of Economic Studies*, **72**, 716–24.

Hersh, Richard H., and Merrow, John (eds.) (2005), *Declining by Degrees: Higher Education at Risk*, New York: Palgrave Macmillan.

Hoffman, E. (1997), "Labor Economics and Labor Markets," Industrial Relations Research Association, Proceedings of the 49th annual meeting, New Orleans, 347–52.

Holbrook, Todd (2010), "More Healthcare Hubbub," April 15, Center for College Affordability and Productivity, Washington, DC.

Holmstrom, Bengt (1999), "Managerial Incentive Problems: A Dynamic Perspective," *Review of Economic Studies*, **66**(1), 169–82.

Holmstrom, Bengt, and Milgrom, P. (1991), "Multitask Principal–Agent Analyses: Incentive Contracts, Asset Ownership, and Job Design," *Journal of Law, Economics, and Organization*, **7**, 24–52.

Hörner, Johannes (2002), "Reputation and Competition," *American Economic Review*, **92**(3), 644–63.

Hoxby, Caroline M. (2004), "Productivity in Education: The Quintessential Upstream Industry," *Southern Economic Journal*, **71**(2), 209–31.

Hoxby, Caroline M. (2009), "The Changing Selectivity of American Colleges," NBER working paper.

Ikenberry, Stanley, and Hartle, Terry W. (2000), *Taking Stock: How Americans Judge Quality, Affordability, and Leadership at U.S. Colleges and Universities*, Washington, DC: American Council on Education.

Immerwahr, John, and Johnson, Jean (2010), *Squeeze Play 2010: Continued Public Anxiety on Cost, Harsher Judgments on How Colleges Are Run*, San Jose, CA and New York: National Center for Public Policy and Higher Education and Public Agenda.

Intercollegiate Studies Institute, American Civic Literacy Program (2010), "The Shaping of the American Mind: The Diverging Influences of the College Degree and Civic Learning on American Beliefs," http://www.americancivicliteracy.org/report/pdf/02-10-10/civic_literacy_report_2010.pdf.

Iyigun, Murat F. (1999), "Public Education and Intergenerational Economic Mobility," *International Economic Review*, **40**(3), 697–710.

James, Estelle (1990), "Decision Processes and Priorities in Higher Education," in Stephen A. Hoenack and Eileen L. Collins (eds.), *The Economics of American Universities*, Buffalo: State University of New York Press.

Johnes, Geraint (1997), "Costs and Industrial Structure in Contemporary British Higher Education," *Economic Journal*, **107**, 727–37.

Jovanovic, Boyan (1979), "Job Matching and the Theory of Turnover," *Journal of Political Economy*, **87**, 972–90.

Kelly, Andrew P., and Aldeman, Chad (2010), *False Fronts? Behind Higher Education's Voluntary Accountability Systems*, March, Washington, DC: Education Sector and American Enterprise Institute.

Kipp, Samuel M., Price, Derek V., and Wohlford, Jill K. (2002), *Unequal Opportunity: Disparities in College Access among the 50 States*, Indianapolis, IN: Lumina Foundation.

Kirp, David L. (2003), *Shakespeare, Einstein, and the Bottom Line: The Marketing of Higher Education*, Cambridge, MA: Harvard University Press.

Kirp, David L. (2005), "This Little Student Went to Market," in Richard H. Hersh and John Merrow (eds.), *Declining by Degrees: Higher Education at Risk*, New York: Palgrave Macmillan.

Kirp, David L., and Berman, Elizabeth Popp (2003), "A Good Deal of Collaboration: The University of California, Berkeley," in David L. Kirp (ed.), *Shakespeare, Einstein, and the Bottom Line: The Marketing of Higher Education*, Cambridge, MA: Harvard University Press.

Klein, B., and Leffler, K.B. (1981), "The Role of Market Forces in Assuring Contractual Performance," *Journal of Political Economy*, **89**, 615–41.

Koshal, R.K., and Koshal, M. (1995), "Quality and Economies of Scale in Higher Education," *Applied Economics*, **27**(8), 773–8.

Koshal, R.K., and Koshal, M. (2000), "Do Liberal Arts Colleges Exhibit Economies of Scale and Scope?," *Education Economics*, **8**(3), 209–20.

Kuh, George (1999), "How Are We Doing? Tracking the Quality of the Undergraduate Experience, 1960s to the Present," *Review of Higher Education*, **22**, 99–119.

Larson, Erik (2001), "Why College Costs Too Much," *Time*, June 24.

Lazear, Edward P. (1981), "Agency Earnings Profiles, Productivity and Hours Restrictions," *American Economic Review*, **41**, 606–20.

Lazear, Edward P. (1986), "Raids and Offer Matching," *Research in Labor Economics*, **8**(Part A), 141–65.

Lederman, Doug (2009), "Rankings Rancor at Clemson," *Inside Higher Ed*, June 4.

Levitt, Stephen D., and Dubner, Stephen J. (2009), *SuperFreakonomics: Global Cooling, Patriotic Prostitutes, and Why Suicide Bombers Should Buy Life Insurance*, New York: William Morrow.

Lewis, Harry R. (2006), *Excellence without a Soul: Does Liberal Education Have a Future?*, New York: PublicAffairs.

Liebeskind, Julia, and Rumelt, Richard P. (1989), "Markets for Experience Goods with Performance Uncertainty," *RAND Journal of Economics*, **20**(4), 601–21.

Light, Audrey, and Strayer, Wayne (2000), "Determinants of College Completion: School Quality or Student Ability?," *Journal of Human Resources*, **35**(2), 299–332.

Lutz, Nancy A. (1989), "Warranties as Signals under Consumer Moral Hazard," *RAND Journal of Economics*, **20**(2), 239–55.

MacLeod, W. Bentley, and Urquiola, Miguel (2009), "Anti-Lemons: School Reputation and Educational Quality," Working Paper 15112, National Bureau of Economic Research.

Maeroff, Gene I. (2005), "The Media: Degrees of Coverage," in Richard Hersch and John Merrow (eds.), *Declining by Degrees: Higher Education at Risk*, New York: Palgrave Macmillan.

Malanga, Steve (2010), 'You Don't Have To Be a Professor,' *Minding the Campus: Reforming Our Universities*, February 11.

Marsh, Herbert W., and Hattie, John (2002), "The Relation between Research Productivity and Teaching Effectiveness: Complementary, Antagonistic, or Independent Constructs?," *Journal of Higher Education*, **73**(5), 603–41.

Martin, Robert E. (1986), "On Judging Quality by Price: Price Dependent Expectations, Not Price Dependent Preferences," *Southern Economic Journal*, **52**(3), 665–72.

Martin, Robert E. (2005), *Cost Control, College Access, and Competition in Higher Education*, Cheltenham, UK and Northampton, MA, USA: Edward Elgar Publishing.

Martin, Robert E. (2009), 'The Revenue-to-Cost Spiral in Higher Education,' Pope Center Series on Higher Education, July, John William Pope Center for Higher Education Studies, Raleigh, NC.

Mas-Colell, Andreu, Whinston, Michael D., and Green, Jerry G. (1995), *Microeconomic Theory*, New York: Oxford University Press.

Massy, William F. (2003), *Honoring the Trust: Quality and Cost Containment in Higher Education*, Boston, MA: Anker Publishing Company.

Massy, William F., and Zemsky, Robert M. (1994), "Faculty Discretionary Time: Departments and the Academic Ratchet," *Journal of Higher Education*, **65**, 1–22.

McCormick, Robert E., and Tinsley, Maurice (1987), "Athletics versus Academics? Evidence from SAT Scores," *Journal of Political Economy*, **95**(5), 1103–16.

Mehta, Shailendra Raj (2000), "Quality of Education, Productivity Changes, and Income Distribution," *Journal of Labor Economics*, **18**(2), 252–81.

Mincer, Jacob (1974), *Schooling, Experience, and Earnings*, New York: Columbia University Press.

Moore, William J., Newman, Robert J., and Turnbull, Geoffrey K. (1998), "Do Academic Salaries Decline with Seniority?," *Journal of Labor Economics*, **16**(2), 352–66.

Nalebuff, Barry (2004), "Bundling as an Entry Barrier," *Quarterly Journal of Economics*, **119**, 159–87.

National Center for Education Statistics (NCES) (2006), *National Assessment of Adult Literacy*, Washington, DC: NCES.

National Center for Education Statistics (2008), *Digest of Education Statistics*, Washington, DC: NCES.

National Center for Education Statistics (2009), *University Hiring in 2009*, Washington, DC: NCES.

National Center for Public Policy and Higher Education (NCPPHE) (2002), *Losing Ground: A National Status Report on the Affordability of American Higher Education*, San Jose, CA: NCPPHE.

National Center for Public Policy and Higher Education (2008), *Measuring Up 2008: The National Report Card on Higher Education*, San Jose, CA: NCPPHE.

National Commission on the Cost of Higher Education (1998), *Straight*

Talk about College Costs and Prices, Report of the National Commission on the Cost of Higher Education, Phoenix, AZ: Oryx Press.

Nelson, Phillip (1970), "Information and Consumer Behavior," *Journal of Political Economy*, **78**, 311–29.

O'Brien, Darcy (1979), "A Generation of 'Lost' Scholars," *New York Times*, March 18.

Oi, Walter (1962), "Labor as a Quasi-Fixed Factor," *Journal of Political Economy*, **70**, December, 538–55.

O'Keefe, Bryan, and Vedder, Richard (2008), *Griggs v. Duke Power: Implications for College Credentialing*, Washington, DC and Raleigh, NC: Center for College Affordability and Productivity, and John William Pope Center for Higher Education Policy.

Oyer, Paul (2006), "Initial Labor Market Conditions and Long-Term Outcomes for Economists," *Journal of Economic Perspectives*, **20**(3), 143–60.

Ransom, Michael R. (1993), "Seniority and Monopsony in the Academic Labor Market," *American Economic Review*, **83**(1), 221–33.

Robertson, J., and Bond, C.H. (2001), "Experiences of the Relation between Teaching and Research: What Do Academics Value?," *Higher Education Research and Development*, **20**(1), 5–19.

Rojstaczer, Stuart, and Healy, Christopher (2009), "Grade Inflation in American Colleges and Universities," GradeInflation.com.

Rolnick, Arthur J., and Weber, Warren E. (1986), "Gresham's Law or Gresham's Fallacy?," *Journal of Political Economy*, **94**(1), 185–99.

Rothschild, Michael, and White, Lawrence J. (1995), "The Analytics of Pricing in Higher Education and Other Services in which Customers Are Inputs," *Journal of Political Economy*, **103**, 573–86.

Roy, A.D. (1951), "Some Thoughts on the Distribution of Earnings," *Oxford Economic Papers*, **3**, 235–46.

Salop, Joanne, and Salop, Steven (1976), "Self Selection and Turnover in the Labor Market," *Quarterly Journal of Economics*, **90**, November, 619–27.

Schmalensee, Richard (1982), "Commodity Bundling by Single-Product Monopolies," *Journal of Law and Economics*, **25**(1), 67–71.

Schwartz, Steven (2004), "How to Tame Grade Inflation," *Guardian*, October 21.

Shapiro, Carl (1983), "Premiums for High Quality Products as Returns to Reputations," *Quarterly Journal of Economics*, **98**(4), 659–79.

Sorokina, Olga V. (2003), "Executive Compensation: The Case of Liberal Arts College Presidents," *Issues in Political Economy*, **12**, 1–16.

Spence, Michael (1977), "Consumer Misperception, Product Failure and Producer Liability," *Review of Economic Studies*, **44**, 561–72.

Sperber, Murray (2001), *Beer and Circus: How Big-Time College Sports Is Crippling Undergraduate Education*, New York: Henry Holt & Company.

Sperber, Murray (2005), "How Undergraduate Education Became College Lite – and a Personal Apology," in Richard H. Hersh and John Merrow (eds.), *Declining by Degrees: Higher Education at Risk*, New York: Palgrave Macmillan.

Stecklow, Steve (1995), "Cheat Sheets: Colleges Inflate SATs and Graduation Rates in Popular Guidebook," *Wall Street Journal*, April 5, A1.

Stigler, George J. (1967), "Imperfections in the Capital Market," *Journal of Political Economy*, **75**(3), 287–92.

Tavares, Stephanie (2009), "UNLV President Garners Praise, Catches a Break," *Las Vegas Sun*, July 8.

Tracy, Joseph, and Waldfogel, Joel (1997), "The Best Business Schools: A Market-Based Approach," *Journal of Business*, **70**(1), 1–31.

Triplett, Jack E., and Bosworth, Barry P. (2003), "Productivity Measurement Issues in Service Industries: 'Baumol's Disease' has been Cured," *FRBNY Economic Policy Review*, **9**(3), 23–33.

Tuchman, Gaye (2009), *Wannabe U: Inside the Corporate University*, Chicago: University of Chicago Press.

Turner, Sarah E. (2004), "Going to College and Finishing College: Explaining Different Educational Outcomes," in Caroline M. Hoxby (ed.), *College Choices: The Economics of Where to Go, When to Go, and How to Pay for It*, Chicago: University of Chicago Press.

Varian, Hal R. (2006), *Intermediate Microeconomics*, 7th edn., New York: W.W. Norton & Company.

Vedder, Richard (2010), "Students Be Damned," January 14, Center for College Affordability and Productivity, Washington DC.

Von Hoffman, Nicholas (2006), "College Presidents High on the Hog," *Nation*, October 31.

Wadsworth, Deborah (2005), "Ready or Not? Where the Public Stands on Higher Education Reform," in Richard Hersch and John Merrow (eds.), *Declining by Degrees: Higher Education at Risk*, New York: Palgrave Macmillan.

Wang, Penelope (2008), "Is College Still Worth the Price?," *Money*, September, 87–94.

Washburn, Jennifer (2005), *University Inc.: The Corporate Corruption of Higher Education*, New York: Basic Books.

Waugh, William L. (2003), "Issues in University Governance: More 'Professional' and Less Academic," *Annals of the American Academy of Political and Social Science*, **585**, January, 84–96.

Weisbrod, Burton A. (ed.) (1998), *To Profit or Not to Profit: The Commercial Transformation of the Nonprofit Sector*, Cambridge: Cambridge University Press.

Winston, Gordon (1999), "Subsidies, Hierarchy, and Peers: The Awkward Economics of Higher Education," *Journal of Economic Perspectives*, **13**, 13–36.

Wolfe, Tom (2004), *I Am Charlotte Simmons*, Toronto: HarperCollins Publishers, Ltd.

Wolinsky, Asher (1983), "Prices as Signals of Product Quality," *Review of Economic Studies*, **50**(4), 647–58.

Zemsky, Robert M. (1989), *Structure and Coherence: Measuring the Undergraduate Curriculum*, Washington, DC: American Association of Colleges.

Zemsky, Robert M. (2007), "The Rise and Fall of the Spellings Commission," *Chronicle of Higher Education*, **53**(21), January, B6.

Zemsky, Robert M. (2009), *Making Reform Work: The Case for Transforming American Higher Education*, New Brunswick, NJ: Rutgers University Press.

Index